# CAT

## Intermediate
## Paper 4
### ACCOUNTING FOR COSTS

**PRACTICE & REVISION KIT**

---

**In this January 2009 new edition**

- **Do you know?** Checklists to test your knowledge and understanding of topics

- A question and answer bank

- The ACCA's June 2008 and December 2008 CAT examination papers as mock exams

BPP's **i-Pass** product also supports this paper.

---

FOR EXAMS IN 2009

**BPP**
LEARNING MEDIA

First edition 2004
Sixth edition January 2009

ISBN 9780 7517 6310 2 (previous ISBN 9780 7517 4798 0)

British Library Cataloguing-in-Publication Data
A catalogue record for this book
is available from the British Library

Published by

BPP Learning Media Ltd
BPP House, Aldine Place
London W12 8AA

www.bpp.com/learningmedia

Printed in the United Kingdom

We are grateful to the Association of Chartered Certified
Accountants for permission to reproduce past
examination questions and some official answers. The
answers to remaining past examination questions have
been prepared by BPP Learning Media Ltd.

# Contents

## Review form & free prize draw

# Question index

LEARNING MEDIA

### Mock exam 1

June 2008 exam

### Mock exam 2

December 2008 exam

# Topic index

Listed below are the key Paper 4 syllabus topics and the numbers of the questions in this Kit covering those topics.

If you need to concentrate your practice and revision on certain topics or if you want to attempt all available questions that refer to a particular subject, you will find this index useful.

# Using your BPP Practice and Revision Kit

To provide the practice to help you succeed in both the paper based and computer based examinations for Paper 4 *Accounting for Costs*.

To pass the examination you need a thorough understanding in all areas covered by the syllabus and teaching guide.

## Recommended approach

- Make sure you are able to answer questions on **everything** specified by the syllabus and teaching guide. You cannot make any assumptions about what questions may come up on your paper. The examiners aim to discourage 'question spotting'. In a paper that has objective test questions or a number of shorter questions, the examiner has the opportunity to test a wide area of the syllabus. Where there are long questions, a number of different issues can be brought in. And an area that has been tested in one sitting can still be tested again in the next sitting.

- Learning is an **active** process. Use the **DO YOU KNOW?** Checklists to test your knowledge and understanding of the topics covered in Paper 4 *Accounting for Costs* by filling in the blank spaces. Then check your answers against the **DID YOU KNOW?** Checklists. Do not attempt any questions if you are unable to fill in any of the blanks - go back to your **BPP Interactive Text** and revise first.

- When you are revising a topic, think about the mistakes that you know that you should avoid by writing down **POSSIBLE PITFALLS** at the end of each **DO YOU KNOW**? Checklist.

- Once you have completed the checklists successfully, you should attempt the questions on that topic. Each section has a selection of **OBJECTIVE TEST QUESTIONS** and **COMPULSORY WRITTEN QUESTIONS**. Make good use of the **HELPING HANDS** provided to help you answer the questions. On questions that have been in past exam papers, we report **'what the examiner said'**. This shows you how students who sat the exam coped with the question and tells you what the pitfalls were and what the examiner was looking for.

- There is a mark allocation for each compulsory written question. Each mark carries with it a time allocation of 1.2 minutes (including time for selecting and reading questions). A 15 mark question therefore should be completed in 18 minutes.

- Once you have completed all of the questions in the body of this Practice & Revision Kit, you should attempt the **MOCK EXAMS** under examination conditions. These are the latest actual exams. Check your answers against our answers and apply the ACCA's Official marking scheme to find out how well you did.

# Passing your CAT 4 exam

CAT 4 builds on what you learnt in CAT 2. There is a lot to learn, but none of it is particularly difficult and a good grasp of these topics will help you in higher level management accounting in CAT 7.

## The exam

You can take this exam as a written paper or by CBE. All questions in the exam are compulsory. This means you cannot avoid any topic, but also means that you do not need to waste time in the exam deciding which questions to attempt. There are twenty MCQs and four longer questions in the paper-based exam and a mixture of MCQs and other types of OTQ in the CBE. This means that the examiner is able to test most of the syllabus at each sitting, and that is what he aims to do. So you need to have revised right across the syllabus for this exam.

## Revision

This kit has all the latest exam questions, so if you just worked through it to the end you would be very well prepared for the exam. It is important to tackle questions under exam conditions. Allow yourself just the number of minutes shown next to the question in the index and don't look at the answer until you have finished. Then correct your answer and go back to the study text for any topic you are really having trouble with. Try the same question again a week later – you will be surprised how much better you are getting. Doing the questions like this will really show you what you know, and will make the exam experience less worrying.

## Doing the exam

If you have honestly done your revision you can pass this exam. There are certain points which you must bear in mind:

- Read the question properly, particularly the longer questions. You don't want to waste time doing something that has not been asked for. It is worth reading a longer question through twice.

- Make your workings clear and legible. This helps you to deal with the question and it helps the marker to give you marks. If your answer is wrong but you used the correct method in your workings you can still get marks – if the marker can read them.

- Don't spend more than the allotted time on each question. If you are having trouble with an MCQ leave it and carry on. You can come back to it at the end. If there is part of a question that you can't do, leave it and do the rest.

# Approach to examining the Syllabus

Paper 4 is a two-hour paper. It can be taken as a written paper or a computer based examination. The questions in the computer based examination are objective test questions – multiple choice, number entry and multiple response. (See page (xiii) for frequently asked questions about computer based examinations.)

The written examination consists of two sections, structured as follows:

|  |  | *No of marks* |
|---|---|---|
| Section A | 20 compulsory multiple choice questions of 2 marks each | 40 |
| Section B | 4 compulsory written questions of between 10 and 20 marks each | 60 |
|  | Total | 100 |

## Analysis of past papers

**Marks**

### December 2008

*Section A*

Twenty multiple choice questions covering various accounting for costs topics | 40

*Section B*
| | | |
|---|---|---|
| 1 | Net cash flows; net present value; internal rate of return | 16 |
| 2 | Profit centre and break-even sales revenue | 11 |
| 3 | Process costing | 15 |
| 4 | Labour expenses | 18 |

### June 2008

*Section A*

Twenty multiple choice questions covering various accounting for costs topics | 40

*Section B*

| | | |
|---|---|---|
| 1 | Inventory valuation | 13 |
| 2 | Process costing | 13 |
| 3 | Absorption costing and overhead apportionment | 15 |
| 4 | Limiting factors and production planning | 19 |

### December 2007

*Section A*

Twenty multiple choice questions covering various accounting for costs topics | 40

*Section B*

| | | |
|---|---|---|
| 1 | Absorption costing profit statement. Marginal costing, contribution, net profit, break-even sales revenue. Comparison of absorption and marginal costing | 19 |
| 2 | Calculation of total cost and cost and profit per unit | 20 |
| 3 | Overhead absorption rates | 10 |
| 4 | Process costing and joint costs | 11 |

# June 2007

*Section A*

Twenty multiple choice questions covering various accounting for costs topics | 40

*Section B*

| | | |
|---|---|---|
| 1 | Graphical representation of present values | 16 |
| 2 | Raw material inventory management | 18 |
| 3 | Understanding and application of cost-volume-profit analysis | 10 |
| 4 | Overhead apportionment and absorption | 16 |

# December 2006

*Section A*

Twenty multiple choice questions covering various accounting for costs topics | 40

*Section B*

| | | |
|---|---|---|
| 1 | Cost centres, profit centres, investment centres | 10 |
| 2 | Labour costing | 15 |
| 3 | Overhead absorption | 16 |
| 4 | Relevant costing; NPV | 19 |

# June 2006

*Section A*

Twenty multiple choice questions covering various accounting for costs topics | 40

*Section B*

| | | |
|---|---|---|
| 1 | Job costing | 14 |
| 2 | Break even; contribution/sales ratio | 13 |
| 3 | Coding systems; apportionment | 17 |
| 4 | Process costing – joint products; further processing | 16 |

# December 2005

*Section A*

Twenty multiple choice questions covering various accounting for costs topics | 40

*Section B*

| | | |
|---|---|---|
| 1 | Compound interest formula; NPV | 16 |
| 2 | Overhead apportionment and absorption | 14 |
| 3 | Information; cost function formula and calculation | 12 |
| 4 | Profit/volume chart; contribution | 18 |

# June 2005

*Section A*

| | | |
|---|---|---|
| 1 | Twenty multiple choice questions covering various accounting for costs topics | 40 |

*Section B*

| | | |
|---|---|---|
| 1 | Absorption costing and marginal costing | 14 |
| 2 | Cost per unit of normal output and process account | 14 |
| 3 | Stock costs and EOQ | 15 |
| 4 | Break even and profit/volume | 17 |

## December 2004

*Section A*

Twenty multiple choice questions covering various accounting for costs topics 40

*Section B*

| | | |
|---|---|---|
| 1 | Labour costs | 16 |
| 2 | Process costing – joint products | 14 |
| 3 | Service costing | 16 |
| 4 | Decision making and limiting factor analysis | 14 |

## June 2004

*Section A*

Twenty multiple choice questions covering various accounting for costs topics 40

*Section B*

| | | |
|---|---|---|
| 1 | Inventory control | 12 |
| 2 | Absorption costing and job costing | 14 |
| 3 | Job costing and process costing | 19 |
| 4 | Capital investment appraisal | 15 |

## Pilot paper

*Section A*

Twenty multiple choice questions covering various accounting for costs topics 40

*Section B*

| | | |
|---|---|---|
| 1 | Marginal costing and absorption costing | 17 |
| 2 | Job costing | 13 |
| 3 | Process costing: joint products | 12 |
| 4 | Discounted cash flow | 18 |

# The Computer Based Examination

The ACCA has introduced a computer based examination (CBE) for CAT Papers 1–4 (in addition to the conventional paper based examination).

Computer based examinations must be taken at an ACCA CBE Licensed Centre.

## How does CBE work?

- Questions are displayed on a monitor

- Candidates enter their answer directly onto the computer

- Candidates have two hours to complete the examination

- When the candidate has completed their examination, the computer automatically marks the file containing the candidate's answers

- Candidates are provided with a certificate showing their results before leaving the examination room

- The CBE Licensed Centre uploads the results to the ACCA (as proof of the candidate's performance) within 48 hours

## Benefits

- **Flexibility** as a CBE can be sat at any time.

- **Resits** can also be taken at any time and there is no restriction on the number of times a candidate can sit a CBE.

- **Instant feedback** as the computer displays the results at the end of the CBE.

- Results are notified to ACCA **within 48 hours**.

- **Extended closing date periods** (see ACCA website for further information)

## CBE question types

- Multiple choice – choose one answer from four options

- Multiple response 1 – select more than one response by clicking the appropriate tick boxes

- Multiple response 2 – select a response to a number of related part questions by choosing one option from a number of drop down menus

- Number entry – key in a numerical response to a question

## CAT CBE

You will have two hours in which to answer a number of questions, which are worth a total of 100 marks. See the ACCA website for a demonstration and up to date information (www.acca.org.uk/colleges/cbe_demo).

# Tackling Multiple Choice Questions

Of the total marks available for the paper based exam, multiple choice questions (MCQs) comprise 50 per cent. MCQs also feature in the computer based exam.

The MCQs in your exam contain four possible answers. You have to **choose the option that best answers the question**. The three incorrect options are called distracters. There is a skill in answering MCQs quickly and correctly. By practising MCQs you can develop this skill, giving you a better chance of passing the exam.

You may wish to follow the approach outlined below, or you may prefer to adapt it.

**Step 1**      Skim read all the MCQs and identify what appear to be the easier questions.

**Step 2**      Attempt each question – **starting with the easier questions** identified in Step 1. Read the question **thoroughly**. You may prefer to work out the answer before looking at the options, or you may prefer to look at the options at the beginning. Adopt the method that works best for you.

**Step 3**      Read the four options and see if one matches your own answer. Be careful with numerical questions as the distracters are designed to match answers that incorporate common errors. Check that your calculation is correct. Have you followed the requirement exactly? Have you included every stage of the calculation?

**Step 4**      You may find that none of the options matches your answer.

- Re-read the question to ensure that you understand it and are answering the requirement
- Eliminate any obviously wrong answers
- Consider which of the remaining answers is the most likely to be correct and select the option

**Step 5**      If you are still unsure make a note and continue to the next question

**Step 6**      Revisit unanswered questions. When you come back to a question after a break you often find you are able to answer it correctly straight away. If you are still unsure have a guess. You are not penalised for incorrect answers, so **never leave a question unanswered!**

After extensive practice and revision of MCQs, you may find that you recognise a question when you sit the exam. Be aware that the detail and/or requirement may be different. If the question seems familiar read the requirement and options carefully – do not assume that it is identical.

# Using your BPP products

This Kit gives you the question practice and guidance you need in the exam. Our other products can also help you pass:

- **Learning to Learn Accountancy** gives further valuable advice on revision

- **Passcards** provide you with clear topic summaries and exam tips

- **Success CDs** help you revise on the move

- **i-Pass CDs** offer tests of knowledge against the clock

- **Learn Online** is an e-learning resource delivered via the Internet, offering comprehensive tutor support and featuring areas such as study, practice, email service, revision and useful resources

You can purchase these products by visiting www.bpp.com/mybpp.

Visit our website www.bpp.com/cat/learnonline to sample aspects of Learn Online free of charge.

# Questions

# Do you know? – Management information and information technology

Check that you can fill in the blanks in the statements below before you attempt any questions. If in doubt, you should go back to your BPP Interactive Text and revise first.

- The raw material for data processing is known as ......... and when it is processed it is known as ..................... .

- Features of useful management information include the following.

    - ..................................
    - ..................................
    - ..................................
    - ..................................

    - ..................................
    - ..................................
    - ..................................
    - ..................................

- ............. involves establishing objectives for a company and developing ................. in order to achieve those objectives.

- ........................... are prepared for individuals external to an organisation.............................. ..................... are prepared for internal managers.

- The main features of a management information report are a follows.

    - ..................................................
    - ..................................................
    - ..................................................
    - ..................................................
    - ..................................................
    - ..................................................

- The three stages of data input are as follows.

    (1) ....................................................
    (2) ....................................................
    (3) ....................................................

- Common document reading methods include the following.

    - ..................................................
    - ..................................................
    - ..................................................
    - ..................................................
    - ..................................................

- Card reading devices include ................................................ cards and ................. cards.

- Data storage methods include the following.

    - ..................................................
    - ..................................................
    - ..................................................
    - ..................................................

    TRY QUESTIONS 1 and 2

- *Possible pitfalls*

    *Write down the mistakes you know you should avoid.*

# Did you know? – Management information and information technology

Could you fill in the blanks? The answers are in bold. Use this page for revision purposes as you approach the exam.

- The raw material for data processing is known as **data** and when it is processed it is known as **information.**

- Features of useful management information include the following.

  | | |
  |---|---|
  | – **Relevant** | – **Manageable volume** |
  | – **Complete** | – **Timely** |
  | – **Accurate** | – **Cost less than value of benefits** |
  | – **Clear** | – **User has confidence in it** |

- **Planning** involves establishing objectives for a company and developing **strategies** in order to achieve those objectives

- **Financial accounts** are prepared for individuals external to an organisation. **Management accounts** are prepared for internal managers.

- The main features of a management information report are a follows.

  - **Title**
  - **To – who is the report for?**
  - **Date**
  - **Subject**
  - **Appendix**
  - **From**

- The three stages of data input are as follows.

  (1) **Origination of data**
  (2) **Transcription of data**
  (3) **Data input**

- Common document reading methods include the following.

  - **MICR**
  - **OMR**
  - **Scanners and OCR**
  - **Bar coding and EPOS**
  - **EFTPOS**

- Card reading devices include **magnetic stripe** cards and **smart** cards.

- Data storage methods include the following.

  - **Disks**
  - **Tape**
  - **CD-ROM**
  - **DVD-ROM**

  TRY QUESTIONS 1 and 2

- *Possible pitfalls*

  - **Confusing internal sources and external sources of management information**
  - **Confusing primary and secondary sources of management information**
  - **Not remembering the main features of a management information report**

# 1 Objective test questions: Management information and information technology

1 Which of the following would be included in the financial accounts, but may be excluded from the cost accounts?

    A    Direct material costs
    B    Depreciation of storeroom handling equipment
    C    Bank interest and charges
    D    Factory manager's salary

2 A management information system is

    A    A system which measures and corrects the performance of activities of subordinates in order to make sure that the objectives of an organisation are being met and the plans devised to attain them are being carried out

    B    A system by which managers ensure that information is obtained and used effectively and efficiently in the accomplishment of the organisation's objectives

    C    A system which involves selecting appropriate information so that management can prepare a long-term plan to attain the objectives of the organisation

    D    A collective term for the hardware and software used to drive a database system with the outputs, both to screen and print, being designed to provide easily assimilated information for management

3 Management accounts are prepared for the following individuals.

    ☐    Shareholders

    ☐    Inland Revenue

    ☐    Internal managers of an organisation

4 When visiting your local supermarket, the items that you have purchased are scanned by a device which acts as a cash register. This device is known as

    A    MICR
    B    OCR
    C    OMR
    D    EPOS

5 Printers which print a whole page at a time are known as:

    A    Bubble jet printers
    B    Daisy wheel printers
    C    Dot matrix printers
    D    Laser printers

6 Which one of the following is a common feature of cost accounting but not financial accounting?

    A    Control accounts
    B    Cost classification
    C    Marginal costing
    D    Periodic stocktaking

7    Consider the following incomplete statements relating to management information:

(i)     clear to the user
(ii)    detailed and completely accurate
(iii)   provided whatever the cost
(iv)    relevant for purpose

Which of the above are necessary features of useful management information?

A    (i) and (ii)
B    (i) and (iv)
C    (ii) and (iv)
D    (i), (ii) and (iii)

8    Features of computer systems include:

(i)     icons
(ii)    keyboard
(iii)   optical mark reading
(iv)    pull-down menu

Which of the above are features of graphical user interfaces?

A    (i) and (iv)
B    (ii) and (iii)
C    (i), (iii) and (iv)
D    (i), (ii) and (iv)

9    What is the purpose of management information?

A    Planning only
B    Planning and control only
C    Planning, control and decision-making only
D    Planning, control, decision-making and research and development

10   Which of the following are used for the capture and storage of management accounting data by computer?

(i)     Bar code
(ii)    Disk
(iii)   Printer
(iv)    Tape

A    (i) and (ii) only
B    (i), (ii) and (iv) only
C    (i), (iii) and (iv) only
D    (ii), (iii) and (iv) only

# 2 Compulsory written question: Management information and information technology
17 mins

(a)    The data used to prepare financial accounts and management accounts are the same. The differences between the financial accounts and the management accounts arise because the data is analysed differently.

*Required*

Identify the ways in which financial accounts and management accounts differ.    (8 marks)

(b)    Explain briefly the meaning and role of the following in the context of information technology.

(i)     MICR
(ii)    OMR
(iii)   EPOS
    (6 marks)

    **(14 marks)**

# Do you know? – Cost classification and cost behaviour

Check that you can fill in the blanks in the statements below before you attempt any questions. If in doubt, you should go back to your BPP Interactive Text and revise first.

- Costs can be divided into the following three elements:

    - ...............................................
    - ...............................................
    - ...............................................

- There are a number of different ways in which costs can be classified.

    - ............ and ............ (or overhead) costs

    - ............. costs (production costs, distribution and selling costs, administration

    - costs and financing costs)

    - Fixed and ............ costs

- A ............. is a unit of product or service which has costs attached to it. ............. are the essential 'building blocks' of a costing system, and they act as a collecting place for certain costs before they are analysed further. A ............ is similar to a cost centre but is accountable for both costs and revenues.

- Cost behaviour patterns demonstrate the way in which costs are affected by changes in the level of activity. Costs which are affected by the level of activity are ............. costs, and those which are not affected by the level of activity are .......... costs or ........... costs.

- Costs which are fixed in nature within certain levels of activity are .............. costs. Some costs are partly fixed and partly variable (and therefore only partly affected by activity level changes), such costs are known as............ costs (semi-variable/semi-fixed costs).

- The basic principle of cost behaviour is that as the level of activity rises, costs will usually ..........

- The effect of increasing activity levels on unit costs is as follows. (Tick as appropriate)

|  | Rises | Falls | Remains constant |
|---|---|---|---|
| Variable cost per unit |  |  |  |
| Fixed cost per unit |  |  |  |
| Total cost per unit |  |  |  |

- The fixed and variable elements of semi-variable costs can be determined by the ......................... method.

TRY QUESTIONS 3 to 6

- *Possible pitfalls*

    *Write down the mistakes you know you should avoid.*

# Did you know? – Cost classification and cost behaviour

**Could you fill in the blanks? The answers are in bold. Use this page for revision purposes as you approach the exam.**

- Costs can be divided into the following three elements:

  - **Materials**
  - **Labour**
  - **Expenses**

- There are a number of different ways in which costs can be classified.

  - **Direct** and **indirect** (or overhead) costs

  - **Functional** costs (production costs, distribution and selling costs, administration

  - costs and financing costs)

  - Fixed and **variable** costs

- A **cost unit** is a unit of product or service which has costs attached to it. **Cost centres** are the essential 'building blocks' of a costing system, and they act as a collecting place for certain costs before they are analysed further. A **profit centre** is similar to a cost centre but is accountable for both costs and revenues.

- Cost behaviour patterns demonstrate the way in which costs are affected by changes in the level of activity. Costs which are affected by the level of activity are **variable** costs, and those which are not affected by the level of activity are **fixed** costs or **period** costs.

- Costs which are fixed in nature within certain levels of activity are **step** costs. Some costs are partly fixed and partly variable (and therefore only partly affected by activity level changes), such costs are known as **mixed** costs (semi-variable/semi-fixed costs).

- The basic principle of cost behaviour is that as the level of activity rises, costs will usually **rise**.

- The effect of changing activity levels on unit costs is as follows. (Tick as appropriate)

| | Rises | Falls | Remains constant |
|---|---|---|---|
| Variable cost per unit | | | ✓ |
| Fixed cost per unit | | ✓ | |
| Total cost per unit | | ✓ | |

- The fixed and variable elements of semi-variable costs can be determined by the **high-low** method.

  TRY QUESTIONS 3 to 5

- *Possible pitfalls*

  - **Not being able to define key terms encountered in the Interactive Text**
  - **Being unable to distinguish between variable, fixed, step and mixed costs**

# 3 Objective test questions: Cost classification and cost behaviour

1   A cost unit is

    A   The cost per hour of operating a machine
    B   The cost per unit of electricity consumed
    C   A unit of product or service in relation to which costs are ascertained
    D   A measure of work output in a standard hour

2   A cost centre is

    A   A unit of product or service in relation to which costs are ascertained

    B   An amount of expenditure attributable to an activity

    C   A production or service location, function, activity or item of equipment for which costs are accumulated

    D   A centre for which an individual budget is drawn up

3   Prime cost is

    A   All costs incurred in manufacturing a product
    B   The total of direct costs
    C   The material cost of a product
    D   The cost of operating a department

4   Which of the following costs are part of the prime cost for a manufacturing company?

    A   Cost of transporting raw materials from the supplier's premises
    B   Wages of factory workers engaged in machine maintenance
    C   Depreciation of lorries used for deliveries to customers
    D   Cost of indirect production materials

5   Which of the following are indirect costs?

    (i)     The depreciation of maintenance equipment
    (ii)    The overtime premium incurred at the specific request of a customer
    (iii)   The hire of a tool for a specific job

    A   Item (i) only
    B   Items (i) and (ii) only
    C   Items (ii) and (iii) only
    D   All of them

6   A company has to pay a royalty of $1 per unit to the designer of a product which it manufactures and sells.

    The royalty charge would be classified in the company's accounts as:

    ☐   A direct expense

    ☐   A production overhead

    ☐   An administrative overhead

    ☐   A selling overhead

7 Which of the following items might be a suitable cost unit within the credit control department of a company?

☐ Telephone expense

☐ Cheque received and processed

☐ Customer account

8 Which one of the following would be classed as indirect labour?

☐ Machine operators in a company manufacturing washing machines

☐ A stores assistant in a factory store

☐ Plumbers in a construction company

☐ A committee in a firm of management consultants

9 The following is a graph of cost against level of activity

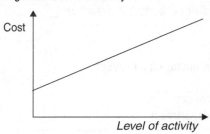

To which one of the following costs does the graph correspond?

A Electricity bills made up of a standing charge and a variable charge
B Bonus payment to employees when production reaches a certain level
C Sales commissions payable per unit up to a maximum amount of commission
D Bulk discounts on purchases, the discount being given on all units purchased

10 Which of the following graphs depicts supervisor salary costs, where one supervisor is needed for every five employees added to the staff.

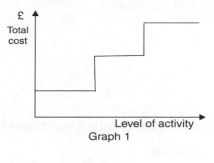

Graph 1

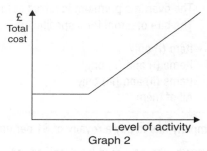

Graph 2

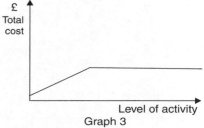

Graph 3

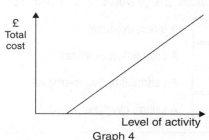

Graph 4

A       Graph 1
B       Graph 2
C       Graph 3
D       Graph 4

11      The following data have been collected for four cost types – W, X, Y, Z – at two activity levels:

| Cost type | Cost @ 100 units $ | Cost @ 140 units $ |
| --- | --- | --- |
| W | 8,000 | 10,560 |
| X | 5,000 | 5,000 |
| Y | 6,500 | 9,100 |
| Z | 6,700 | 8,580 |

Where V = variable, SV = semi-variable and F = fixed, assuming linearity, the four cost types W, X, Y and Z are respectively

| | W | X | Y | Z |
| --- | --- | --- | --- | --- |
| A | V | F | SV | V |
| B | SV | F | V | SV |
| C | V | F | V | V |
| D | SV | F | SV | SV |

12      A production worker is paid a salary of $650 per month, plus an extra 5 pence for each unit produced during the month. This labour cost is best described as:

A       A variable cost
B       A fixed cost
C       A step cost
D       A semi-variable cost

13      A hotel has recorded that the laundry costs incurred were $570 when 340 guests stayed for one night. They know that the fixed laundry cost is $400 per night. What is the variable laundry cost per guest-night (to the nearest penny)?

A       $0.50
B       $1.18
C       $1.68
D       Impossible to calculate from the information available

14      Which of these graphs represents a linear variable cost – when the vertical axis represents total cost incurred?

Graph 1

Graph 2

Graph 3

Graph 4

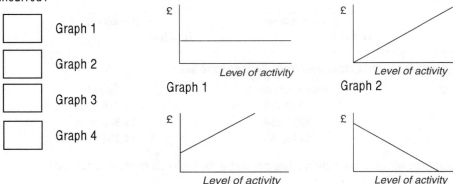

Graph 1

Graph 2

Graph 3

Graph 4

15    Which of these graphs represents a fixed cost – when the vertical axis represents total cost incurred?

Graph 1

Graph 2

Graph 3

Graph 4

---

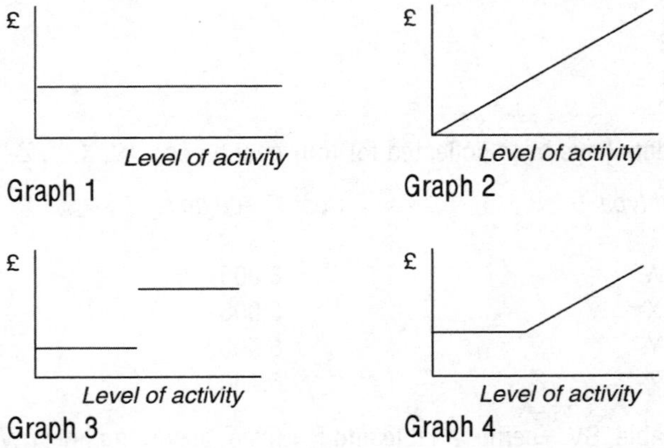

16    Which of these graphs represents a semi-variable or mixed cost – when the vertical axis represents total cost incurred (tick all that are correct)?

Graph 1

Graph 2

Graph 3

Graph 4

---

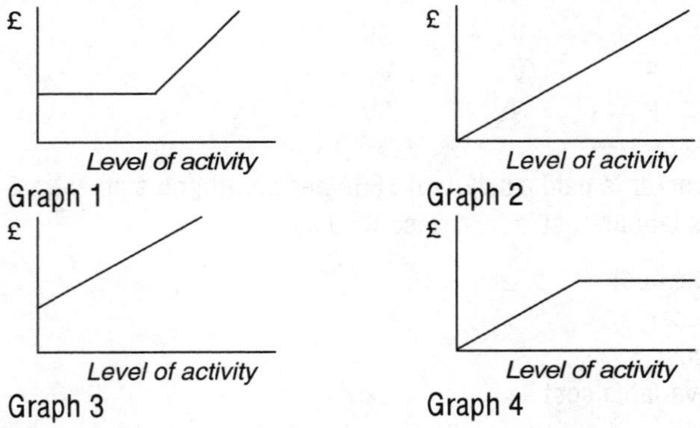

17    Which of these graphs represents a step fixed cost – when the vertical axis represents total cost incurred?

Graph 1

Graph 2

Graph 3

Graph 4

---

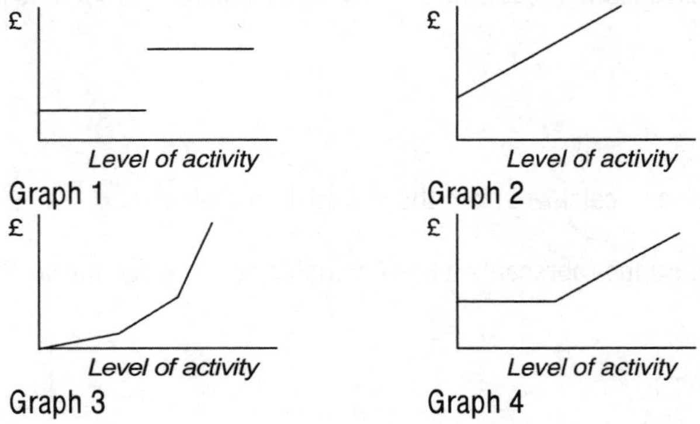

18    Total production cost costs and output over three periods have been:

| Period | Production costs | Output |
| --- | --- | --- |
| 1 | $230,485 | 12,610 units |
| 2 | $254,554 | 14,870 units |
| 3 | $248,755 | 14,350 units |

What are the estimated variable production costs per unit if the high-low method is applied?

A    $10.50
B    $10.65
C    $11.15
D    $15.50

19    The following table details the total cost Y, a step cost, for different production levels of Product X.

| Units of Product X | Cost Y ($'000) |
|---|---|
| 0 | 100 |
| 10 | 100 |
| 20 | 100 |
| 30 | 150 |
| 40 | 150 |

What could have been the cause for the increase in the cost?

A    Increased storage requirements
B    Pay increase for direct labour
C    Loss of material discounts
D    Temporarily employing extra delivery drivers on hourly pay rates

20

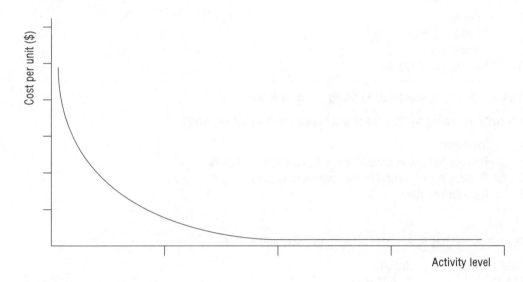

Which description best fits the cost curve?

A    Direct material cost per unit
B    Fixed production cost per unit
C    Direct labour cost per unit
D    Variable production cost per unit

21    A particular cost is fixed in total for a period.

What is the effect on cost per unit of a reduction in activity of 50%?

A    Cost per unit increases by 50%
B    Cost per unit reduces by 50%
C    Cost per unit increases by 100%
D    Cost per unit is unchanged

22    The table shows the total of Cost Y at different production levels of Product X:

| Units of Product X | Total cost Y ($'000) |
|---|---|
| 50 | 60 |
| 100 | 60 |
| 150 | 60 |
| 200 | 90 |
| 250 | 90 |

What could have been the cause of the increase in cost?

A     Increased fuel and maintenance costs for delivery vehicles
B     Increased storage requirements
C     Loss of discounts on raw materials
D     Pay increase for direct labour

23    The following classifications may be applied to costs:

(i)     direct
(ii)    fixed
(iii)   period
(iv)   production

Which of the above classifications could be applied to the cost of raw materials used by a company in the manufacture of its range of products?

A     (i) only
B     (i) and (iv) only
C     (ii) and (iii) only
D     (ii), (iii) and (iv) only

24    A particular cost is classified as being 'semi-variable'.

If activity increases by 10% what will happen to the cost per unit?

A     Increase
B     Reduce but not in proportion to the change in activity
C     Reduce in proportion to the change in activity
D     Remain constant

25    The following data is available relating to costs and activity:

| Total cost | Activity |
| --- | --- |
| $28,420 | 11,600 units |
| $29,294 | 12,440 units |
| $29,764 | 12,880 units |

Using the high-low method, what is the variable cost per unit (to the nearest penny)?

A     $0.95
B     $1.04
C     $1.05
D     $1.07

# 4 Compulsory written question: Cost classification and cost behaviour (12/01, amended)

**19 mins**

(a) Define the terms 'cost centre' and 'cost unit'. (3 marks)

(b) Avocet Limited has produced an overhead budget for next year based on two levels of activity, 10,000 units and 12,000 units. It needs to calculate budgeted figures based on an activity level of 15,000 units. The budgeted figures for activity levels of 10,000 and 12,000 are shown below.

**Avocet Limited – budgeted overheads for the year ending 31 December 20X2**

| Production (units) | Type of cost | 10,000 | 12,000 |
|---|---|---|---|
| | | $ | $ |
| Factory rent | Fixed | 5,000 | 5,000 |
| Machine depreciation | Fixed | 7,500 | 7,500 |
| Indirect labour | Variable | 20,000 | 24,000 |
| Indirect materials | Variable | 12,000 | 14,400 |
| Electricity | Semi-variable | 8,000 | 9,000 |
| Inventory insurance | Semi-variable | 9,500 | 11,000 |
| Total | | 62,000 | 70,900 |

*Required*

Calculate the budgeted cost for each of the six types of overheads at an activity level of 15,000 units giving consideration to the fact that some overheads are fixed costs, some are variable and some are semi-variable.

(13 marks)

**(16 marks)**

# 5 Compulsory written question: Information and cost function (12/05)

**14 mins**

(a)     Describe fully FOUR features of useful information.                                                                (6 marks)

(b)     A firm's cost function may be expressed as:

y = a + bx

Where:

        y is the total cost
        a is the total fixed cost
        b is the variable cost per unit
        x is the number of units of output

The total cost for output of 8,400 units in a period is $106,250 and the total period fixed cost is $41,990.

*Required*

Using the above information and formula, calculate:

(i)     The variable cost per unit;                                                                              (2 marks)
(ii)    The total cost for output of 8,660 units in a period;                                              (2 marks)
(iii)   The cost per unit for output of 8,500 units in a period.                                          (2 marks)
                                                                                                         **(12 marks)**

# Do you know? – Materials, labour and expenses

**Check that you can fill in the blanks in the statements below before you attempt any questions. If in doubt, you should go back to your BPP Interactive Text and revise first.**

- FIFO prices materials issues at the prices of the newest/oldest items in inventory, and values closing inventory at the value of the most recent/oldest items in inventory. (Delete as appropriate)

- LIFO prices materials issues at the prices of the newest/oldest items in inventory and values closing inventory at the value of the most recent/oldest items. (Delete as appropriate)

- ..............................is usually carried out annually, when all items of inventory are counted on a specific date. ....................................... involves counting and checking a number of inventory items on a regular basis so that each item is checked at least once a year.

- Inventory control levels are calculated in order to maintain inventory at the optimum level. The four critical control levels are as follows.

  - .......................... (maximum usage × maximum lead time)

  - .......................... (quantity of inventory to be reordered when inventory reaches reorder level)

  - .......................... (reorder level – (average usage × average lead time))

  - .......................... (reorder level + reorder quantity – (min usage × min lead time))

- The ............................... is the ordering quantity which minimises inventory costs (holding costs and ordering costs), and is calculated as follows.

  $$Q = \sqrt{\frac{2cd}{h}}$$ Where h = .........................................

  c = .........................................
  d = .........................................
  Q = .........................................

- Labour attendance time is recorded on an ................... or on a ................... Job time is recorded on the following documents:

  - ...................
  - ...................
  - ...................
  - ...................

- The labour cost of work done by pieceworkers is recorded on a ......................... (operation card). Piecework, time-saved bonus, discretionary bonus, group bonus scheme and profit-sharing are all different types of ...................... scheme.

- Expenditure which results in the acquisition of fixed assets is known as ............. expenditure, and is charged to the income statement via a .............................. over a period of time. Expenditure which is incurred for the purpose of the trade of the business or in order to maintain the existing earning capacity of fixed assets is known as ................. expenditure.

- In a job costing system................ expenses are recorded by coding them to the appropriate job or client. .............. expenses are initially allocated to appropriate cost centres and then spread out or ................... to the cost centres that have benefited from the expense.

  TRY QUESTIONS 7 TO 15

- *Possible pitfalls*

  *Write down the mistakes you know you should avoid.*

# Did you know? – Materials, labour and expenses

Could you fill in the blanks? The answers are in bold. Use this page for revision purposes as you approach the exam.

- FIFO prices materials issues at the prices of the ~~newest~~/oldest items in inventory, and values closing inventory at the value of the most recent/~~oldest~~ items in inventory.

- LIFO prices materials issues at the prices of the newest/~~oldest~~ items in inventory and values closing inventory at the value of the most ~~recent~~/oldest items.

- **Periodic inventory taking** is usually carried out annually, when all items of inventory are counted on a specific date. **Continuous inventory taking** involves counting and checking a number of inventory items on a regular basis so that each item is checked at least once a year.

- Inventory control levels are calculated in order to maintain inventory at the optimum level. The four critical control levels are as follows.
  - **Reorder level** (maximum usage × maximum lead time)
  - **Reorder quantity** (quantity of inventory to be reordered when inventory reaches reorder level)
  - **Minimum inventory level** (reorder level – (average usage × average lead time))
  - **Maximum inventory level** (reorder level + reorder quantity – (min usage × min lead time))

- The **economic order quantity** is the ordering quantity which minimises inventory costs (holding costs and ordering costs), and is calculated as follows.

$$Q = \sqrt{\frac{2cd}{h}}$$   Where   h  = **holding costs of one unit of inventory for one year**

   c  = **cost of ordering a consignment**
   d  = **annual demand**
   Q  = **economic order quantity**

- Labour attendance time is recorded on an **attendance card** or on a **clock card.** Job time is recorded on the following documents.
  - **Daily time sheets**
  - **Weekly time sheets**
  - **Job cards**
  - **Route cards**

- The labour cost of work done by pieceworkers is recorded on a **piecework ticket** (operation card). Piecework, time-saved bonus, discretionary bonus, group bonus scheme and profit-sharing are all different types of **incentive** scheme.

- Expenditure which results in the acquisition of fixed assets is known as **capital** expenditure, and is charged to the income statement via a **depreciation charge** over a period of time. Expenditure which is incurred for the purpose of the trade of the business or in order to maintain the existing earning capacity of fixed assets is known as **revenue** expenditure.

- In a job costing system **direct** expenses are recorded by coding them to the appropriate job or client. **Indirect** expenses are initially allocated to appropriate cost centres and then spread out or **apportioned** to the cost centres that have benefited from the expense.

  TRY QUESTIONS 7 to 15

- *Possible pitfalls*
  - **Confusing FIFO with LIFO**
  - **Not being able to reproduce the inventory control formulae**
  - **Confusing the meaning of 'c', 'd', and 'h' in the economic order quantity equation**

# 6 Objective test questions: Materials

1    In the context of calculating inventory control levels, what is meant by the term 'lead time'?

    A    The time between raising a purchase requisition and the relevant materials being received into inventory

    B    The time between materials inventory reaching the minimum level and a stockout occurring

    C    The time between placing an order for materials and the relevant materials being received into inventory

    D    The time between the current date and the date at which a stockout will occur at current levels of usage

2    In the context of inventory control, what is the reorder level?

    A    The amount of inventory to be ordered on each occasion that an order is placed with a supplier

    B    A inventory level which actual stockholdings should not exceed

    C    A inventory level below which stockholding should not fall

    D    A inventory level at which a replenishment order should be placed

3    A component has a safety inventory of 280, a reorder quantity of 1,200 and a rate of demand which varies between 100 and 400 per day. The average inventory of the component is approximately

    A    800
    B    880
    C    920
    D    1,480

4    Fall Limited wishes to minimise its inventory costs. Order costs are $10 per order and holding costs are $0.10 per unit per month. Fall Limited estimates annual demand to be 5,400 units.

    The economic order quantity is ☐ units.

## The following information applies to Question 5 and 6

The re-order level of Material M is 1,600 kg and the order quantity is 1,400 kg. Lead times and usage are as follows:

| Lead time: | minimum | 1 week |
| | average | 1.5 weeks |
| | maximum | 2 weeks |
| Usage: | average | 600 kg per week |
| | minimum | 700 kg per week |
| | maximum | 800 kg per week |

5    What is the maximum inventory control level of Material M?

    A    1,400 kg
    B    1,950 kg
    C    2,400 kg
    D    3,000 kg

6    What is the minimum inventory level of Material M?

    A    Nil
    B    350 kg
    C    550 kg
    D    1,000 kg

7   The following relate to the management of raw materials:

(i)    holding costs per unit of inventory would increase;
(ii)   the economic order quantity would decrease
(iii)  average inventory levels would increase
(iv)   total ordering costs would decrease

Which of the above would result from the introduction of buffer (safety) inventory?

A    (iii) only
B    (ii) and (iii) only
C    (ii), (iii) and (iv) only
D    (i), (ii), (iii) and (iv)

---

8   2,400 units of component C, valued at a price of $6 each, were in inventory on 1 March. The following receipts and issues were recorded during March.

3 March      Received     4,000 units @ $6.20 per unit
12 March     Received     2,000 units @ $6.86 per unit
23 March     Issued       5,100 units

Using the weighted average price method of inventory valuation, the total value of the components

remaining in inventory on 23 March was $ ☐

---

9   In a period of rising prices, which one of the following will be true with a first in first out (FIFO) system of pricing inventory issues?

☐   Product costs are overstated and profits understated

☐   Product costs are overstated and profits overstated

☐   Product costs are understated and profits understated

☐   Product costs are understated and profits overstated

---

10   2,400 units of component C, valued at a price of $6 each, were in inventory on 1 March. The following receipts and issues were recorded during March.

3 March      Received     4,000 units @ $6.20 per unit
12 March     Received     2,000 units @ $6.86 per unit
23 March     Issued       5,100 units

Using the FIFO method of inventory valuation, the total value of the components issued on 23 March

was $ ☐

---

11   XYZ Ltd had an opening inventory value of $880 (275 units valued at $3.20 each) on 1 April.

The following receipts and issues were recorded during April.

8 April      Receipts     600 units     $3.00 per unit
15 April     Receipts     400 units     $3.40 per unit
30 April     Issues       900 units

Using the FIFO method, the total value of the issues on 30 April is $ ☐

12    The following information is available for part LP42.

| Minimum usage per day | 300 units |
|---|---|
| Average usage per day | 400 units |
| Maximum usage per day | 600 units |
| Lead time for replenishment | 3-4 days |
| Reorder quantity | 1,900 units |

The maximum level of inventory is ☐ units

---

13    A company uses the first-in, first-out (FIFO) method to price issues of raw material to production and to value its closing inventory.

Which of the following statements best describes the first-in, first-out method?

A      The last materials received will be the first issued to production
B      The first materials issued will be priced at the cost of the most recently received materials
C      The last materials issued will be those that were most recently received
D      The first materials issued will be priced at the cost of the earliest goods still in inventory

---

14    A company uses two very similar types of fixing bracket, Z99 and Z100. The brackets are purchased from an outside supplier. When the company undertakes a inventory check it finds some differences as show below.

| Product | Inventory record | Inventory count |
|---|---|---|
| Z99 | 100 | 79 |
| Z100 | 80 | 101 |

What is the most likely reason for the differences between the inventory record and the inventory count for each bracket?

A      Production was higher than expected
B      Some brackets were damaged during production
C      A customer asked the company to supply some extra brackets of both types
D      Some brackets were put in the incorrect storage racks

---

15    If FIFO rather than LIFO was used when material prices are falling, which of the following combinations would be correct?

| | Production costs | Profits |
|---|---|---|
| A | will be lower | will be higher |
| B | will be higher | will be lower |
| C | will be lower | will be lower |
| D | will be higher | will be higher |

---

16    Which of the following costs would be needed in order to calculate the economic order quantity?

1      The cost of storing materials
2      The cost of interest incurred in financing materials
3      The cost of ordering materials
4      The cost of insuring materials

A      Items 1 and 2 only
B      Items 3 and 4 only
C      Items 1, 3 and 4 only
D      Items 1, 2, 3 and 4

# The following information relates to questions 17 and 18

Shown below are the inventory movements for Material X for the year ended 30 November 20X2.

| Date | Detail | Units | Unit price $ | Value $ |
|---|---|---|---|---|
| 01 Jan 20X2 | Opening inventory | 100 | 10.00 | 1,000 |
| 28 Feb 20X2 | Receipt | 600 | 10.50 | 6,300 |
| 03 May 20X2 | Issue | 430 | | |
| 06 Jul 20X2 | Receipt | 350 | 11.00 | 3,850 |
| 17 Sep 20X2 | Issue | 550 | | |
| 28 Oct 20X2 | Receipt | 600 | 11.40 | 6,840 |
| 11 Nov 20X2 | Issue | 510 | | |

17    The total value of the three issues shown above if the company had used the last-in, first-out (LIFO) basis is

$ [          ]

18    The total value of the three issues shown above if the company had used the first-in, first-out (FIFO) basis is

$ [          ]

19    If materials already issued but not required for one job can be used for another job in progress, there is no point in returning the materials to the warehouse, so instead a ........................................ note can be raised. This prevents one job being charged with too many materials and another with too little.

20    The following are statements relating to raw material pricing in a situation where raw material prices are rising consistently.

1    Production costs will be lower using weighted average pricing rather than LIFO
2    Profit will be higher using LIFO pricing rather than FIFO
3    Inventory values will be lower using FIFO pricing rather than weighted average

Are the statements true or false?

A    Statement 1 is true but Statements 2 and 3 are false
B    Statements 1 and 2 are true but Statement 3 is false
C    Statements 1 and 3 are true but Statement 2 is false
D    Statements 2 and 3 are true but Statement 1 is false

# The following information relates to questions 21 and 22

| Day | Transaction | Units | Unit price $ | Value $ |
|---|---|---|---|---|
| 1 | Balance b/f | 100 | 5.00 | 500 |
| 3 | Issue | 40 | | |
| 4 | Receipt | 50 | 5.50 | 275 |
| 6 | Receipt | 50 | 6.00 | 300 |
| 7 | Issue | 70 | | |

21    If the first-in, first-out method of pricing is used what is the value of the issue on Day 7?

A    $350
B    $355
C    $395
D    $420

22    If the last-in, first-out method is used what is the value of the issue on Day 7?

A    $350
B    $395
C    $410
D    $420

23    A company orders a particular raw material in order quantities of 250 units. No safety inventory is held, the inventory holding cost is $3 per unit per annum and the annual demand is 2,500 units.

What is the total annual inventory holding cost of the material?

A    $375
B    $750
C    $3,750
D    $7,500

24    Which of the following is NOT relevant to the calculation of the economic order quantity of a raw material?

A    Ordering cost
B    Purchase price
C    Inventory holding cost
D    Usage

25    The order quantity of a raw material is 2,000 kg. Safety inventory of 1,200 kg is held. The inventory holding cost of the raw material is $1.20 per kg per annum.

What is the total annual inventory holding cost of the raw material?

A    $1,200
B    $1,920
C    $2,640
D    $3,840

# 7 Compulsory written question: Materials I (6/04)    15 mins

A company uses Material M in the manufacture of its products. The order quantity of the material is 1,000 kg. Average usage is 400 kg per week and a safety inventory of 500 kg is kept. Lead time between order and receipt is two weeks.

Receipts and issues of Material M over a three week period were:

|         |       |            | Kg    | Total cost ($) |
|---------|-------|------------|-------|----------------|
| Week 1: | Day 1 | Balance b/f | 900   | 10,800         |
|         | Day 3 | Issue      | 400   |                |
|         | Day 5 | Receipt    | 1,000 | 12,600         |
| Week 2: | Day 2 | Issue      | 260   |                |
|         | Day 4 | Issue      | 170   |                |
| Week 3: | Day 3 | Issue      | 370   |                |

*Required*

Calculate in relation to Material M the:

(i)     re-order level;                                                                                     (3 marks)

(ii)    total cost of the four issues in the three week period if the weighted average method is applied when each issue occurs;                                                                              (5 marks)

(iii)   cost of the inventory remaining at the end of the three week period if the Last-in First-out (LIFO) method is applied.                                                                                    (4 marks)
                                                                                                      **(12 marks)**

# 8 Compulsory written question: Materials II (6/05)    18 mins

Many manufacturing organisations hold raw material inventory.

*Required*

(a)    List three examples of holding costs.                                                    (3 marks)
(b)    List two examples of stockout costs.                                                     (2 marks)

A manufacturing organisation uses 20,000 kilograms (kg) of a raw material evenly over a period. The material is purchased for £2.50 per kg, the cost of placing an order with the supplier is £60 and the cost of holding one kg of the material in inventory for the period is 15% of the purchase price.

*Required*

(c)    Calculate the economic order quantity (EOQ) of the raw material (to the nearest kg).       (5 marks)

(d)    Calculate the total holding costs of the raw material in the period if the order quantity is 3,000 kg and buffer inventory is 1,000 kg.                                                                   (5 marks)
                                                                                          **(15 marks)**

# 9 Compulsory written question: Materials III (6/07)    22 mins

(a)    Material X is used by a company in the manufacture of one of its products, Product Z. Demand for Product Z for the next year is forecast to be 26,000 units.

Each finished unit of Product Z contains 0·72 kilograms of Material X. There is a preparation loss of 10% of material used. It is not planned to change the stock-holding of Product Z in the year ahead but a reduction of 1,000 kilograms in the stock of Material X is planned.

*Required*

Calculate the quantity of Material X that needs to be purchased in the year ahead.            (4marks)

(b)    Material Y is also used in the manufacture of Product Z and in several other products. The total annual requirement for Material Y is 120,000 litres, used evenly over each year.

The costs of ordering stock and holding stock are as follows:

Ordering                            $45 per order
Holding                             $0.30 per litre per annum

A safety inventory of 2,500 litres of Material Y is held and the average lead time (the interval between placing an order for materials and having them delivered) is 1·5 weeks.

*Required*

Calculate for Material Y the:

(i)     Economic order quantity, using the formula $\sqrt{[(2CoD) \div Ch]}$;                        (4 marks)
(ii)    Reorder level (assume 1 year = 50 weeks);                                             (4 marks)
(iii)   Total annual cost of ordering inventory;                                              (3 marks)
(iv)    Total annual cost of holding inventory.                                               (3 marks)

                                                                                          **(18 marks)**

# 10 Objective test questions: Labour

1 Gross wages incurred in department 1 in June were $54,000. The wages analysis shows the following summary breakdown of the gross pay.

| | Paid to direct labour $ | Paid to indirect labour $ |
|---|---|---|
| Ordinary time | 25,185 | 11,900 |
| Overtime: basic pay | 5,440 | 3,500 |
| Premium | 1,360 | 875 |
| Shift allowance | 2,700 | 1,360 |
| Sick pay | 1,380 | 300 |
| | 36,065 | 17,935 |

What is the direct wages cost for department 1 in June?

- A $25,185
- B $30,625
- C $34,685
- D $36,065

2 Which of the following would be classed as indirect labour?

- A A coach driver in a transport company
- B Machine operators in a milk bottling plant
- C A maintenance assistant in a factory maintenance department
- D Plumbers in a construction company

3 Which of the following is not a cost of labour turnover?

- A The cost of recruiting new employees to replace those leaving
- B The cost of increased wastage due to lack of expertise among new staff
- C The contribution forgone on the output lost due to slower working
- D The salary paid to the personnel manager

4 Which of the following statements is/are true about group bonus schemes?

- (i) Group bonus schemes are appropriate when increased output depends on a number of people all making extra effort
- (ii) With a group bonus scheme, it is easier to reward each individual's performance
- (iii) Non-production employees can be rewarded as part of a group incentive scheme

- A (i) only
- B (i) and (ii) only
- C (i) and (iii) only
- D all of them

5 Guilt Trips Ltd budgets to make 50,000 units of output (in eight hours each) during a budget period of 400,000 hours.

Actual output during the period was 54,000 units which took 480,000 hours to make.

The efficiency and capacity ratios are:

| | Efficiency ratio | Capacity ratio |
|---|---|---|
| A | 90% | 83% |
| B | 90% | 120% |
| C | 111% | 83% |
| D | 111% | 120% |

6    A manufacturing firm has temporary production problems and overtime is being worked.

The amount of overtime premium contained in direct wages would normally be classed as which one of the following:

☐    Direct expenses

☐    Production overheads

☐    Direct labour costs

☐    Administrative overheads

---

7    An employee is paid $8 per piecework hour produced. In a 40 hour week he produces the following output.

| | Piecework time allowed per unit |
|---|---|
| 6 units of Product X | 2 hours |
| 10 units of Product Z | 4 hours |

The employee's pay for the week is (to 2 decimal places) $ ☐

---

8    A company operates a piecework scheme to pay its staff. The staff receive $0.20 for each unit produced. However, the company guarantees that every member of staff will receive at least $15 per day.

Shown below is the number of units produced by Operator A during a recent week.

| Day | Monday | Tuesday | Wednesday | Thursday | Friday |
|---|---|---|---|---|---|
| Units produced | 90 | 70 | 75 | 60 | 90 |

What are Operator A's earnings for the week?

A    $75
B    $77
C    $81
D    $152

---

9    Which of the following statements is correct?

A    Idle time cannot be controlled because it is always due to external factors
B    Idle time is always controllable because it is due to internal factors
C    Idle time is always due to inefficient production staff
D    Idle time is not always the fault of production staff

---

10    A company makes a product for which the standard labour time is 2 hours per unit. The budgeted production hours for a given week were 820. During the week the production staff were able to produce 380 units of product. Staff worked and were paid for 800 hours. During the week 20 production hours were lost due to a shortage of material.

The efficiency ratio was therefore:

A    95.00%
B    95.12%
C    97.44%
D    97.50%

---

11    A company has calculated that its activity ratio is 103.5% and that its efficiency ratio is 90%.

Therefore its capacity ratio will be:

A    86.96%
B    93.15%
C    115.00 %
D    193.50%

12    A company employs 20 direct production operatives and 10 indirect staff in its manufacturing department. The normal operating hours for all employees is 38 hours per week and all staff are paid $5 per hour. Overtime hours are paid at the basic rate plus 50%.

      During a particular week all employees worked for 44 hours. What amount would be charged to production overhead?

      A    $2,650
      B    $2,350
      C    $450
      D    $300

13    A company has planned to produce 5,200 units of Product X next month and has allowed a total standard time for this level of production of 325 hours. The actual output for the month was 5,616 units, which was actually achieved in 357 hours.

      What was the efficiency ratio (to the nearest two places of decimals)?

      A    91.04%
      B    98.32%
      C    101.71%
      D    109.85%

14    Employee A works a normal working week of 36 hours at a basic rate of $3.60 per hour. A premium of 50% of the basic hourly rate is paid for all hours worked in excess of 36 hours per week. Employee A worked for a total of 42 hours last week. The reasons for the overtime were:

      –    machine breakdown                                         4 hours
      –    completion of a special job at the request of a customer   2 hours

      How much of Employee A's earnings for the last week should be treated as direct wages?

      A    $129.60
      B    $140.40
      C    $151.20
      D    $162.00

15    A company pays direct operatives a basic wage of $8.50 per hour plus a productivity bonus. The bonus is calculated as:

      [(time allowed – time taken) × (basic rate per hour ÷ 3)]

      The time allowed is 2.4 minutes per unit of output. An operative produced 1,065 units in a 37.5 hour week.

      What were the total earnings of the operative in the week?

      A    $318.75
      B    $333.20
      C    $340.40
      D    $362.10

16    The following items are some of the costs incurred by a company:

      (i)     training of direct operatives
      (ii)    wages of distribution staff
      (iii)   normal idle time in the factory
      (iv)    productive time of direct operatives
      (v)     sales personnel salaries

      Which of the above items will usually be treated as production overhead costs?

      A    (i) and (ii) only
      B    (i) and (iii) only
      C    (i), (iii) and (iv) only
      D    (ii), (iv) and (v) only

17  A differential piecework scheme has a basic rate of $0.50 per unit. Output in addition to 500 units is paid at higher rates. The premiums over and above the basic rate, which apply only to additional units over the previous threshold, are:

| Output (units) | Premium (per unit) |
|---|---|
| 501–600 | $0.05 |
| above 600 | $0.10 |

What is the total amount paid if output is 620 units?

A  $317
B  $318
C  $322
D  $372

---

18  Labour costs may include:

(i)    overtime hours of direct operatives at basic rate
(ii)   overtime premiums of factory employees
(iii)  productive time of direct operatives
(iv)   training of direct operatives

Which of the above items will usually be treated as a direct cost?

A  (i) and (ii)
B  (i) and (iii)
C  (ii) and (iv)
D  (i), (iii) and (iv)

---

# 11 Compulsory written question: Labour I (12/01, amended)

### 13 mins

Amalgamated Limited is a manufacturer of a product used in the motor industry. The product is assembled from various parts and the production operatives are paid on a piecework basis. The piecework scheme to be applied to all good production in a week is as follows.

| 0 – 100 units: | $0.40 per unit |
|---|---|
| 101 – 200 units: | $0.48 per unit |
| 201 – 300 units: | $0.56 per unit |
| Over 300 units: | $0.64 per unit |

Rejected production does not qualify for payment.

It should also be noted that only additional units qualify for the higher rates.

The following output was achieved by three operatives during the week ending 31 October 20X1.

| Operative | A | B | C |
|---|---|---|---|
| Output (including rejects) | 520 units | 600 units | 480 units |
| Rejects | 19 units | 62 units | 10 units |

Required

(a)  Calculate separately the earnings of each of operatives A, B and C for the week ending 31 October 20X1.

(9 marks)

(b)  What is one advantage to an employer if they use a piecework scheme?

(1 mark)

(c)  What is one disadvantage to an employer if they use a piecework scheme?

(1 mark)

**(11 marks)**

# 12 Compulsory written question: Labour II (12/04)    20 mins

(a)    Costs relating to labour turnover may be classified as:

    (i)     replacement costs
    (ii)    preventative costs

*Required*

Give TWO examples of costs within EACH of the above classifications and state a formula used to calculate the rate of labour turnover.    (6 marks)

(b)    A company manufactures a single product at the rate of 25 units per direct labour hour. 660 direct labour hours were budgeted to be worked in a period during which 640 hours were actually worked and 16,390 units were manufactured.

*Required*

Calculate the following ratios for the period:

    (i)     efficiency
    (ii)    capacity
    (iii)   production volume    (10 marks)
    **(16 marks)**

# 13 Compulsory written question: Labour III (12/06)    18 mins

A company manufactures a single product. Currently, the company employs a team of six direct operatives who produce a total of 2,500 units of the product in a 40-hour week. The hourly rate of pay for all operatives is $8.00.

In an effort to improve productivity, and thus to increase output in the normal 40-hour week, an incentive scheme has been suggested. The scheme, which the six operatives have agreed to trial over a 4-week period, provides for differential piecework payments in addition to a reduced basic rate per hour. Details of the scheme are:

Basic hourly rate    $4.00 per hour

Differential piecework rates:

First 2,500 units of output in a week    $0.375 per unit
Output 2,501 to 3,000 units in a week    $0.45 per unit on additional units over 2,500
Output over 3,000 units in a week  $0.60 per unit on additional units over 3,000

In the first week of the trial, total output was 3,080 units in the 40 hours worked.

*Required*

(a)    For the existing time rate payment system, calculate:

    (i)     The labour cost per unit, based on the current weekly output of 2,500 units.    (2 marks)

    (ii)    The % change in the labour cost per unit if weekly output in the 40 hours worked could be increased to 2,750 units.    (2 marks)

(b)    For the incentive scheme, calculate:

    (i)     The labour cost per unit, based on the results of the first week of the trial.    (6 marks)

    (ii)    The level of output in a 40 hour week at which total labour cost would be the same as under the existing time rate payment system.    (5 marks)
    **(15 marks)**

# 14 Objective test questions: Expenses

1 Which of the following are examples of capital expenditure?

   (i)     Purchase of a building
   (ii)    Extension to a building
   (iii)   Fixing broken windows
   (iv)    Replacing missing roof tiles

   A    (i) and (ii)
   B    (i) and (iii)
   C    (i) and (iv)
   D    (i), (ii), (iii) and (iv)

2 During 20X0, Joe Ltd bought new machinery for $40,000 and built an extension on its head office at a cost of $20,000. Machinery was maintained at a cost of $4,000 during the year and the head office was repainted at a cost of $5,000.

   Joe Ltd's capital expenditure in 20X0 is

   A    $40,000
   B    $60,000
   C    $64,000
   D    $69,000

3 New England plc purchases an asset for $20,000 which is depreciated over four years using the straight line method. Assume a zero residual value after four years.

   What is the net book value of the asset after three years?

   A    $5,000
   B    $10,000
   C    $15,000
   D    $20,000

4 New England plc purchases another asset for $60,000 which is depreciated at a rate of 20% per annum on the reducing balance. What is the net book value of the asset after four years?

   A    $12,000
   B    $19,661
   C    $24,576
   D    $30,720

5 The process by which whole cost items are charged direct to a cost unit or a cost centre is known as

   A    Allocation
   B    Obsolescence
   C    Depreciation
   D    Expenditure

6 Capital expenditure is charged to the profit and loss account (income statement) at the end of an accounting period.

   ☐  True
   ☐  False

7    Which of the following are items of revenue expenditure?

☐    Administration expenses

☐    Plant maintenance costs

☐    Purchase of a new factory

☐    Purchase of managing director's second-hand car

---

8    When an asset loses value because it has been superseded due to the development of a technically superior asset, this is known as ☐

---

9    A machine costs $200,000 and it is estimated that it will be sold as scrap for $10,000 at the end of its useful life. Such machines have been seen to run for approximately 40,000 hours before they wear out.

If the machine was used for 3,000 hours in year 1, the depreciation charge for the year (to the nearest $) is

$ ☐

---

10   The following cost centres are used in Pelion Ltd's cost accounting records.

| Code | Description |
|------|-------------|
| 400  | Department X |
| 410  | Department Y |
| 880  | Rent |

The rent of the shared premises is to be split evenly between department X and department Y. Complete the following table of the weekly costs showing how the costs will **initially** be coded.

|                                              | $     | Code |
|----------------------------------------------|-------|------|
| Supervisors' wages Department X              | 2,000 | ☐    |
| Supervisors' wages Department Y              | 3,000 | ☐    |
| Rent of premises shared by Departments X and Y | 1,500 | ☐  |

---

11   A new machine has an estimated five year life and a nil disposal value at the end of its life. Depreciation methods being considered are:

(i)   Reducing balance at 25% per annum
(ii)  Straight line

Which of the following statements is correct?

A    Depreciation in each year would be greater using the reducing balance method

B    Depreciation in each year would be greater using the straight-line method

C    Depreciation would be greater in year 1 but less in year 5 if the reducing balance method, rather than the straight line method, was used

D    Depreciation would be greater in year 1 but less in year 5 if the straight line method, rather than the reducing balance method, was used

12    Which chart shows the unit cost behaviour of straight-line depreciation costs?

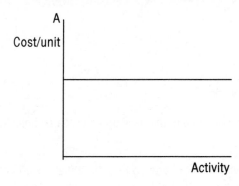

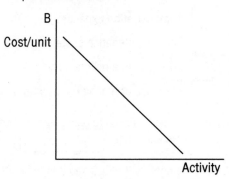

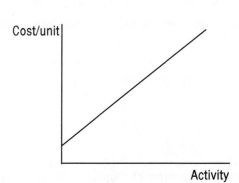

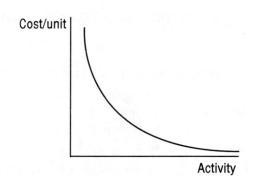

A    Chart A
B    Chart B
C    Chart C
D    Chart D

---

13    A fixed asset has an expected life of 10 years with a nil residual value. The asset is due to be depreciated using the straight-line method.

Which of the following statements is correct regarding the use of the reducing balance method instead?

A    Depreciation will be higher in each year using 20% reducing balance
B    Depreciation will be higher in each of years 1, 2 and 3 using 25% reducing balance
C    Depreciation will be lower in each year using 15% reducing balance
D    Depreciation will be lower in year 2 using 18% reducing balance

---

14    The following statements relate to depreciation:

1    Using the reducing balance method, product unit costs decline from year to year if output stays the same.

2    Using the straight-line method, product unit costs decline as output increases.

Are the statements TRUE or FALSE?

         Statement 1      Statement 2
A        True             True
B        False            False
C        True             False
D        False            True

---

# Do you know? – Absorption costing and marginal costing

**Check that you can fill in the blanks in the statements below before you attempt any questions. If in doubt, you should go back to your BPP Interactive Text and revise first.**

- Costs incurred during production or while providing a service that cannot be traced directly and in full to the product or service are known as ........................, and the four main types of ................. are production, administration, .................... and distribution.

- The three stages of calculating the costs of overheads to be charged to manufactured output are as follows: ............................. ; ............................. ; and .............................

- The procedure whereby indirect costs (overheads) are spread fairly between cost centres is known as ............................... Service cost centres may be apportioned to production cost centres by the ........................... method or by the .................... method of reapportionment.

- The three main types of overhead absorption rate are as follows.

    - ............................................................ (calculated by dividing budgeted overhead by budgeted level of activity)

    - ............................................................ (or blanket overhead absorption rate, which is used throughout a factory for all jobs and units of output irrespective of the department in which they were produced)

    - ............................................................ (a fairer rate which is representative of the costs of the resources put into making products)

- Under and over absorption of overhead occurs when actual overhead incurred is different to absorbed overhead. ...............-absorbed overhead occurs when actual overhead is less than absorbed overhead, and therefore too ................. overhead has been charged to production. .........-absorbed overhead occurs when actual overhead is greater than absorbed overhead, and therefore too ........... overhead has been charged to production. Under or over absorption of overheads occurs because the predetermined overhead absorption rates are based on forecasts (estimates).

- Marginal cost is the ..................... cost of one unit of product or service. ................... is the difference between the sales value and the marginal cost of one unit of product or service.

- In marginal costing, fixed production costs are treated as ............... costs and are written off as they are incurred. In absorption costing fixed production costs are ........................ the cost of units and are carried forward in inventory to be charged against the sales revenue for the next period. Inventory values using absorption costing are therefore ............... than those calculated using marginal costing.

- Marginal costing and absorption costing will report different profit figures if there is any change in the volume of inventory during the period. If closing inventory is greater than opening inventory, absorption costing will report a ............. profit than marginal costing. If opening inventory is greater than closing inventory (ie inventory levels ................), then absorption costing will report a ............... profit than marginal costing.

TRY QUESTIONS 16 to 23

- *Possible pitfalls*

    *Write down the mistakes you know you should avoid.*

# Did you know? – Absorption costing and marginal costing

Could you fill in the blanks? The answers are in bold. Use this page for revision purposes as you approach the exam.

- Costs incurred during production or while providing a service that cannot be traced directly and in full to the product or service are known as **overheads**, and the four main types of **overhead** are production, administration, **selling** and distribution.

- The three stages of calculating the costs of overheads to be charged to manufactured output are as follows: **allocation;** apportionment; and **absorption.**

- The procedure whereby indirect costs (overheads) are spread fairly between cost centres is known as **apportionment**. Service cost centres may be apportioned to production cost centres by the **direct** method or by the **step down** method of reapportionment.

- The three main types of overhead absorption rate are as follows.

    – **Predetermined overhead absorption rate** (calculated by dividing budgeted overhead by budgeted level of activity)

    – **Single factory-wide absorption rate** (or blanket overhead absorption rate, which is used throughout a factory for all jobs and units of output irrespective of the department in which they were produced)

    – **Separate departmental overhead absorption rate** (a fairer rate which is representative of the costs of the resources put into making products)

- Under and over absorption of overhead occurs when actual overhead incurred is different to absorbed overhead. **Over**-absorbed overhead occurs when actual overhead is less than absorbed overhead, and therefore too **much** overhead has been charged to production. **Under**-absorbed overhead occurs when actual overhead is greater than absorbed overhead, and therefore too **little** overhead has been charged to production. Under or overabsorption of overheads occurs because the predetermined overhead absorption rates are based on forecasts (estimates).

- Marginal cost is the **variable** cost of one unit of product or service. **Contribution** is the difference between the sales value and the marginal cost of one unit of product or service.

- In marginal costing, fixed production costs are treated as **period** costs and are written off as they are incurred. In absorption costing fixed production costs are **absorbed into** the cost of units and are carried forward in inventory to be charged against the sales revenue for the next period. Inventory values using absorption costing are therefore **greater** than those calculated using marginal costing.

- Marginal costing and absorption costing will report different profit figures if there is any change in the volume of inventory during the period. If closing inventory is greater than opening inventory, absorption costing will report a **higher** profit than marginal costing. If opening inventory is greater than closing inventory (ie inventory levels **decrease**), then absorption costing will report a **lower** profit than marginal costing.

    TRY QUESTIONS 16 to 23

- *Possible pitfalls*

    – **Including an element of fixed overheads in the inventory valuation in marginal costing statements**

    – **Selecting inappropriate bases when calculating overhead absorption rates**

    – **Confusing under recovery and over recovery of overheads**

# 15 Objective test questions: Overheads and absorption costing

1    A method of overhead cost data involves spreading common costs over cost centres on the basis of benefit received. This is known as

    A      Overhead absorption
    B      Overhead apportionment
    C      Overhead allocation
    D      Overhead analysis

2    The following extract of information is available concerning the four cost centres of EG Ltd.

|  | Production cost centres | | | Service cost centre |
|---|---|---|---|---|
|  | *Machinery* | *Finishing* | *Packing* | *Canteen* |
| Number of direct employees | 7 | 6 | 2 | - |
| Number of indirect employees | 3 | 2 | 1 | 4 |
| Overhead allocated and apportioned | $28,500 | $18,300 | $8,960 | $8,400 |

The overhead cost of the canteen is to be re-apportioned to the production cost centres on the basis of the number of employees in each production cost centre. After the re-apportionment, the total overhead cost of the packing department, to the nearest $, will be

    A      $1,200
    B      $9,968
    C      $10,080
    D      $10,160

3    Which of the following bases of apportionment would be **most** appropriate for apportioning heating costs to production cost centres?

    A      Floor space occupied (square metres)
    B      Volume of space occupied (cubic metres)
    C      Number of employees
    D      Labour hours worked

4    Over-absorbed overheads occur when

    A      Absorbed overheads exceed actual overheads
    B      Absorbed overheads exceed budgeted overheads
    C      Actual overheads exceed budgeted overheads
    D      Budgeted overheads exceed absorbed overheads

5    The production overhead of department D is absorbed using a machine hour rate. Budgeted production overheads for the department were $280,000 and the actual machine hours were 70,000. Production overheads were under absorbed by $9,400.

If actual production overheads were $295,000 what was the overhead absorption rate per machine hour (to the nearest cent)?

    A      $4.00
    B      $4.08
    C      $4.21
    D      $4.35

6    Overhead apportionment is used to (tick the correct answer):

   ☐ Charge whole items of costs to cost centres

   ☐ Charge cost units with an appropriate share of overheads

   ☐ Charge whole items of costs to cost units

   ☐ Spread common costs over cost centres

   ☐ Ensure budgeted overheads are not exceeded

---

7    A vehicle repair company recovers overheads on the basis of labour hours. Budgeted overheads were $615,000 and actual labour hours were 48,225. Overheads were over absorbed by $35,000.

   If actual overheads were $640,150, the budgeted overhead absorption rate per hour was $ ☐

---

8    Actual overheads      $496,980
     Actual machine hours  16,566
     Budgeted overheads    $475,200

   Based on the data above, and assuming that the budgeted overhead absorption rate was $32 per hour, the

   number of machine hours (to the nearest hour) budgeted to be worked were ☐ hours.

---

9    An overhead absorption rate is used to (tick the correct answer):

   ☐ Share out common costs over benefiting cost centres

   ☐ Find the total overheads for a cost centre

   ☐ Charge overheads to products

   ☐ Control overheads

---

10   A company has two production departments, Cutting and Finishing. The budgeted overheads and operating hours for the two departments for next year are:

   Cutting      $210,000      60,000 machine hours      4,000 labour hours
   Finishing    $200,000       5,000 machine hours     14,000 labour hours

   From the information given the pre-determined overhead absorption rates for the departments should

   A    Both be based on machine hours
   B    Both be based on labour hours
   C    Be based on machine hours for the cutting department and labour hours for the finishing department
   D    Be based on labour hours for the cutting department and machine hours for the finishing department

---

11   A company absorbs production overheads using a machine hour basis. In order to calculate any over or under absorbed overheads which of the following would be needed, in addition to the pre-determined machine hour rate?

   A    Budgeted overheads and actual overheads incurred
   B    Budgeted overheads and actual hours worked
   C    Actual overheads incurred and budgeted hours
   D    Actual overheads incurred and actual hours worked

---

12    Which of the following are acceptable bases for absorbing production overheads?

1    direct labour hours
2    machine hours
3    as a percentage of prime cost
4    per unit

A    Method 1 and 2 only
B    Method 3 and 4 only
C    Method 1, 2, 3 and 4
D    Method 1, 2 or 3 only

## The following information relates to questions 13 and 14

Knight Ltd has two service departments serving two production departments. Overhead costs apportioned to each department are as follows.

| Production 1 | Production 2 | Service 1 | Service 2 |
|---|---|---|---|
| $ | $ | $ | $ |
| 45,000 | 60,000 | 9,000 | 8,000 |

Service department 1 is expected to work a total of 40,000 hours for the other departments, divided as follows.

|  | Hours |
|---|---|
| Production 1 | 20,000 |
| Production 2 | 10,000 |
| Service 2 | 10,000 |

Service 2 is expected to work a total of 10,000 hours for the other departments, divided as follows.

|  | Hours |
|---|---|
| Production 1 | 4,000 |
| Production 2 | 4,000 |
| Service 1 | 2,000 |

13    Using the direct method of reapportionment, the total overheads apportioned to production department 1 =

$ [        ]

14    Using the step down method of reapportionment, the total overheads apportioned to production department

2 = $ [        ]

(*Note.* Apportion the overheads of service department 1 first.)

15    A company had the following budgeted and actual production overhead costs in its two production cost centres, Machining and Assembly.

|  | Budget | Actual |
|---|---|---|
| Machining | $210,000 | $212,000 |
| Assembly | $136,000 | $134,000 |

Which statement is true?

A    From the data available it is not possible to determine over/under absorption
B    Machining overheads were over-absorbed: Assembly overheads were under-absorbed
C    Machining overheads were over-absorbed: Assembly overheads were over-absorbed
D    Machining overheads were under-absorbed: Assembly overheads were over-absorbed

16  The following production overhead costs relate to a production cost centre:

Budget      $124,000
Actual      $126,740
Absorbed    $125,200

Which of the following statements is true?

A   Overheads were over-absorbed by $1,200
B   Overheads were over-absorbed by $1,540
C   Overheads were under-absorbed by $1,200
D   Overheads were under-absorbed by $1,540

---

17  There are two production cost centres and two service cost centres in a factory. Production overheads have been allocated and apportioned to cost centres and now require re-apportionment from service cost centres to production cost centres. Relevant details are:

| | Service cost Centre A | Service cost Centre B |
|---|---|---|
| Total overhead | $42,000 | $57,600 |
| % to Production Cost Centre X | 40 | 55 |
| % to Production Cost Centre Y | 60 | 45 |

What is the total re-apportionment to Production Cost Centre Y?

A   $42,720
B   $48,480
C   $51,120
D   $56,880

---

18  Overheads are absorbed at a pre-determined rate based on direct labour hours. The following additional information is available for a period:

| | | |
|---|---|---|
| Budget | $164,000 overhead expenditure | 10,000 direct labour hours |
| Actual | $158,000 overhead expenditure | 9,800 direct labour hours |

What was the overhead over/under-absorption in the period?

A   $2,720 over-absorbed
B   $3,224 over-absorbed
C   $3,280 under-absorbed
D   $6,000 under-absorbed

---

19  A company uses absorption costing. In a period, 34,000 units of the company's single product were manufactured and 33,000 units were sold.

Consider the following two statements:

1.   Fixed production overheads would be over-absorbed.
2.   Profit would be higher than in the previous period.

Are the statements true in relation to the situation described or is it not possible to determine whether or not they are true?

| | Statement 1 | Statement 2 |
|---|---|---|
| A | Cannot determine | Cannot determine |
| B | Cannot determine | True |
| C | True | Cannot determine |
| D | True | True |

20    Which of the following would be the most appropriate basis for reapportioning the cost of personnel services in a factory?

   A    Floor space occupied
   B    Hours worked by direct operatives
   C    Number of direct operatives
   D    Number of employees

21    An overhead absorption rate of $12.00 per direct labour hour was established based on a budget of 2,100 hours. Actual direct labour hours worked were 2,180 and actual overhead expenditure was $25,470.

   What was the over/under absorption of overhead?

   A    $270 under absorbed
   B    $690 over absorbed
   C    $960 over absorbed
   D    $960 under absorbed

22    Machine hours are used to absorb overheads in a production cost centre. Overheads allocated and apportioned to the cost centre are:

|  | $ |
|---|---|
| Allocated | 13,122 |
| Apportioned | 7,920 |
| Reapportioned from service cost centers | 2,988 |

   216,000 units of product are manufactured at a rate of 120 units per machine hour.

   What is the overhead absorption rate per machine hour?

   A    $7.29
   B    $11.13
   C    $11.69
   D    $13.35

# 16 Compulsory written question: Overheads and absorption costing I (12/05)                    17 mins

(a)    State an appropriate basis of apportionment for each of the following production overhead costs:

   (i)    Factory rent;
   (ii)   Staff canteen.                                                                    (4 marks)

(b)    Overheads allocated, apportioned and re-apportioned to two production cost centres in a factory for a period were:

|  | Production cost centre | |
|---|---|---|
|  | X | Y |
| Budget | $161,820 | $97,110 |
| Actual | $163,190 | $96,330 |

Overheads are absorbed using predetermined rates. A machine hour rate is used in Production Cost Centre X and a direct labour rate in Production Cost Centre Y. Machine and direct labour activity in each production cost centre is:

|  | Production cost centre | |
|---|---|---|
|  | X | Y |
| Machine hours: |  |  |
|     Budget | 8,700 | 1,760 |
|     Actual | 8,960 | 1,725 |
| Direct labour hours: |  |  |
|     Budget | 6,220 | 8,300 |
|     Actual | 6,276 | 7,870 |

*Required*

Calculate for each production cost centre for the period:

| | | |
|---|---|---|
| (i) | The predetermined production overhead absorption rate; | (3 marks) |
| (ii) | The production overheads absorbed; | (3 marks) |
| (iii) | The over/under absorption of production overhead. | (4 marks) |
| | | **(14 marks)** |

# 17 Compulsory written question: Overheads and absorption costing II (12/06)                           20 mins

A company has three production departments (X, Y and Z) in its factory. After completion of all overhead allocation and apportionment, the production department budgets for Year 6 included the following:

| | Department | | |
|---|---|---|---|
| | X | Y | Z |
| Overhead costs | $51,240 | $87,120 | $66,816 |
| Direct labour hours | - | - | 11,520 |
| Machine hours | 4,200 | 5,280 | - |

A predetermined overhead absorption rate is established for each production department each year.

Actual data for Month 1 of Year 6 included:

| | Department | | |
|---|---|---|---|
| | X | Y | Z |
| Overhead costs | $4,410 | $7,190 | $5,610 |
| Direct labour hours | - | - | 985 |
| Machine hours | 340 | 426 | - |

*Required*

(a)   Calculate, from the data provided, an appropriate predetermined overhead absorption rate for each production department for Year 6.                                                                          (4 marks)

(b)   Calculate the amount of the over/under absorption of overhead in Month 1 in each production department and in total for the factory.                                                                    (9 marks)

(c)   Suggest two general causes of overhead under absorption.                                      (3 marks)
                                                                                              **(16 marks)**

# 18 Compulsory written question: Overheads and absorption costing III (12/07)                           12 mins

The following information is available for two production cost centres in a factory for a period

| | Cost centre X | Cost centre Y |
|---|---|---|
| Budgeted costs | $28,556 | $56, 264 |
| Budgeted hours | 1,210 machine hours | 6,460 labour hours |
| Predetermined absorption rate | $23.60 per machine hour | $8.4 per labour hour |
| Actual costs | $29,609 | $52,567 |
| Actual hours | 1,235 machine hours | 6,395 labour hours |

*Required*

(a)   Calculate the over or under absorption of overhead for the period in each cost centre.      (6 marks)

(b)   Explain two advantages of using predetermined, as opposed to actual, overhead absorption rates.  (4 marks)
                                                                                              **(10 marks)**

# 19 Compulsory written question: Coding systems and overhead apportionment (6/06)

**20 mins**

(a)  (i)  Explain briefly what a coding system is and why coding systems are used.  (3 marks)

(ii)  List TWO features of an efficient and effecting coding system.  (3 marks)

(b)  There are two production cost centres (P1 and P2) and two service cost centres (Materials Store and Employee Facilities) in a factory. Estimated overhead costs for the factory for a period, requiring apportionment to cost centres, are:

|  | $ |
|---|---|
| Buildings depreciation and insurance | 42,000 |
| Management salaries | 27,000 |
| Power to operate machinery | 12,600 |
| Other utilities | 9,400 |

In addition, the following overheads have been allocated to cost centres:

| | | Cost Centre | |
|---|---|---|---|
| P1 | P2 | Materials store | Employee facilities |
| $107,000 | $89,000 | $68,000 | $84,000 |

Further information:

| | P1 | P2 | Cost centre Materials store | Employee facilities | Total |
|---|---|---|---|---|---|
| Floor area (m²) | 4,560 | 5,640 | 720 | 1,080 | 12,000 |
| Number of employees | 18 | 24 | 6 | 6 | 54 |
| Share of other utilities o/hd | 35% | 45% | 10% | 10% | 10% |
| Machine hours | 6,200 | 5,800 | | | 12,000 |
| Share of Materials Store o/hds | 40% | 60% | | | 100% |

**Required**

(i)  Prepare a schedule showing the allocated and apportioned factory overhead costs for each cost centre.  (7 marks)

(ii)  Re-apportion the service cost centre overheads.  (4 marks)

**(17 marks)**

# 20 Objective test questions: Marginal costing and absorption costing

1  The overhead absorption rate for product Y is $2.50 per direct labour hour. Each unit of Y requires 3 direct labour hours. Stock (inventory) of product Y at the beginning of the month was 200 units and at the end of the month was 250 units. What is the difference in the profits reported for the month using absorption costing compared with marginal costing?

A    The absorption costing profit would be $375 less
B    The absorption costing profit would be $125 greater
C    The absorption costing profit would be $375 greater
D    The absorption costing profit would be $1,875 greater

2    A company produces a single product for which cost and selling price details are as follows.

| | $ per unit | $ per unit |
|---|---|---|
| Selling price | | 28 |
| Direct material | 10 | |
| Direct labour | 4 | |
| Variable overhead | 2 | |
| Fixed overhead | 5 | |
| | | 21 |
| Profit per unit | | 7 |

Last period, 8,000 units were produced and 8,500 units were sold. The opening stock (inventory) was 3,000 units and profits reported using marginal costing were $60,000. The profits reported using an absorption costing system would be

A    $47,500
B    $57,500
C    $59,500
D    $62,500

---

3    A company had opening stock (inventory) of 48,500 units and closing stock (inventory) of 45,500 units. Profits based on marginal costing were $315,250 and on absorption costing were $288,250. What is the fixed overhead absorption rate per unit?

A    $5.94
B    $6.34
C    $6.50
D    $9.00

---

4    Which of the following are arguments in favour of the use of absorption costing?

(i)    Closing stock (inventory) is valued in accordance with accounting standards
(ii)    There is no under or over absorption of overheads
(iii)    When sales fluctuate but production is constant, absorption costing smooths out profit fluctuations.

A    (i) only
B    (i) and (ii) only
C    (i) and (iii) only
D    (ii) and (iii) only

---

5    A company currently uses absorption costing. The following information relates to Product X for Month 1:

| | |
|---|---|
| Opening stock (inventory) | Nil |
| Production | 900 units |
| Sales | 800 units |

If the company had used marginal costing, which of the following combinations would be true?

| | Profit | Stock (inventory) valuation |
|---|---|---|
| A | would be higher | would be higher |
| B | would be higher | would be lower |
| C | would be lower | would be higher |
| D | would be lower | would be lower |

---

6    A firm had opening stocks (inventory) of 33,480 units and closing stocks (inventory) of 25,920 units. Profits using marginal costing were $228,123 and using absorption costing were $203,931.

The fixed overhead absorption rate per unit (to the nearest penny) was $ ☐

7    When opening stocks (inventory) were 8,500 litres and closing stocks (inventory) 6,750 litres, a firm had a profit of $27,400 using marginal costing.

Assuming that the fixed overhead absorption rate was $2 per litre, the profit using absorption costing would be $ ▢

8    In a period where opening stocks (inventory) were 5,000 units and closing stocks (inventory) 8,000 units, a firm had a profit of $130,000 using absorption costing. If the fixed overhead absorption rate was $4 per unit,

the profit using marginal costing would be $ ▢

9    In the context of reporting the profit for a given period, which of the following statements is/are true?

▢ If stock (inventory) levels reduce, absorption costing will report a lower profit than marginal costing.

▢ If stock (inventory) levels reduce, marginal costing will report a lower profit than absorption costing.

▢ If production and sales volumes are equal, marginal costing and absorption costing will report the same profit figure.

10   A company manufactures a single product. Production and sales quantities for a period were:

|  | Production | Sales |
| --- | --- | --- |
| Budget | 100,000 units | 102,000 units |
| Actual | 97,000 units | 96,000 units |

The fixed production overhead absorption rate is $1.40 per unit.

If marginal costing had been used instead of absorption costing how would the profit for the period have differed?

A    $1,400 less using marginal costing
B    $1,400 more using marginal costing
C    $4,200 less using marginal costing
D    $4,200 more using marginal costing

11   A company sold 82,000 units of its single product in a period in which 84,000 units were manufactured.

Consider the following statements:

1.    Stock (inventory) value at the end of the period would be higher than at the beginning of the period.

2.    Stock (inventory) values both at the beginning and at the end of the period would be higher using absorption rather than marginal costing.

Are the statements true or false in relation to the situation described?

|  | Statement 1 | Statement 2 |
| --- | --- | --- |
| A | False | False |
| B | False | True |
| C | True | False |
| D | True | True |

12   What distinguishes absorption costing from marginal costing?

A    Product costs include both prime cost and production overhead
B    Product costs include both production and non-production costs
C    Stock (inventory) valuation includes a share of all production costs
D    Stock (inventory) valuation includes a share of all costs

13    A company uses a marginal costing system. 10,000 units of its single product were manufactured in a period during which 9,760 units were sold.

If absorption costing is applied instead what would be the effect on profit?

A    Higher by (240 units × fixed production overhead cost per unit)

B    Lower by (240 units × fixed production overhead cost per unit)

C    Higher by [240 units × (fixed production overhead cost per unit + fixed non-production overhead cost per unit)]

D    Lower by [240 units × (fixed production overhead cost per unit + fixed non-production overhead cost per unit)]

# 21 Compulsory written question: Marginal costing and absorption costing I (Pilot paper)                    20 mins

A company manufactures a single product with a selling price of $28 per unit. Variable production costs per unit of product are:

Direct material          $6.10
Direct labour            $5.20
Variable overhead        $1.60

Fixed production overheads are $30,000 per month. Administration overheads are semi-variable in nature: variable costs are 5% of sales and fixed costs are $13,000 per month.

Production and sales quantities over a two month period are:

|         | Production   | Sales       |
|---------|--------------|-------------|
| Month 1 | 4,000 units  | 3,500 units |
| Month 2 | 3,600 units  | 3,800 units |

There is no finished goods inventory at the beginning of Month 1.

The company has prepared the following profit statement for each of the two months using the absorption costing method.

Profit statement

|                          | Month 1 | | Month 2 | |
|--------------------------|---------|---------|---------|---------|
|                          | $ | $ | $ | $ |
| Sales                    |  | 98,000 |  | 106,400 |
| Production cost of sales: |  |  |  |  |
| Opening inventory        |  |  | 10,200 |  |
| Cost of production       | 81,600 |  | 76,440 |  |
| Closing inventory*       | (10,200) |  | (6,370) |  |
|                          |  | 71,400 |  | 80,270 |
| Gross profit             |  | 26,600 |  | 26,130 |
| Administration overhead  |  | 17,900 |  | 18,320 |
| Net profit               |  | 8,700 |  | 7,810 |

\* Inventory valuation:     end Month 1     $81,600 × (500 ÷ 4,000 units)
                            end Month 2     $76,440 × (300 ÷ 3,600 units)

Required

(a)    Prepare a profit statement for each of the two months using the marginal costing method.          (10 marks)

(b)    Provide a reconciliation of the absorption costing and marginal costing profits for Month 2, supported by a full explanation of the difference.                                                              (7 marks)
                                                                                                     **(17 marks)**

# 22 Compulsory written question: Marginal costing and absorption costing II (6/05)

**17 mins**

A company has the following costs for its single product, based on planned production and sales of 46,000 litres in a period:

|  | $ per litre |
|---|---|
| Prime costs | 5.20 |
| Production overhead – all fixed | 2.80 |
| Non-production overhead | |
| – variable | 0.65 |
| – fixed | 1.70 |
| | $10.35 |

Actual production and sales in the period were:

| Production | 46,000 litres | |
|---|---|---|
| Sales | 45,600 litres | (at $12.00 per litre) |

There was no finished inventory at the beginning of the period. Variable costs per litre and total fixed costs in the period were as planned. Variable non-production overheads vary in total with the number of litres sold.

*Required*

(a)   Prepare a profit statement for the period using absorption costing.          (8 marks)

(b)   Explain fully why, and calculate by how much, the profits for the period would be different if marginal costing was used instead.          (6 marks)

**(14 marks)**

# Do you know? – Cost bookkeeping

**Check that you can fill in the blanks in the statements below before you attempt any questions. If in doubt, you should go back to your BPP Interactive Text and revise first.**

- An account which controls total cost is called a ............... account. For example, the wages ............. account acts as a sort of ....................... for net wages paid and deductions made from gross pay. The gross pay is then usually analysed between ............ wages (which will be debited to the........................... account) and ........... wages (which will be debited to the ....................................... account).

- There are two types of cost bookkeeping system, the interlocking and the integrated.

  - The ..................... accounts system combines the financial and cost accounts in one set of self-balancing ledger accounts.

  - An interlocking system features two ledgers: the ............ ledger; and the ......... ledger.

- The accounting entries for the various stages of the production process are as follows.

  - Resources (direct materials, labour and expenses) are allocated to work in progress by ................... the work in progress control account and ............... the resource accounts.

  - Indirect materials, labour and expenses (overheads incurred) are allocated to production by ............. the raw materials and wages and salaries accounts and ............. the production overhead account.

  - The amount of overhead absorbed is .............. to the work in progress account, and ................... to the production overhead account. Overheads incurred have therefore been ..................... to the production overhead account, and those absorbed have been ................... to the production overhead account. If overhead absorbed differs from overhead incurred, the difference is written off to an ..................................................... account.

  - The production of finished goods is recorded by debiting the ........................... account and crediting the ...............................................account.

  - The cost of goods sold is established by transferring the balance on the ....................... account to the cost of sales account.

- There are a number of advantages and limitations associated with both interlocking and integrated systems.

  TRY QUESTIONS 24 and 25

- *Possible pitfalls*

  *Write down the mistakes you know you should avoid.*

# Did you know? – Cost bookkeeping

**Could you fill in the blanks? The answers are in bold. Use this page for revision purposes as you approach the exam.**

- An account which controls total cost is called a **control** account. For example, the wages **control** account acts as a sort of **collecting place** for net wages paid and deductions made from gross pay. The gross pay is then usually analysed between **direct** wages (which will be debited to the **work in progress** account) and **indirect** wages (which will be debited to the **production overhead** account).

- There are two types of cost bookkeeping system, the interlocking and the integrated.

    - The **integrated** accounts system combines the financial and cost accounts in one set of self–balancing ledger accounts.

    - An interlocking system features two ledgers: the **financial** ledger; and the **cost** ledger.

- The accounting entries for the various stages of the production process are as follows.

    - Resources (direct materials, labour and expenses) are allocated to work in progress by **debiting** the work in progress control account and **crediting** the resource accounts.

    - Indirect materials, labour and expenses (overheads incurred) are allocated to production by **crediting** the raw materials and wages and salaries accounts and **debiting** the production overhead account.

    - The amount of overhead absorbed is **debited** to the work in progress account, and **credited** to the production overhead account. Overheads incurred have therefore been **debited** to the production overhead account, and those absorbed have been **credited** to the production overhead account. If overhead absorbed differs from overhead incurred, the difference is written off to an **under-/over-absorbed overhead** account.

    - The production of finished goods is recorded by debiting the **finished goods** account and crediting the **work in progress** account.

    - The cost of goods sold is established by transferring the balance on the **finished goods** account to the cost of sales account.

- There are a number of advantages and limitations associated with both interlocking and integrated systems.

    TRY QUESTIONS 24 and 25

- *Possible pitfalls*

    - **Posting debit entries as credits and credit entries as debits when completing interlocking and integrated accounts**

    - **Being unable to identify which costs are indirect costs when preparing the production overhead account**

# 23 Objective test questions: Cost bookkeeping

1    A company's accounting system operates so that the cost accounts are independent of the financial accounts. The two sets of accounts are reconciled on a regular basis to keep them continuously in agreement. This type of accounting system is known as

     A     Independent accounts
     B     Interlocking accounts
     C     Reconciled accounts
     D     Integrated accounts

2    M Limited operates a system of interlocking accounts. A reconciliation is currently being prepared to reconcile the cost accounting profit with the financial accounting profit. Which of the following items would be included in the reconciliation statement?

     (i)     The differences between the inventory valuations used in the cost accounts and those used in the financial accounts

     (ii)    The amount paid for rent of the factory premises

     (iii)   The interest received for some cash deposited in the bank

     A     (i) only
     B     (i) and (ii) only
     C     (i) and (iii) only
     D     (i), (ii) and (iii)

3    Which of the following statements about integrated accounts is/are correct?

     (i)     Integrated systems save time and administrative effort

     (ii)    Integrated systems maintain two separate sets of accounts: one for financial accounts and one for cost accounts

     (iii)   Integrated systems avoid the need for periodic profit reconciliations

     A     (i) only
     B     (i) and (ii) only
     C     (i) and (iii) only
     D     (ii) and (iii) only

4    The wages control account for A Limited for February is shown below.

WAGES CONTROL ACCOUNT

| | $ | | $ |
|---|---|---|---|
| Bank | 128,400 | Work in progress control | 79,400 |
| Balance c/d | 12,000 | Production overhead control | 61,000 |
| | 140,400 | | 140,400 |
| | | Balance b/d | 12,000 |

Which of the following statements about wages for February is *not* correct?

     A     Wages paid during February amounted to $128,400
     B     Wages for February were prepaid by $12,000
     C     Direct wages cost incurred during February amounted to $79,400
     D     Indirect wages cost incurred during February amounted to $61,000

5    The material stores control account for J Limited for March looks like this:

MATERIAL STORES CONTROL ACCOUNT

| | $ | | $ |
|---|---|---|---|
| Balance b/d | 12,000 | Work in progress | 40,000 |
| Creditors | 49,000 | Overhead control | 12,000 |
| Work in progress | 18,000 | Balance c/d | 27,000 |
| | 79,000 | | 79,000 |
| Balance b/d | 27,000 | | |

Which of the following statements are correct?

(i)     Issues of direct materials during March were $18,000
(ii)    Issues of direct materials during March were $40,000
(iii)   Issues of indirect materials during March were $12,000
(iv)   Purchases of materials during March were $49,000

A    (i) and (iv) only
B    (ii) and (iv) only
C    (ii), (iii) and (iv) only
D    All of them

6    When materials are purchased on credit and put into raw materials inventory, the relevant cost bookkeeping entries are (tick correct boxes):

| | Debit | Credit | No entry in this a/c |
|---|---|---|---|
| Work in progress | | | |
| Materials inventory | | | |
| Cost of sales | | | |
| Cash | | | |
| Creditors | | | |

7    A record of total actual expenditure incurred on indirect costs and the amount absorbed into individual units, jobs or processes is known as a:

☐  Stores control account
☐  Wages control account
☐  Work in progress control account
☐  Production overhead control account

8    In an integrated cost and financial accounting system, the accounting entries at the end of the period for production overhead over-absorbed would be (tick the correct boxes):

| | Debit | Credit | No entry in this a/c |
|---|---|---|---|
| Overhead control account | | | |
| Work in progress account | | | |
| Income statement | | | |

9    In a typical cost ledger, the double entry for indirect labour cost incurred is:

|  | DR | Wages control | CR | Overhead control |
|  | DR | WIP control | CR | Wages control |
|  | DR | Overhead control | CR | Wages control |
|  | DR | Wages control | CR | WIP control |

10   An interlocking system features two ledgers.

(a)   The [          ] ledger contains asset, liability, revenue, expense and appropriation accounts.

(b)   The [          ] ledger is where cost information is analysed in more detail.

11   Which one of the following may be included in the cost accounts but excluded from the financial accounts?

A    Depreciation of equipment
B    Distribution expenses
C    Factory manager's salary
D    Notional rent

12   In an interlocking system, what would be the entry for the issue of indirect material from inventory?

| | Account debited | Account credited |
|---|---|---|
| A | Material inventory | Production overhead |
| B | Material inventory | Work-in-progress |
| C | Production overhead | Material inventory |
| D | Work-in-progress | Material inventory |

13   In a cost bookkeeping system what would be the entry for the absorption of production overhead?

| | Debit | Credit |
|---|---|---|
| A | Cost Ledger Control Account | Production Overhead Account |
| B | Production Overhead Account | Work-in-Progress Account |
| C | Work-in-Progress Account | Cost Ledger Control Account |
| D | Work-in-Progress Account | Production Overhead Account |

14   In an integrated cost and financial accounting system what would be the entry to record direct labour costs being charged to production?

| | Debit | Credit |
|---|---|---|
| A | Financial ledger control | Work-in-progress |
| B | Production overhead | Wages control |
| C | Finished goods | Work-in-progress |
| D | Work-in-progress | Wages control |

# 24 Compulsory written question: Cost bookkeeping   24 mins

Ten Days Early is a company which operates an interlocking cost accounting system, which is not integrated with the financial accounts. At the beginning of February 20X1, the opening balances in the cost ledger were as follows.

|  | $ |
|---|---|
| Stores ledger control account | 36,400 |
| Work in progress control account | 23,000 |
| Finished goods control account | 15,700 |
| Cost ledger control account | 75,100 |

During February 20X1 the following transactions took place.

|  | $ |
|---|---|
| Materials purchased | 28,700 |
| Materials issued to: | |
|   Production | 21,300 |
|   Service departments | 4,200 |
| Gross factory wages paid | 58,900 |

Of these gross wages, $19,500 were indirect wages.

|  | $ |
|---|---|
| Production overheads incurred (excluding the items shown above) | 1,970 |
| Raw material inventory written off, damaged | 1,200 |
| Selling overheads incurred and charged to cost of sales | 10,500 |
| Sales | 88,000 |
| Material and labour cost of goods sold | 52,800 |

At the end of February 20X1 stocks (inventory) of work in progress were $7,640 higher than at the beginning of the month. The company operates a marginal costing system.

*Required*

Prepare the following accounts to record these transactions in February 20X1.

(a) Cost ledger control account
(b) Stores ledger control account
(c) Factory wages control account
(d) Production overhead control account
(e) Work in progress (WIP) control account
(f) Finished goods control account
(g) Selling overhead control account
(h) Sales account
(i) Cost of sales account
(j) Costing income statement

**(20 marks)**

**Helping hand**

The key to answering this type of question is to tackle the problem methodically. You should find the following approach helpful.

**Step 1.**   *Draw up proforma control accounts for the stores ledger, work in progress, finished goods and cost ledger and enter the balances given in the question.*

**Step 2.**   *Draw up the relevant accounts and record the February 20X1 transactions as follows.*

- **Materials purchased** – Debit the stores ledger control account and credit the cost ledger control account with the value of materials purchased.

- **Materials issued to production** – Debit the WIP control account and credit the stores ledger control account with the value of the materials issued to production.

- **Materials issued to service departments** – Debit the production overhead control account and credit the stores ledger control account with the value of materials issued to service departments.

- **Gross factory wages paid** – Debit the factory wages control account and credit the cost ledger control account with the gross factory wages paid.

- **Indirect wages** – Debit the production overhead control account and credit the factory wages control account with value of the indirect wages.

- **Production overheads incurred** – Debit the production overhead control account and credit the cost ledger control account with the value of the production overheads incurred.

- **Raw materials inventory written off/damaged** – Debit the costing income statement and credit the stores ledger control account with the value of written off/damaged raw materials inventory.

- **Selling overheads** – Debit the selling overhead control account and credit the cost ledger control account with the value of selling overheads.

- **Sales** – Credit the sales account and debit the cost ledger control account with the value of the sales.

- **Material and labour cost of goods sold** – Debit the cost of sales account and credit the finished goods control account.

**Step 3.**   *Balance off the ledger accounts remembering the following.*

- The balance on the factory wages control account is transferred to the WIP control account.

- The balances on the production overhead control account and the sales account are transferred to the costing income statement.

- The balance on the selling overhead control account is transferred to the cost of sales account.

- The balance on the cost of sales account is transferred to the costing income statement.

**Step 4.**   *Balance the costing income statement in order to determine the profit/loss for the period.*

# Do you know? – Job, batch and service costing

**Check that you can fill in the blanks in the statements below before you attempt any questions. If in doubt, you should go back to your BPP Interactive Text and revise first.**

- Job costing is the costing method used where each cost unit is separately identifiable. Costs for each job are collected on a ........................... or ............. Overhead is absorbed into the cost of jobs using the .................................................. rate.

- The usual method of fixing prices within a jobbing concern is ...........................

- Batch costing is similar to job costing in that each batch of similar articles is separately identifiable. The cost per unit manufactured in a batch is calculated by dividing the ...................................... by the .................................... in the batch.

- Service costing is used by companies operating in a service industry or by companies wishing to establish the cost of services carried out by some of their departments.

- Characteristics of services ⎯⎡ .............................
  ⎢ .............................
  ⎢ .............................
  ⎣ .............................

- If a service is a function of two activity variables, a ................. cost unit might be appropriate.

- A difficulty with service costing is the selection of an appropriate cost unit. The cost per unit is calculated by dividing the ........................................ for the period by the ............................................. in the period.

  TRY QUESTIONS 26 to 29

- *Possible pitfalls*

  *Write down the mistakes you know you should avoid.*

# Did you know? – Job, batch and service costing

**Could you fill in the blanks? The answers are in bold. Use this page for revision purposes as you approach the exam.**

- Job costing is the costing method used where each cost unit is separately identifiable. Costs for each job are collected on a **job cost sheet** or **job card**. Overhead is absorbed into the cost of jobs using the **predetermined overhead absorption** rate.

- The usual method of fixing prices within a jobbing concern is **cost plus pricing**.

- Batch costing is similar to job costing in that each batch of similar articles is separately identifiable. The cost per unit manufactured in a batch is calculated by dividing the **total batch cost** by the **number of units** in the batch.

- Service costing is used by companies operating in a service industry or by companies wishing to establish the cost of services carried out by some of their departments.

- Characteristics of services
  - **Intangibility**
  - **Simultaneity**
  - **Perishability**
  - **Heterogeneity**

- If a service is a function of two activity variables, a **composite** cost unit might be appropriate.

- A difficulty with service costing is the selection of an appropriate cost unit. The cost per unit is calculated by dividing the **total costs** for the period by the **number of service units** in the period.

TRY QUESTIONS 26 to 29

- *Possible pitfalls*

  - **Posting amounts brought forward (plant on site, materials on site, work in progress) as credits instead of debits in the contract account**

  - **Forgetting to include accruals brought forward and carried forward in the contract account**

# 25 Objective test questions: Job, batch and service costing

1  Which of the following is a feature of job costing?

  A    Production is carried out in accordance with the wishes of the customer
  B    Associated with continuous production of large volumes of low-cost items
  C    Establishes the cost of services rendered
  D    Costs are charged over the units produced in the period

2  A firm uses job costing and recovers overheads as a percentage of direct labour cost.

  Three jobs were worked on during a period, the details of which are as follows.

|                          | Job 1 | Job 2  | Job 3  |
| ------------------------ | ----- | ------ | ------ |
|                          | $     | $      | $      |
| Opening work in progress | 8,500 | 0      | 46,000 |
| Material in period       | 17,150 | 29,025 | 0      |
| Labour for period        | 12,500 | 23,000 | 4,500  |

  The overheads for the period were exactly as budgeted, $140,000.

  Job 3 was completed during the period and consisted of 2,400 identical circuit boards. The firm adds 50% to total production costs to arrive at a selling price.

  What is the selling price of a circuit board?

  A    It cannot be calculated without more information
  B    $31.56
  C    $41.41
  D    $55.21

3  P Limited manufactures ring binders which are embossed with the customer's own logo. A customer has ordered a batch of 300 binders. The following data illustrate the cost for a typical batch of 100 binders.

|                  | $  |
| ---------------- | -- |
| Direct materials | 30 |
| Direct wages     | 10 |
| Machine set up   | 3  |
| Design and artwork | 15 |
|                  | 58 |

  Direct employees are paid on a piecework basis.

  P Limited absorbs production overhead at a rate of 20 per cent of direct wages cost. Five per cent is added to the total production cost of each batch to allow for selling, distribution and administration overhead.

  P Limited requires a profit margin of 25 per cent of sales value.

  The selling price for a batch of 300 binders (to the nearest cent) will be

  A    $189.00
  B    $193.20
  C    $201.60
  D    $252.00

4      JC operates a job costing system. The company's standard net profit margin is 20 per cent of sales value.

The estimated costs for job B124 are as follows.

Direct materials     3 kg @ $5 per kg
Direct labour         4 hours @ $9 per hour

Production overheads are budgeted to be $240,000 for the period, to be recovered on the basis of a total of 30,000 labour hours.

Other overheads, related to selling, distribution and administration, are budgeted to be $150,000 for the period. They are to be recovered on the basis of the total budgeted production cost of $750,000 for the period.

The price to be quoted for job B124 is $ ☐

---

5      In which of the following situation(s) will job costing normally be used?

☐    Production is continuous

☐    Production of the product can be completed in a single accounting period

☐    Production relates to a single special order

---

6      State which of the following are characteristics of service costing.

(i)     High levels of indirect costs as a proportion of total costs
(ii)    Use of composite cost units
(iii)   Use of equivalent units

A    (i) only
B    (i) and (ii) only
C    (ii) only
D    (ii) and (iii) only

---

7      Which of the following would be appropriate cost units for a transport business?

(i)     Cost per tonne-kilometre
(ii)    Fixed cost per kilometre
(iii)   Maintenance cost of each vehicle per kilometre

A    (i) only
B    (i) and (ii) only
C    (i) and (iii) only
D    All of them

---

8      Which of the following organisations should *not* be advised to use service costing.

A    Distribution service
B    Hospital
C    Maintenance division of a manufacturing company
D    A light engineering company

---

9      Calculate the most appropriate unit cost for a distribution division of a multinational company using the following information.

| | |
|---|---|
| Miles travelled | 636,500 |
| Tonnes carried | 2,479 |
| Number of drivers | 20 |
| Hours worked by drivers | 35,520 |
| Tonne/miles carried | 375,200 |
| Costs incurred | $562,800 |

A    $0.88
B    $1.50
C    $15.84
D    $28,140

10    The formula used to calculate the cost per service unit is:

Cost per service unit = $\dfrac{A}{B}$

A    [                    ]

B    [                    ]

11    Match up the following services with their typical cost units.

| *Service* | *Cost unit* |
|---|---|
| Hotels | [  ] |
| Education | [  ] |
| Hospitals | [  ] |
| Catering organisations | [  ] |

A = Meal served
B = Patient day
C = Full-time student
D = Occupied bed-night

12    Service costing has four specific characteristics.

1 =

2 =

3 =

4 =

13    A small engineering company that makes generators specifically to customers' own designs has had to purchase some special tools for a particular job. The tools will have no further use after the work has been completed and will be scrapped.

The cost of these tools should be treated as

A    Variable production overheads
B    Fixed production overheads
C    Indirect expenses
D    Direct expenses

# The following information relates to questions 14 and 15.

Happy Returns operates a haulage business with three vehicles. During week 26 it is expected that all three vehicles will be used at a total cost of $10,390; 3,950 kilometres will be travelled (including return journeys when empty) as shown in the following table.

| Journey | Tonnes carried (one way) | Kilometres (one way) |
|---------|--------------------------|----------------------|
| 1 | 34 | 180 |
| 2 | 28 | 265 |
| 3 | 40 | 390 |
| 4 | 32 | 115 |
| 5 | 26 | 220 |
| 6 | 40 | 480 |
| 7 | 29 | 90 |
| 8 | 26 | 100 |
| 9 | 25 | 135 |
|   | 280 | 1,975 |

14    The total of tonne-kilometres in week 26 = [        ]

15    The average cost per tonne-kilometre for week 26 = $ [        ] per tonne-kilometre (to the nearest cent).

16    Job XX has been completed at a total production cost of $3,633. Administration and selling overheads are applied at 20% of production cost. The selling price of each job is established so as to provide a GROSS profit margin of 30%.

What is the selling price of Job XX?

A    $4,723
B    $5,190
C    $5,668
D    $6,228

17    The following items are recorded in a costing system:

(i)     Actual direct material cost
(ii)    Actual direct labour cost
(iii)   Actual manufacturing overheads
(iv)    Absorbed manufacturing overheads

Which of the items are contained in a typical job cost?

A    (i) and (ii) only
B    (i), (ii) and (iii) only
C    (i), (ii) and (iv) only
D    All four items

# 26 Compulsory written question: Job costing I (Pilot paper)

16 mins

A company manufactures carpet for the hotel industry. No finished stocks (inventory) are carried as the company only manufactures specifically to customer order. At the end of Month 6, one incomplete job (Job X124) remained in progress. Production costs incurred on the job to the end of Month 6 were:

| | |
|---|---|
| Direct material | $7,220 |
| Direct labour | $6,076 |
| Production overhead | $10,416 |

During Month 7, the company accepted two further jobs (Job X125 and Job X126) and incurred prime costs as follows.

| | Job X124 | Job X125 | Job X126 |
|---|---|---|---|
| Direct material issued from stores | $6,978 | $18,994 | $12,221 |
| Direct material returned to stores | Nil | ($700) | ($2,170) |
| Direct material transfers | Nil | $860 | ($860) |
| Direct labour hours | 780 | 2,364 | 1,510 |

Direct labour is paid at a rate of $7.00 per hour. Production overheads are absorbed at a rate of $12.00 per direct labour hour.

During Month 7, Jobs X124 and X125 were completed. On completion of a job, 20% of the total production cost is added in order to recover distribution, selling and administration costs. The amounts invoiced to customers during Month 7 for the completed jobs were:

| | |
|---|---|
| Job X124 | $60,000 |
| Job X125 | $79,000 |

*Required*

(a) For each of the jobs calculate the following total costs:

    (i) direct materials (3 marks)
    (ii) direct labour (3 marks)
    (iii) production overhead (3 marks)

(b) Calculate the total cost and profit/(loss) of each of Job X124 and Job X125. (4 marks)

**(13 marks)**

# 27 Compulsory written question: Job costing II (6/06)

17 mins

Company X is preparing a job cost estimate that will be used to provide a quote for a potential customer. Estimated costs for the job are to be based on the following:

Direct materials $2,893

Direct labour 210 hours at a basic rate of $8.00 per hour

Direct production staff also receive a bonus each period. The bonus is paid on actual hours worked at a rate per hour calculated using the following formula:

{[(time allowed − time worked) ÷ time allowed] × basic rate per hour}

The bonus to be included currently in the costing of all jobs is based on the following estimates for the period:

Total time worked 3,400 labour hours
Total time allowed 4,000 labour hours

Production overheads Absorbed at 20% of prime cost (including labour bonus) + $9.00 per direct labour hour

Non-production overheads Absorbed at 25% of total production cost

Quoted prices are calculated to provide Company X with a net profit margin of 20% of sales.

*Required*

(a) Calculate the total estimated PRODUCTION cost of the job. (10 marks)
(b) Calculate the price that should be quoted for the job. (4 marks)
**(14 marks)**

# 28 Compulsory written question: Service costing (12/04)

19 mins

(a) Describe the main ways in which the costing of services differs from the costing of manufactured products. (6 marks)

(b) A transport business operates a fleet of 10 vehicles. Operating data are as follows:

Purchase of vehicles
   (depreciated on a straight line basis over 4 years) $460,000 (for 10 vehicles)
Vehicle disposal value (after 4 years) $4,000 (per vehicle)
Road fund licence and insurance $2,290 (per vehicle per year)
Tyres (8 per vehicle renewed every 40,000 kilometres) $210 (per tyre)
Servicing (every 16,000 kilometres) $650 (per vehicle service)
Fuel (consumption of 1 litre per 3.2 kilometres) $0.80 (per litre)
Vehicle usage 80,000 kilometres (per vehicle per year)
Drivers (1 driver per vehicle) $18,000 (per driver per year)

*Required*

Calculate the total vehicle operating costs per kilometre (to four decimal places of $). (10 marks)
**(16 marks)**

# Do you know? – Process costing

**Check that you can fill in the blanks in the statements below before you attempt any questions. If in doubt, you should go back to your BPP Interactive Text and revise first.**

- Process costing is a costing method used where it is not possible to identify separate units of production usually because of the continuous nature of the production processes involved.

- Three reasons why losses occur include the following.

    (1)  .......................

    (2)  .......................

    (3)  .......................

- ................... loss is the loss expected during a process and it is not given a cost. If it has a scrap value then it is valued at this amount.

- ................... loss is the extra loss resulting when actual loss is greater than the loss anticipated. It is given a cost.

- Loss may have a scrap value. Revenue from normal scrap is treated as a reduction in costs.

- When dealing with process costing questions, the following four-step approach should be used.

    **Step 1** .................................................................................................

    **Step 2** .................................................................................................

    **Step 3** .................................................................................................

    **Step 4** .................................................................................................

- When there is closing work in progress at the end of a period, it is necessary to calculate the ......................................... of production in order to determine the cost of a completed unit.

- The costs of labour and overhead are sometimes referred to as ..................... costs.

- ............. products are two or more products separated in a process, each of which has a significant value compared to the other.

- A ............................. is an incidental product from a process which has an insignificant value compared to the main product.

- The point at which joint and by-products become separately identifiable is known as the .................................................. or the ...................................... point.

TRY QUESTIONS 30 to 35

- *Possible pitfalls*
  *Write down the mistakes you know you should avoid.*

# Did you know? – Process costing

**Could you fill in the blanks? The answers are in bold. Use this page for revision purposes as you approach the exam.**

- Process costing is a costing method used where it is not possible to identify separate units of production usually because of the continuous nature of the production processes involved.

- Three reasons why losses occur include the following.

    (1) **Wastage**
    (2) **Spoilage**
    (3) **Evaporation**

- **Normal** loss is the loss expected during a process and it is not given a cost. If it has a scrap value then it is valued at this amount.

- **Abnormal** loss is the extra loss resulting when actual loss is greater than the loss anticipated. It is given a cost.

- Loss may have a scrap value. Revenue from normal scrap is treated as a reduction in costs.

- When dealing with process costing questions, the following four-step approach should be used.

    ## Step 1    Determine output and losses

    ## Step 2    Calculate cost per unit of output, losses and WIP

    ## Step 3    Calculate total cost of output, losses and WIP

    ## Step 4    Complete accounts

- When there is closing work in progress at the end of a period, it is necessary to calculate the **equivalent units** of production in order to determine the cost of a completed unit.

- The costs of labour and overhead are sometimes referred to as **conversion** costs.

- **Joint** products are two or more products separated in a process, each of which has a significant value compared to the other.

- A **by-product** is an incidental product from a process which has an insignificant value compared to the main product.

- The point at which joint and by-products become separately identifiable is known as the **point of separation** or the **split-off** point.

TRY QUESTIONS 30 to 35

- *Possible pitfalls*

    – **Forgetting that units arising from abnormal loss are included as equivalent units, whereas those arising from normal loss are not**

    – **Not using the suggested four-step approach when answering process costing questions**

# 29 Objective test questions: Process costing

1       What is an equivalent unit?

    A       A unit of output which is identical to all others manufactured in the same process
    B       Notional whole units used to represent uncompleted work
    C       A unit of product in relation to which costs are ascertained
    D       The amount of work achievable, at standard efficiency levels, in an hour

## The following information relates to questions 2 and 3

Patacake Ltd produces a certain food item in a manufacturing process. On 1 November, there was no opening inventory of work in process. During November, 500 units of material were input to the process, with a cost of $9,000. Direct labour costs in November were $3,840. Production overhead is absorbed at the rate of 200% of direct labour costs. Closing inventory on 30 November consisted of 100 units which were 100% complete as to materials and 80% complete as to labour and overhead. There was no loss in process.

2       The full production cost of completed units during November was

    A       $10,400
    B       $16,416
    C       $16,800
    D       $20,520

3       The value of the closing work in progress on 30 November is

    A       $2,440
    B       $3,720
    C       $4,104
    D       $20,520

4       In process costing, a joint product is

    A       A product which is later divided into many parts

    B       A product which is produced simultaneously with other products and is of similar value to at least one of the other products

    C       A product which is produced simultaneously with other products but which is of a greater value than any of the other products

    D       A product produced jointly with another organisation

5       What is a by-product?

    A       A product produced at the same time as other products which has no value

    B       A product produced at the same time as other products which requires further processing to put it in a saleable state

    C       A product produced at the same time as other products which has a relatively low volume compared with the other products

    D       A product produced at the same time as other products which has a relatively low value compared with the other products

6       In process costing, if an abnormal loss arises, the process account is generally

    A       debited with the scrap value of the abnormal loss units
    B       debited with the full production cost of the abnormal loss units
    C       credited with the scrap value of the abnormal loss units
    D       credited with the full production cost of the abnormal loss units

7   A company makes a product, which passes through a single process.

Details of the process for the last period are as follows.

Materials             5,000 kg at 50c per kg
Labour                $700
Production overheads  200% of labour

Normal losses are 10% of input in the process, and without further processing any losses can be sold as scrap for 20c per kg.

The output for the period was 4,200 kg from the process.

There was no work in progress at the beginning or end of the period.

The value credited to the process account for the scrap value of the normal loss for the period will be $ ☐

8   A company makes a product, which passes through a single process.

Details of the process for the last period are as follows.

Materials             5,000 kg at 50c per kg
Labour                $700
Production overheads  200% of labour

Normal losses are 10% of input in the process, and without further processing any losses can be sold as scrap for 20c per kg.

The output for the period was 4,200 kg from the process.

There was no work in progress at the beginning or end of the period.

The value of the abnormal loss for the period is $ ☐

9   A product is manufactured as a result of two processes, 1 and 2. Details of process 2 for the latest period were as follows.

Opening work in progress              Nil
Materials transferred from process 1  10,000 kg valued at $40,800
Labour and overhead costs             $8,424
Output transferred to finished goods  8,000 kg
Closing work in progress              900 kg

Normal loss is 10% of input and losses have a scrap value of $0.30 per kg.

Closing work in progress is 100% complete for material, and 75% complete for both labour and overheads.

The value of the closing work in progress for the period was $ ☐

10  A company manufactures product Q, in a single process. At the start of the month there was no work in progress. During the month 300 litres of raw material were input into the process at a total cost of $6,000. Conversion costs during the month amounted to $4,500. At the end of the month 250 litres of product Q were transferred to finished goods inventory. Normal process loss is 5% of input, abnormal loss was 5 litres and the remaining work in process was 100% complete with respect to materials and 50% complete with respect to conversion costs.

The equivalent units for closing work in progress at the end of the month would have been:

Material          ☐   equivalent litres

Conversion costs  ☐   equivalent litres

11   A company makes a product, which passes through a single process.

Details of the process for the last period are as follows:

Materials                 5,000 kg at 50c per kg
Labour                    $700
Production overheads      200% of labour

Normal losses are 10% of input in the process, and without further processing any losses can be sold as scrap for 20c per kg.

The output for the period was 4,200 kg from the process.

There was no work in progress at the beginning or end of the period.

The value of the output for the period is $ ☐

12   In process costing the 'Point of separation' is relevant to which of the following?

A    Abnormal losses
B    Normal losses
C    Joint products
D    Abnormal gains

13   A company discovers, at the end of a process, that abnormal losses had occurred.

At what value would a unit of abnormal loss be recorded in the process account?

A    The total cost per unit of normal output
B    Scrap value
C    The direct cost per unit of normal output
D    Nil value

14   What are conversion costs?

☐    Rework costs

☐    Direct costs only

☐    Indirect costs only

☐    Production costs excluding direct materials

15   340 litres of Chemical X were produced in a period. There is a normal loss of 10% of the material input into the process. There was an abnormal loss in the period of 5% of the material input.

How many litres of material were input into the process during the period?

A    357 litres
B    374 litres
C    391 litres
D    400 litres

16   What basis is used to credit abnormal losses in a process account?

A    Raw material cost per unit
B    Nil value
C    Production cost per unit of actual output
D    Production cost per unit of normal output

17  A company manufactures Chemical Z in a single process. No losses occur in the process. There was no work-in-progress at the start of a period during which 300 litres of raw material were input to the process. 250 litres of the finished chemical were output from the process in the period. The work-in-progress remaining was 100% complete with respect to materials and 50% complete with respect to conversion costs.

What were the equivalent units for costing work-in-progress at the end of the period?

|   | Material | Conversion costs |
|---|----------|------------------|
| A | 25 litres | 25 litres |
| B | 25 litres | 50 litres |
| C | 50 litres | 25 litres |
| D | 50 litres | 50 litres |

---

18  How are abnormal GAINS recorded in a process account?

A   Credited at a cost per unit based on total production cost divided by actual output
B   Credited at a cost per unit based on total production cost divided by normal output
C   Debited at a cost per unit based on total production cost divided by actual output
D   Debited at a cost per unit based on total production cost divided by normal output

---

19  Products A and B are manufactured in a joint process. The following data is available for a period:

| | | |
|---|---|---|
| Joint process costs | | $30,000 |
| Output: | Product A | 2,000 kg |
| | Product B | 4,000 kg |
| Selling price | Product A | $12 per kg |
| | Product B | $18 per kg |

What is Product B's share of the joint process costs if the sales value method of cost apportionment is used?

A   $7,500
B   $18,000
C   $20,000
D   $22,500

---

20  The following statements relate to process costing:

1.  The higher the net realisable value of normal losses the lower will be the cost per unit of normal output

2.  The higher the abnormal losses the higher will be the cost per unit of normal output.

Are the statements true or false?

|   | Statement 1 | Statement 2 |
|---|-------------|-------------|
| A | False | False |
| B | False | True |
| C | True | False |
| D | True | True |

---

21  Raw materials costing $12,800 were input to a process during a period. Conversion costs totalled $18,430. There was no work-in-progress at the beginning of the period and no process losses during the period. 3,600 units of the product were completed in the period with 400 units remaining in the process at the end of the period, complete for materials and with 70% of the conversion costs applied.

What was the production cost per unit?

A   $7.81
B   $7.95
C   $8.05
D   $8.68

22    In a production process the percentage completion of the work-in-progress (WIP) at the end of a period is found to have been understated.

When this is corrected what will be the effect on the cost per unit and the total value of WIP?

|   | Cost per unit | Total value of WIP |
|---|---------------|--------------------|
| A | Decrease      | Decrease           |
| B | Decrease      | Increase           |
| C | Increase      | Decrease           |
| D | Increase      | Increase           |

23    Products A and B are manufactured jointly. Production costs in the joint process totalled $102,000 in a period and output was:

Product A    12,000 units (sold at $6.00 per unit)
Product B    22,000 units (sold at $4.00 per unit)

Joint costs are apportioned on the basis of realisable value.

What share of the joint costs in the period would be apportioned to Product B?

A    $40,800
B    $45,900
C    $56,100
D    $66,000

24    12,00 kg of a material were input to a process in a period. The normal loss is 10% of input. There is no opening or closing work-in-progress. Output in the period was 10,920 kg.

What was the abnormal gain/loss in the period?

A    Abnormal gain of 120 kg
B    Abnormal loss of 120 kg
C    Abnormal gain of 1,080 kg
D    Abnormal loss of 1,080 kg

25    In process costing what are equivalent units?

A    Production output expressed as expected performance
B    Production of homogeneous product
C    Notional whole units representing incomplete work
D    Units produced in more than one process

# 30 Compulsory written question: Process costing I
# (Pilot paper)
**14 mins**

Chemicals X, Y and Z are produced from a single joint process. The information below relates to the period just ended:

Input to process:    Direct materials    3,200 litres, cost $24,000
                     Direct labour       $48,000

                     Factory overheads are absorbed at 120% of prime cost

Output from process: Chemical X    1,440 litres
                     Chemical Y    864 litres
                     Chemical Z    576 litres

                     Scrap  10% of input, credited to the process account at sales value as it occurs

| Selling prices: | Chemical X | $100 per litre |
| | Chemical Y | $80 per litre |
| | Chemical Z | $60 per litre |
| | Scrap | $16 per litre |

*Required*

Calculate for the period just ended:

(a)   The joint process costs to be apportioned to the joint products;                                  (4 marks)

(b)   The total sales value of the output of the three products;                                         (2 marks)

(c)   The share of the joint process costs charged to Chemical X, using the volume of output method of apportionment;                                                                                          (3 marks)

(d)   The share of the joint process costs charged to Chemical Y, using the sales value method of apportionment.
                                                                                                        (3 marks)
                                                                                                       **(12 marks)**

# 31 Compulsory written question: Process costing II (6/04)

## 23 mins

(a)   (i)    Give an example of a business where job costing may be applied and describe the features of this type of business which make the costing method appropriate;                                        (4 marks)

      (ii)   Give an example of a business where process costing may be applied and describe the features of this type of business which make the costing method appropriate.                                     (4 marks)

(b)   A company manufactures a product by means of two successive processes, Process 1 and Process 2. The following relates to the period just ended:

| | *Process 2* | |
| | Units | Cost ($) |
| Opening work in process | Nil | Nil |
| Transfer from Process 1 | 2,160 | 22,032 |
| Material added | | 5,295 |
| Conversion costs | | 8,136 |
| Transfer to finished goods warehouse | 1,950 | |
| Closing work-in progress | 210 | |

The work-in-progress at the end of the period was 80% complete with respect to material added and 40% complete with respect to conversion costs in Process 2.

*Required*

Calculate for the period the:

(i)    Production cost per equivalent unit of the product;                                               (6 marks)
(ii)   Value of the transfer to the finished goods warehouse;                                            (2 marks)
(iii)  Value of the closing work-in-progress in Process 2.                                               (3 marks)
                                                                                                       **(19 marks)**

# 32 Compulsory written question: Process costing III (6/05)

**17 mins**

600 tonnes of raw material, costing $430,032, were input to a process in a period. Conversion costs totaled $119,328. Losses, in the form of reject product, are normally 12% of input. Reject product is sold for $260.00 per tonne.

521 tonnes of finished product passed inspection in the period. The remaining output was sold as reject product. There was no work-in-progress either at the beginning or the end of the period.

*Required*

For the period:

(a) Calculate the cost per unit of normal output. (8 marks)
(b) Prepare the process account, including any abnormal losses/gains. (6 marks)

**(14 marks)**

# 33 Compulsory written question: Process costing IV (6/06)

**19 mins**

(a) Two products (Y and Z) are jointly produced in a single process. Joint costs for a period totalled $52,000. Output of the two products in the period was:

| | |
|---|---|
| Product Y | 2,000 units |
| Product Z | 3,500 units |

There was no opening or closing work-in-progress or finished goods inventory.

Both products are currently sold without further processing for:

| | |
|---|---|
| Product Y | $12.00 per unit |
| Product Z | $16.00 per unit |

Sales values are used as the basis for apportioning joint costs.

*Required*

Prepare a statement showing the gross profit (in total and per unit) for each product in the period.

(9 marks)

(b) In another process operation joint products A and B are produced. Joint costs, apportioned on the basis of weight of output, are $9.80 per kg. Product A can be sold at the split-off point for $9.00 per kg. Alternatively the product can be processed further, at an incremental cost of $2.10 per kg, and sold as Product AA at a price of $11.50 per kg.

*Required*

Comment on EACH of the following statements concerning Product A:

(i) The product should be processed further because if sold as Product A the selling price is below cost. (3 marks)

(ii) The product should be processed further because profit would increase.

(Show calculations clearly to support your comment.) (4 marks)

**(16 marks)**

# 34 Compulsory written question: Process costing V (12/07)

**13 mins**

The following summary shows the selling prices, costs and output of joint products JP1 and JP2 from a manufacturing process

|  | Product JP1 | Product JP2 |
|---|---|---|
| Selling price | $20.00 per kg | $10.00 per kg |
| Share of joint costs | $12.00 per kg | $12.00 per kg |
| Profit/(loss) | $8.00 per kg | ($2.00) per kg |
| Output | 100kg | 120kg |

Both products can be sold at the split-off point but Product JP1 can also be further processed to form Product FP1. Relevant selling price, cost and output information for Product FP1 is:

|  | Product FP1 |
|---|---|
| Selling price | $25.00 per kg |
| Further processing cost | $3.50 per kg |
| Output | 100kg |

*Required*

(a)  Calculate the total joint costs for the period and state the method used to apportion them in the situation above.                                                                                (3 marks)

(b)  Comment on each of the following statements, justifying your comments with supporting calculations:

    (i)   Product JP2 should be discontinued because it makes a loss of $2·00 per unit;          (4 marks)

    (ii)  Product JP1 should be further processed.                                                (4 marks)

**(11 marks)**

# Do you know? – Cost-volume-profit (CVP) analysis and decision making

**Check that you can fill in the blanks in the statements below before you attempt any questions. If in doubt, you should go back to your BPP Interactive Text and revise first.**

- The number of units of sale required to break even is known as the ................................. .

- The ratio which measures how much contribution is earned from each \$1 of sales is known as the ........................................ or ........................................ ratio.

- The difference between the budgeted sales volume (or revenue) and the breakeven sales volume (or revenue) is known as the .......................................................... .

- The total contribution required for a target profit = required profit + ........................... .

- Breakeven analysis is a useful technique for managers as it can provide simple and quick estimates. A graphical representation of breakeven arithmetic can be provided by a ........................... .

- Future costs, cash flows, incremental costs, differential costs and opportunity costs are all known as ......................... costs.

- A past cost which is not relevant in decision making is known as a ........................... .

- In general, when deciding which costs are relevant to a decision, variable costs will be ............... costs and fixed costs will be .................. to the decision.

- The amount of money that a company would have to receive if it were to continue operating without an asset in order to be no worse off than at present, is known as the ............................. .

- A factor which limits an organisation's activities is known as a ........................................ .

TRY QUESTIONS 36 to 42

- *Possible pitfalls*

  *Write down the mistakes you know you should avoid.*

# Did you know? – Cost-volume-profit (CVP) analysis and decision making

**Could you fill in the blanks? The answers are in bold. Use this page for revision purposes as you approach the exam.**

- The number of units of sale required to break even is known as the **breakeven point**.

- The ratio which measures how much contribution is earned from each $1 of sales is known as the **contribution/sales** or **profit/volume** ratio.

- The difference between the budgeted sales volume (or revenue) and the breakeven sales volume (or revenue) is known as the **margin of safety**.

- The total contribution required for a target profit = required profit + **fixed costs**.

- Breakeven analysis is a useful technique for managers as it can provide simple and quick estimates. A graphical representation of breakeven arithmetic can be provided by a **breakeven chart.**

- Future costs, cash flows, incremental costs, differential costs and opportunity costs are all known as **relevant** costs.

- A past cost which is not relevant in decision making is known as a **sunk cost**.

- In general, when deciding which costs are relevant to a decision, variable costs will be **relevant** costs and fixed costs will be **irrelevant** to the decision.

- The amount of money that a company would have to receive if it were to continue operating without an asset, in order to be no worse off than at present, is known as the **deprival value**.

- A factor which limits an organisation's activities is known as a **limiting factor**.

  TRY QUESTIONS 36 to 42

- *Possible pitfalls*

  - **Classifying sunk costs and committed costs as relevant costs**

  - **Not learning all of the formulae required in order to carry out CVP analysis calculations!**

# 35 Objective test questions: Cost-volume-profit (CVP) analysis

1    A company makes a single product and incurs fixed costs of $30,000 per month. Variable cost per unit is $5 and each unit sells for $15. Monthly sales demand is 7,000 units. The breakeven point in terms of monthly sales units is:

    A    2,000 units
    B    3,000 units
    C    4,000 units
    D    6,000 units

2    Which of the following describes the margin of safety?

    A    actual contribution margin achieved compared with that required to break-even
    B    actual sales compared with sales required to break-even
    C    actual verses budgeted net profit margin
    D    actual verses budgeted sales

## The following information relates to questions 3 to 4

Information concerning K Limited's single product is as follows.

|                            | $ per unit |
|----------------------------|-----------:|
| Selling price              | 6.00       |
| Variable production cost   | 1.20       |
| Variable selling cost      | 0.40       |
| Fixed production cost      | 4.00       |
| Fixed selling cost         | 0.80       |

Budgeted production and sales for the year are 10,000 units.

3    What is the company's breakeven point, to the nearest whole unit?

    A    8,000 units
    B    8,333 units
    C    10,000 units
    D    10,909 units

4    How many units must be sold if K Limited wants to achieve a profit of $11,000 for the year?

    A    2,500 units
    B    9,833 units
    C    10,625 units
    D    13,409 units

5    P Limited manufactures a single product E. Data for the product are as follows.

|                                 | $ per unit |
|---------------------------------|-----------:|
| Selling price                   | 50         |
| Direct material cost            | 7          |
| Direct labour cost              | 8          |
| Variable production overhead cost | 8        |
| Variable selling overhead cost  | 2          |
| Fixed overhead cost             | 10         |
| Profit per unit                 | 15         |

The contribution/sales ratio for product E is [    ] % (to the nearest whole percent).

6  Information concerning a company's single product is as follows.

|                          | $ per unit |
|--------------------------|-----------:|
| Selling price            | 19.50      |
| Variable production cost | 3.90       |
| Variable selling cost    | 0.60       |
| Fixed production cost    | 13.00      |
| Fixed selling cost       | 2.60       |

Budgeted production and sales for the year are 12,000 units.

The required annual sales to achieve a profit of $7,800 is ⬚ units.

7

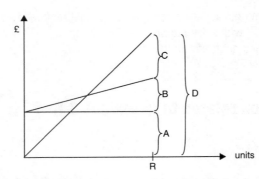

On the above breakeven chart, the contribution at level of activity R can be read as

⬚ less ⬚

8  A Ltd makes a single product which it sells for $10 per unit. Fixed costs are $48,000 per month and the product has a contribution to sales ratio of 40%.

In a month when actual sales were $140,000, A Ltd's margin of safety, in units, was

A  2,000
B  12,000
C  14,000
D  20,000

9  A single product company has a contribution to sales ratio of 40%. Fixed costs amount to $90,000 per annum.

The number of units required to break even is

A  36,000
B  150,000
C  225,000
D  impossible to calculate without further information

10 Z plc makes a single product which it sells for $16 per unit. Fixed costs are $76,800 per month and the product has a contribution to sales ratio of 40%. In a period when actual sales were $224,000, Z plc's margin of safety, in units, was

A  2,000
B  12,000
C  14,000
D  32,000

11    A company's breakeven point is 6,000 units per annum. The selling price is $90 per unit and the variable cost is $40 per unit. What are the company's annual fixed costs?

A    $120
B    $240,000
C    $300,000
D    $540,000

## The following graph relates to questions 12 and 13

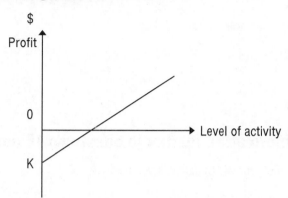

12    Point K on the graph indicates the value of

- semi-variable cost
- total cost
- variable cost
- fixed cost

13    This graph is known as a

- conventional breakeven chart
- contribution breakeven chart
- semi-variable cost chart
- profit/volume chart

14    Windy Ltd manufactures a single product Q, data for which are as follows.

|  | $ per unit |
|---|---|
| Selling price | 60 |
| Direct material cost | 14 |
| Direct labour cost | 12 |
| Variable overhead cost | 19 |
| Fixed overhead cost | 11 |
| Profit | 4 |

The contribution/sales ratio for product Q is ☐ % (to the nearest percent)

15    E Limited manufactures a single product, P. Data for the product are as follows.

|                                   | $ per unit |
|-----------------------------------|-----------|
| Selling price                     | 20        |
| Direct material cost              | 4         |
| Direct labour cost                | 3         |
| Variable production overhead cost | 2         |
| Variable selling overhead cost    | 1         |
| Fixed overhead cost               | 5         |
| Profit per unit                   | 5         |

The contribution/sales ratio for product P is

A    25%
B    50%
C    55%
D    60%

# The following information relates to questions 16 and 17

W Limited sells one product for which data is given below:

|                | $ per unit |
|----------------|-----------|
| Selling price  | 10        |
| Variable cost  | 6         |
| Fixed cost     | 2         |

The fixed costs are based on a budgeted level of activity of 5,000 units for the period.

16    How many units must be sold if W Limited wishes to earn a profit of $6,000 for one period?

A    1,500
B    1,600
C    4,000
D    8,000

17    What is W Limited's margin of safety for the budget period if fixed costs prove to be 20% higher than budgeted?

A    29%
B    40%
C    50%
D    66%

18    B Limited manufactures and sells a single product, with the following estimated costs for next year.

|                     | Unit cost | |
|---------------------|-----------------------------|-----------------------------|
|                     | 100,000 units of output | 150,000 units of output |
|                     | $ | $ |
| Direct materials    | 20.00 | 20.00 |
| Direct labour       | 5.00  | 5.00  |
| Production overheads | 10.00 | 7.50  |
| Marketing costs     | 7.50  | 5.00  |
| Administration costs | 5.00 | 4.00  |
|                     | 47.50 | 41.50 |

Fixed costs are unaffected by the volume of output.

B Limited's management think they can sell 150,000 units per annum if the sales price is $49.50.

The breakeven point, in units, at this price is

A     36,364
B     90,000
C     101,020
D     225,000

19

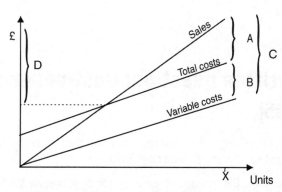

In the above breakeven chart, the contribution at level of activity x can be read as:

A     Distance A
B     Distance B
C     Distance C
D     Distance D

20     A company's single product has a contribution to sales ratio of 20%. The unit selling price is $12. In a period when fixed costs were $48,000 the profit earned was $5,520.

Direct wages were 30% of total variable costs, therefore:

The direct wages cost for the period was $ ⬚

# Questions 21 and 22 are based on the following data:

| | |
|---|---|
| Sales units | 128,000 |
| Sales revenue | $640,000 |
| Variable costs | $384,000 |
| Fixed costs | $210,000 |

21     What sales revenue is required to earn a profit of $65,000?

A     $458,333
B     $590,000
C     $687,500
D     $705,000

22     How many sales units are required to earn a profit of $52,000?

A     52,400 units
B     87,333 units
C     131,000 units
D     160,500 units

23    A company is considering an immediate investment in new machinery. The machinery would cost $100,000 with expected net cash inflows of $30,000 per year starting in Year 1. The disposal value of the machine after five years is expected to be $10,000. $15,000 has already been incurred on development costs.

What is the payback period of the investment based on future incremental cash flows?

A    3.0 years
B    3.3 years
C    3.5 years
D    3.8 years

# 36 Compulsory written question: Cost-volume-profit (CVP) analysis I (6/05)

**20 mins**

A book publisher makes an initial payment of $25,000 to authors for each accepted manuscript, followed by a royalty payment of 15% of the net sales price of each book sold.

The net sales price of a book, which is the revenue received by the publisher, is the listed selling price in bookstores less the bookstore margin of 20% of the listed selling price.

A particular book has a listed selling price of $15.00. Costs incurred on the book by the publisher (excluding initial and royalty payments to the author) are:

Variable costs per copy          $3.20
Total fixed costs          $80,000

*Required*

(a)    Calculate the number of copies of the particular book that need to be sold for the publisher:

    (i)     To break even;                                                                                    (9 marks)
    (ii)    To make a profit of $35,000.                                                               (3 marks)

(b)    Prepare a profit/volume (P/V) chart for the publisher, relating to the particular book publication, covering sales up to 25,000 copies.                                                                        (5 marks)

**(17 marks)**

# 37 Compulsory written question: Cost-volume-profit (CVP) analysis II (12/05)

**22 mins**

(a)    Company A manufactures and sells a single product. The following information is available:

Selling price per unit          $60.00
Variable costs per unit          $36.00
Fixed costs per period          $216,000

*Required*

    (i)     Draw a profit/volume (P/V) chart based on sales up to 14,000 units per period.        (8 marks)
    (ii)    Clearly identify the break-even point, and areas of profit and loss, on the chart.        (2 marks)

(b)    Company B manufactures and sells three products. The following information is available:

|  | Product A | Product B | Product C |
|---|---|---|---|
|  | $ | $ | $ |
| Selling price per unit | 10.00 | 12.50 | 18.70 |
| Variable costs per unit | 5.20 | 7.50 | 9.35 |
|  | Hrs | Hrs | Hrs |
| Machine hours per unit | 0.6 | 0.5 | 1.0 |
| Direct labour hours per unit | 1.0 | 1.2 | 2.5 |

The company wishes to maximise profit each period.

*Required*

(i) Calculate the contribution/sales (C/S) ratio of each of the products. (2 marks)

(ii) List the products in the order of their production priority (ie most profitable product first) in EACH of the following situations:

(1) If machine hours are the limiting factor; (3 marks)

(2) If direct labour hours are the limiting factor. (3 marks)

**(18 marks)**

# 38 Compulsory written question: Cost-volume-profit (CVP) analysis III (6/06)
16 mins

A profit/volume (P/V) chart of two companies (A and B) for a period follows:

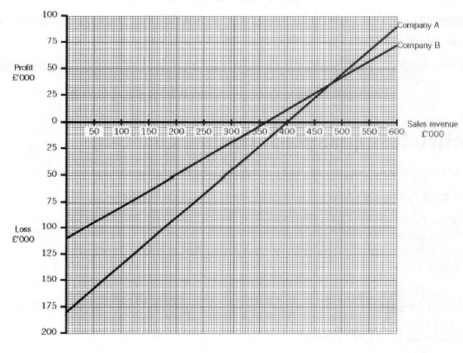

*Required*

(a) By reference to the above chart:

(i) Estimate the break-even sales revenue of Company A. (2 marks)

(ii) Estimate the total fixed costs of Company A. (2 marks)

(iii) State which company has the higher contribution/sales ratio (justify your conclusion). (3 marks)

(iv) Estimate the level of sales at which the profit of the two companies is the same. (2 marks)

(b) Calculate the contribution/sales ratio of Company A and use this to confirm, by calculation, the break-even point identified in (a)(i) above. (4 marks)

**(13 marks)**

# 39 Compulsory written question: Cost-volume-profit (CVP) analysis IV (6/07)

**12 mins**

The variable costs per unit of a company's single product for the period just ended were:

|  | $ |
|---|---|
| Production | 120 |
| Non-production | 16 |

The selling price of the product in the period was $200 per unit and the sales revenue required to break-even was $120,000.

*Required*

(a)     Calculate for the period just ended:

|  |  |  |
|---|---|---|
| (i) | The contribution/sales ratio; | (3 marks) |
| (ii) | The total fixed costs. | (3 marks) |

(b)     In the following period it is expected that fixed costs will total $39,000.

*Required*

Calculate the required contribution per unit in the following period for the break-even point to be 500units.

(4 marks)

**(10 marks)**

# 40 Objective test questions: Decision making

1       In decision making, costs which need to be considered are said to be **relevant costs.**

Which of the following are characteristics associated with relevant costs?

|  |  |
|---|---|
| (i) | Future costs |
| (ii) | Unavoidable costs |
| (iii) | Incremental costs |
| (iv) | Differential costs |

|  |  |
|---|---|
| A | (i) and (iii) only |
| B | (i) and (ii) only |
| C | (i), (iii) and (iv) only |
| D | All of them |

2       Which of the following is *not* a relevant cost?

|  |  |
|---|---|
| A | Differential cost |
| B | Committed cost |
| C | Out-of-pocket cost |
| D | Incremental cost |

3       You are currently employed as a Management Accountant in an insurance company. You are contemplating starting your own business. In considering whether or not to start your own business, your current salary level would be:

|  |  |
|---|---|
| A | A sunk cost |
| B | An incremental cost |
| C | An irrelevant cost |
| D | An opportunity cost |

4    Sue is considering starting a new business and she has already spent $5,000 on market research and intends to spend a further $2,000.

In the assessment of the relevant costs of the decision to set up the business, market research costs are:

A    A sunk cost of $7,000
B    A sunk cost of $5,000 and an incremental cost of $2,000
C    A sunk cost of $2,000 and an incremental cost of $5,000
D    An opportunity cost of $7,000

5    A firm has some material which originally cost $45,000. It has a scrap value of $12,500 but if reworked at a cost of $7,500, it could be sold for $17,500. There is no other foreseen use for the material.

The relevant cost of using the material for a special job is $ [        ]

6    When comparing the costs of different factories, a firm charges rent as an expense in all the factory operating statements even when the particular factory is owned and not rented. In these circumstances the rent is:

[        ]    An avoidable cost

[        ]    A notional cost

[        ]    A fixed cost

[        ]    An incremental cost

7    Which of the following descriptions of a sunk cost is/are correct?

[        ]    A cost which is irrelevant for decision making

[        ]    A cost that has already been incurred

[        ]    A cost that is unaffected by future fluctuations in the level of activity

8    Your company regularly uses material X and currently has in stock (inventory) 500 kgs for which it paid $1,500 two weeks ago. If this were to be sold as raw material, it could be sold today for $2.00 per kg. You are aware that the material can be bought on the open market for $3.25 per kg, but it must be purchased in quantities of 1,000 kgs.

You have been asked to determine the relevant cost of 600 kgs of material X to be used in a job for a customer. The relevant cost of the 600 kgs is

A    $1,325
B    $1,825
C    $1,950
D    $3,250

9    X Limited has 500 kg of material K in stock (inventory) for which it paid $2,000. The material is no longer in use in the company and could be sold for $1.50 per kg.

X Limited is considering taking on a single special order which will require 800 kg of material K. The current purchase price of material K is $5 per kg.

In the assessment of the relevant cost of the decision to accept the special order, the cost of material K is

A    A sunk cost of $2,000
B    A sunk cost of $2,000 and an incremental cost of $1,500
C    An opportunity cost of $750 and an incremental cost of $1,500
D    An incremental cost of $4,000

10   A company is considering the use of Material X in a special order. A sufficient quantity of the material, which is used regularly by the company in its normal business, is available from stock (inventory).

What is the relevant cost per kg of Material X in the evaluation of the special order?

    A    Cost of the last purchase
    B    Nil
    C    Replacement cost
    D    Saleable value

---

11   MF Ltd manufactures three products, the selling price and cost details of which are as follows.

|  | Product M | Product F | Product S |
|---|---|---|---|
|  | $ per unit | $ per unit | $ per unit |
| Selling price | 129 | 137 | 141 |
| Direct material ($8/kg) | 32 | 16 | 40 |
| Direct labour ($6/hour) | 30 | 36 | 24 |
| Variable overhead | 10 | 12 | 8 |
| Fixed overhead | 15 | 20 | 14 |

In a period when direct labour is restricted in supply, the most and least profitable use of direct labour are:

Most profitable product ☐

Least profitable product ☐

---

12   A company makes a single product for which cost details are as follows.

|  | $ per unit |
|---|---|
| Direct material ($8 per litre) | 72 |
| Direct labour ($7 per hour) | 49 |
| Production overhead | 56 |
| Total production cost | 177 |

The product is perishable and no stocks (inventory) are held.

Demand for next period will be 2,000 units but only 16,000 litres of material and 15,000 hours of labour will be available. The limiting factor(s) next period will be:

☐ Material

☐ Labour

---

13   A company is launching a new product. In order to manufacture this new product, two types of labour are required – skilled and semi-skilled. The new product requires 5 hours of skilled labour and 5 hours of semi-skilled labour.

A skilled employee is available and is currently paid $10 per hour. A replacement would, however, have to be obtained at a rate of $9 per hour, for the work which would otherwise be done by the skilled employee. The current rate for semi-skilled workers is $5 per hour and an additional employee would be appointed for this work.

The relevant cost of labour to be used in making one unit of the new product would be

$ ☐ (to the nearest $)

14 A company manufactures three products, details of which are as follows.

| | Product J $ per unit | Product K $ per unit | Product L $ per unit |
|---|---|---|---|
| Selling price | 140 | 122 | 134 |
| Direct materials ($2/kg) | 22 | 14 | 26 |
| Other variable cost | 84 | 72 | 51 |
| Fixed cost | 20 | 26 | 40 |

In a period when direct material is restricted in supply, the ranking of the products in terms of the most profitable use of the material is:

First: product ☐

Second: product ☐

Third: product ☐

---

15 A company produces a single product for which cost details are as follows.

| | $ per unit |
|---|---|
| Direct material ($2 per kg) | 8 |
| Direct labour ($6 per hour) | 18 |
| Production overhead | 9 |
| Total production cost | 35 |

The item is perishable and no stocks (inventory) are held.

Demand for next period will be 6,000 units but only 19,000 hours of labour and 22,000 kg of material will be available. What will be the limiting factor next period?

A Material only
B Labour only
C Material and labour
D Sales demand

---

16 R Limited manufactures three products, the selling price and cost details of which are given below.

| | Product P $ | Product Q $ | Product R $ |
|---|---|---|---|
| Selling price per unit | 150 | 190 | 190 |
| **Costs per unit** | | | |
| Direct materials ($5/kg) | 20 | 10 | 30 |
| Direct labour ($4/hour) | 32 | 48 | 40 |
| Variable overhead | 16 | 24 | 20 |
| Fixed overhead | 48 | 72 | 60 |

In a period when direct materials are restricted in supply, the most and least profitable uses of direct materials are:

| | Most profitable | Least profitable |
|---|---|---|
| A | R | P |
| B | Q | R |
| C | Q | P |
| D | R | Q |

17  Z plc manufactures three products which have the following selling prices and costs per unit.

|  | Z1 | Z2 | Z3 |
|---|---|---|---|
|  | $ | $ | $ |
| Selling price | 15.00 | 18.00 | 17.00 |
| **Costs per unit** |  |  |  |
| Direct materials | 4.00 | 5.00 | 10.00 |
| Direct labour | 2.00 | 4.00 | 1.80 |
| **Overhead** |  |  |  |
| Variable | 1.00 | 2.00 | 0.90 |
| Fixed | 4.50 | 3.00 | 1.35 |
|  | 11.50 | 14.00 | 14.05 |
| Profit per unit | 3.50 | 4.00 | 2.95 |

All three products use the same type of labour.

In a period in which labour is in short supply, the rank order of production is:

|  | Z1 | Z2 | Z3 |
|---|---|---|---|
| A | Third | First | Second |
| B | Second | First | Third |
| C | First | Third | Second |
| D | Second | Third | First |

# The following information relates to questions 18 and 19

Brian Ltd produces three products which have the following unit contributions and labour requirements.

| Product | Unit contribution | Labour requirement |
|---|---|---|
|  | $ | Hours |
| Scratch | 6 | 2 |
| Purr | 7 | 3 |
| Buzz | 8 | 3 |

Due to industrial action only 2,600 labour hours are available in control period 13, when expected demand is 700 units of each product. Fixed costs are $1,700 for the period.

18  What is the profit-maximising product mix?

|  | Scratch | Purr | Buzz |
|---|---|---|---|
|  | Units | Units | Units |
| A | 0 | 166 | 700 |
| B | 700 | 0 | 400 |
| C | 700 | 700 | 700 |
| D | 1,300 | 0 | 0 |

19  What is the maximum profit at the profit-maximising product mix?

A   $5,062
B   $5,700
C   $6,100
D   $13,000

20  An engineering company has been offered the opportunity to bid for a contract which requires a special component. Currently, the company has a component in inventory, which has a net book value of $250. This component could be used in the contract, but would require modification at a cost of $50. There is no other foreseeable use for the component held in inventory. Alternatively, the company could purchase a new specialist component for $280.

The relevant cost of using the component currently held in inventory for this contract is $

21 A company manufactures and sells four products. Sales demand cannot be met owing to a shortage of skilled labour. Details of the four products are:

|  | Product A | Product B | Product C | Product D |
| --- | --- | --- | --- | --- |
| Sales demand (units) | 1,500 | 2,000 | 1,800 | 1,900 |
| Contribution ($/unit) | 2.80 | 2.60 | 1.90 | 2.40 |
| Contribution/sales (%) | 30 | 40 | 50 | 45 |
| Skilled labour (hours/unit) | 1.4 | 1.2 | 0.9 | 1.0 |

In what order should the products be made in order to maximise profit?

A    Product A, Product B, Product D, Product C
B    Product B, Product D, Product C, Product A
C    Product C, Product D, Product B, Product A
D    Product D, Product B, Product C, Product A

22 What term is used to represent the benefit sacrificed when one course of action is chosen in preference to an alternative?

A    Avoidable cost
B    Direct cost
C    Incremental cost
D    Opportunity cost

# 41 Compulsory written question: Decision making I (12/04)

**17 mins**

A company manufactures three products. Sales demand for the products in the next period is estimated to be:

| | |
| --- | --- |
| Product A | 6,200 units |
| Product B | 8,000 units |
| Product C | 11,500 units |

Selling prices and unit costs are:

|  | Product A | Product B | Product C |
| --- | --- | --- | --- |
|  | $ per unit | $ per unit | $ per unit |
| Selling price | 9.70 | 11.10 | 13.80 |
| Costs: | | | |
| Direct materials | 2.80 | 3.90 | 4.92 |
| Direct labour ($8.00 per hour) | 2.40 | 2.40 | 3.20 |
| Variable overhead | 0.90 | 0.90 | 1.20 |
| Fixed overheads | 2.70 | 2.70 | 3.60 |

The company is experiencing a shortage of direct labour and estimates that a maximum of 8,500 hours will be available in the next period.

*Required*

(a)    Demonstrate that the availability of direct labour will be a limiting factor in the next period.          (4 marks)

(b)    Determine the production schedule for the next period that will maximise profit.          (10 marks)
          **(14 marks)**

# 42 Compulsory written question: Decision making II (12/07)

**24 mins**

A passenger transport company operates four coaches, each with a capacity for 25 passengers. The company operates on two routes with two coaches on each route. Each coach on Route A completes 12 journeys per day and on Route B 10 journeys per day. The coaches operate for six days per week and for 52 weeks per year.

The company is analysing performance on each route and has gathered the following route data for the last 52 weeks:

|  | Route A | Route B |
|---|---|---|
| Average numbers of passengers per journey | 13 | 11 |
| Average fair paid per passenger, per journey | $2.26 | $2.80 |
| Route length per journey (kilometres) | 14 | 19 |

Operating cost data for the last 52 week period is as follows:

| | |
|---|---|
| Drivers' wages | $110 per coach per working day |
| Fuel and maintenance | $0.8932 per kilometre |
| Vehicle tax and insurance | $3,870 per coach for the period |
| Apportioned fixed costs | $21,760 per route for the period |

*Required*

Calculate, for the 52 week period, the:

| | | |
|---|---|---|
| (a) | total cost per coach on each route; | (10 marks) |
| (b) | cost per kilometre on each route (to four decimal places of $); | (5 marks) |
| (c) | profit per kilometre on each route. | (5 marks) |
| | | **(20 marks)** |

# Do you know? – Capital investment appraisal

**Check that you can fill in the blanks in the statements below before you attempt any questions. If in doubt, you should go back to your BPP Interactive Text and revise first.**

- The basic principle of ............................. involves calculating the present value of an investment. The present value of an investment is the amount of money which must be invested now (for a number of years) in order to earn a future sum (at a given rate of interest).

- A constant sum of money received or paid each year for a given number of years is known as an ..................... . If this constant sum lasts forever, then it is known as a ......................... .

- Annuity × annuity factor = ...............................................................

- Annuity ÷ interest rate = ...............................................................

- The two main discounted cash flow methods ——⌐— NPV
                                                └— IRR

  - **Net present value (NPV) method**. If an investment has a ............... NPV then it is acceptable. An investment with a ..................... NPV should be rejected.

  - **Internal rate of return (IRR) method**. This method determines the rate of interest at which the NPV of the investment = ..... . The project is viable if the IRR exceeds the minimum acceptable return.

- The IRR formula is as follows.

$$IRR = a\% + \left[ \frac{A}{A-B} \times (b-a) \right]\%$$

  Where a = ..........................................

  b = ..........................................

  A = ..........................................

  B = ..........................................

- The time that is required for the cash inflows from a capital investment project to equal the cash outflows is known as the ................................................. .

  TRY QUESTIONS 43 to 46

- *Possible pitfalls*

  *Write down the mistakes you know you should avoid.*

# Did you know? – Capital investment appraisal

**Could you fill in the blanks? The answers are in bold. Use this page for revision purposes as you approach the exam.**

- The basic principle of **discounting** involves calculating the present value of an investment. The present value of an investment is the amount of money which must be invested now (for a number of years) in order to earn a future sum (at a given rate of interest).

- A constant sum of money received or paid each year for a given number of years is known as an **annuity**. If this constant sum lasts forever, then it is known as a **perpetuity**.

- Annuity × annuity factor = **present value of an annuity**

- Annuity ÷ interest rate = **present value of a perpetuity**

- The two main discounted cash flow methods ⎯⎡⎯ NPV
  ⎣⎯ IRR

  - **Net present value (NPV) method**. If an investment has a **positive** NPV then it is acceptable. An investment with a **negative** NPV should be rejected.

  - **Internal rate of return (IRR) method**. This method determines the rate of interest at which the NPV of the investment = **zero**. The project is viable if the IRR exceeds the minimum acceptable return.

- The IRR formula is as follows.

  $$IRR = a\% + \left[ \frac{A}{A-B} \times (b-a) \right]\%$$

  Where a = **one interest rate**

         b = **the other interest rate**

        A = **NPV at rate a**

        B = **NPV at rate b**

- The time that is required for the cash inflows from a capital investment project to equal the cash outflows is known as the **payback period**.

  TRY QUESTIONS 43 to 46

- *Possible pitfalls*

  - **Not being able to calculate and distinguish between the nominal rate of interest and the effective annual rate of interest**

  - **Not being able to calculate the IRR of an investment, even when given the IRR formula. (You must remember what the symbols in the formula mean so that you can use the correct figures in your calculations.)**

# 43 Objective test questions: Capital investment appraisal

1    A building society adds interest monthly to investors' accounts even though interest rates are expressed in annual terms. The current rate of interest is 6% per annum.

An investor deposits $1,000 on 1 January. How much interest will have been earned by 30 June?

A    $30.00
B    $30.38
C    $60.00
D    $300

2    A one-year investment yields a return of 15%. The cash returned from the investment, including principal and interest, is $2,070. The interest is

A    $250
B    $270
C    $300
D    $310.50

3    If a single sum of $12,000 is invested at 8% per annum with interest compounded quarterly, the amount to which the principal will have grown by the end of year three is approximately

A    $15,117
B    $9,528
C    $15,219
D    $30,924

4    Which is worth most, at present values, assuming an annual rate of interest of 8%?

A    $1,200 in exactly one year from now
B    $1,400 in exactly two years from now
C    $1,600 in exactly three years from now
D    $1,800 in exactly four years from now

5    A bank offers depositors a nominal 4% pa, with interest payable quarterly. What is the effective annual rate of interest?

A    1%
B    4%
C    1.025%
D    4.06%

6    A project requiring an investment of $1,200 is expected to generate returns of $400 in years 1 and 2 and $350 in years 3 and 4. If the NPV = $22 at 9% and the NPV = –$4 at 10%, what is the IRR for the project?

A    9.15%
B    9.85%
C    10.15%
D    10.85%

7    A sum of money was invested for 10 years at 7% per annum and is now worth $2,000. The original amount invested (to the nearest $) was

A    $1,026
B    $1,016
C    $3,937
D    $14,048

8 House prices rise at 2% per calendar month. The annual rate of increase correct to one decimal place is

    A    24%
    B    26.8%
    C    12.7%
    D    12.2%

9 Find the present value of ten annual payments of $700, the first paid immediately and discounted at 8%, giving your answer to the nearest $.

    A    $4,697
    B    $1,050
    C    $4,435
    D    $5,073

10 A firms buys a material on a long-term contract which stipulates a price increase per annum of 6% compound. If the current price is $200 per kg, the price in 5 years, to the nearest penny, will be $☐

11 An investor is to receive an annuity of $19,260 for six years commencing at the end of year 1. It has a present value of $86,400.

The rate of interest (to the nearest whole percent) is ☐ %

12 A company charges depreciation at the rate of 25% per annum on the reducing balance method on an asset which cost $40,000.

At the end of year 4 the written down value will be $☐

State your answer to the nearest penny.

13 How much should be invested now (to the nearest $) to receive $24,000 per annum in perpetuity if the annual rate of interest is 5%?

Answer = $☐

14 The net present value of an investment at 12% is $24,000, and at 20% is −$8,000. The internal rate of return of this investment is ☐ %

State your answer to the nearest whole percent.

## The following data is relevant for questions 15 and 16

Diamond Ltd has a payback period limit of three years and is considering investing in one of the following projects. Both projects require an initial investment of $800,000. Cash inflows accrue evenly throughout the year.

| Project Alpha | | Project Beta | |
|---|---|---|---|
| Year | Cash inflow | Year | Cash inflow |
| | $ | | $ |
| 1 | 250,000 | 1 | 250,000 |
| 2 | 250,000 | 2 | 350,000 |
| 3 | 400,000 | 3 | 400,000 |
| 4 | 300,000 | 4 | 200,000 |
| 5 | 200,000 | 5 | 150,000 |
| 6 | 50,000 | 6 | 150,000 |

The company's cost of capital is 10%.

15 The non-discounted payback period of Project Beta = ☐ years and ☐ months.

16    The discounted payback period of Project Alpha is between [    ] and [    ] years.

17    A capital investment project has an initial investment followed by constant annual returns.

      How is the payback period calculated?

      A     Initial investment ÷ annual profit
      B     Initial investment ÷ annual net cash inflow
      C     (Initial investment – residual value) ÷ annual profit
      D     (Initial investment – residual value) ÷ annual net cash inflow

18    A machine has an investment cost of $60,000 at time 0. The present values (at time 0) of the expected net cash inflows from the machine over its useful life are:

      | Discount rate | Present value of cash inflows |
      |---|---|
      | 10% | $64,600 |
      | 15% | $58,200 |
      | 20% | $52,100 |

      What is the internal rate of return (IRR) of the machine investment?

      A     Below 10%
      B     Between 10% and 15%
      C     Between 15% and 20%
      D     Over 20%

19    An investment project has a positive net present value (NPV) of $7,222 when its cash flows are discounted at the cost of capital of 10% per annum. Net cash inflows from the project are expected to be $18,000 per annum for five years. The cumulative discount (annuity) factor for five years at 10% is 3.791.

      What is the investment at the start of the project?

      A     $61,016
      B     $68,238
      C     $75,460
      D     $82,778

20    The following statements relate to an investment project that has been discounted at rates of 10% and 20%:

      1.    The discounted payback period at 10% will be longer than the discounted payback period at 20%.
      2.    The discounted payback period at 20% will be longer than the discounted payback period at 10%.
      3.    The non-discounted payback period will be longer than the discounted payback period.
      4.    The non-discounted payback period will be shorter than the discounted payback period.

      Which of the statements are true?

      A     1 and 3
      B     1 and 4
      C     2 and 3
      D     2 and 4

21    Which of the following accurately defines the internal rate of return (IRR)?

      A     The average annual profit from an investment expressed as a percentage of the investment sum
      B     The discount rate (%) at which the net present value of the cash flows from an investment is zero
      C     The net present value of the cash flows from an investment discounted at the required rate of return
      D     The rate (%) at which discounted net profits from an investment are zero

22    An investment project has the following discounted cash flows ($'000):

| Year | Discount rate | | |
| | 0% | 10% | 20% |
| --- | --- | --- | --- |
| 0 | (90) | (90) | (90) |
| 1 | 30 | 27.3 | 25.0 |
| 2 | 30 | 24.8 | 29.8 |
| 3 | 30 | 22.5 | 17.4 |
| 4 | 30 | 20.5 | 14.5 |
| | 30 | 5.1 | (12.3) |

The required rate of return on investment is 10% per annum.

What is the discounted payback period of the investment project?

A    Less than 3.0 years
B    3.0 years
C    Between 3.0 years and 4.0 years
D    More than 4.0 years

23    What is the effective annual rate of interest of 2.1% compounded every three months?

A    6.43%
B    8.40%
C    8.67%
D    10.87%

# 44 Compulsory written question: Compound interest formula and NPV (12/06)

**19 mins**

(a)    The future value (S) of a sum invested now can be calculated using the formula:

$S = P(1 + r)^n$

*Required*

(i)    Define each of the other constituents in the formula above (ie P, r and n);    (3 marks)

(ii)    Calculate the value (to the nearest $) after four years of $5,000 invested now at a compound rate of interest of 8% per annum.    (3 marks)

(b)    A company is considering an investment in new machinery. The incremental annual profits (losses) relating to the investment are estimated to be:

| | $'000 |
| --- | --- |
| Year 1 | (11) |
| Year 2 | 3 |
| Year 3 | 34 |
| Year 4 | 47 |
| Year 5 | 8 |

Investment at the start of the project would be $175,000. The investment sum, assuming nil disposal value after five years, would be written off using the straight-line method. The depreciation has been included in the profit estimates above, which should be assumed to arise at each year end.

*Required*

(i)    Calculate the net present value (NPV) of the investment at a discount rate of 10% per annum (the company's required rate of return);

Discount factors at 10% are:

| | |
|---|---|
| Year 1 | 0.909 |
| Year 2 | 0.826 |
| Year 3 | 0.751 |
| Year 4 | 0.683 |
| Year 5 | 0.621 |

(8 marks)

(ii) State, on the basis of your calculations, whether the investment is worthwhile. Justify your statement.

(2 marks)

**(16 marks)**

# 45 Compulsory written question: Minimum contract price and NPV (12/06)

**23 mins**

A company currently has spare labour hours in Department X and spare machine capacity in Department Z, and is considering each of the following independent opportunities:

1 Whether to quote for Contract W which would be completed in the near future.
2 Whether to take on sub-contract work for a period of three years.

1 *Contract W*

The contract would be carried out without the need for any additional direct operatives in Department X where two existing operatives, each paid at a rate of $7.50 per hour for a guaranteed 37-hour week, would work on the contract for a total of 220 hours. In another department, Department Y, additional labour would have to be taken on at a cost of $2,400.

Total material costs for the contract are estimated at $5,740, based on replacement prices. Included in materials is Component M, a quantity of which is in inventory. Component M is no longer used in the company's business. Details of Component M are:

| | |
|---|---|
| Stockholding | 80 units |
| Required for Contract W | 120 units |
| Purchase price of existing inventory | $6.10 per unit |
| Disposal proceeds of existing inventory if sold | $4.60 per unit |
| Replacement price | $6.50 per unit |

Overheads would be absorbed on the contract on the following basis:

Production overheads - 120% of direct labour cost (only 20% of the overheads absorbed would be an incremental cost)

Non-production overheads - 40% of total production cost (none of the overheads absorbed would be an incremental cost)

2 *Sub-contract work*

The sub-contract work would be carried out in Department Z, utilising existing machinery. The machinery is now surplus to requirements and would otherwise be sold. The net book value of the machinery is $140,000 but the current disposal value is only $120,000. If used for three years on the sub-contract work the disposal value would be expected to reduce to $10,000. The remaining net book value of the machinery would be depreciated on a straight-line basis over the three years.

Net cash inflows from the sub-contract work, occurring at the end of each year, are forecast to be:

| | |
|---|---|
| Year 1 | $40,000 |
| Year 2 | $55,000 |
| Year 3 | $60,000 |

*Required*

(a)     Calculate the minimum price that could be quoted for Contract W in order to recover incremental costs only. (Show workings clearly.)                                           (10 marks)

(b)     Calculate the net present value (NPV) for the sub-contract work at a cost of capital of 10% per annum.

        Discount factors at 10%:

        Year 1          0.909
        Year 2          0.826
        Year 3          0.751                                                                        (9 marks)
                                                                                                    **(19 marks)**

# 46 Compulsory written question: NPV and IRR (6/07)     19 mins

(a)     Explain why cash flows are discounted in capital investment project appraisal.              (2 marks)

(b)     Describe how the net present value is calculated and used in capital investment project appraisal.  (6 marks)

(c)     A capital investment project has estimated net cash inflows of $60,000 per annum for six years. Discounting the net cash inflows at 10% and 20% per annum, the present values of the inflows are:

| *Annual discount rate* | *Present value of inflows* |
|---|---|
| 10% | $261,300 |
| 20% | $199,600 |

        The initial investment amount is $224,000.

*Required*

(i)     Plot the net present values of the project, at discount rates of 10% and 20% per annum, on the graph paper provided;                                                           (6 marks)

(ii)    Indicate, on the graph, an estimate of the internal rate of return of the project.           (2 marks)
                                                                                                    **(16 marks)**

# 47 Mixed bank 1 (6/06)

1       The management accountant of X Ltd has written a report assessing the cost savings that could be made if the company was to invest in new technology.

        In which area will the report primarily aid the management of X Ltd?

        A       Budgeting
        B       Control
        C       Decision-making
        D       Monitoring

2       Which of the following only contains essential features of useful management information?

        A       Accurate, clear, presented in report format
        B       Timely, reliable, supported by calculations
        C       Regular, complete, communicated in writing
        D       Clear, accurate, relevant for its purpose

3       What is an interlocking bookkeeping system?

        A       A single, combined system containing both cost accounting and financial accounting records
        B       A system combining cost accounting and management accounting
        C       A system supposed by prime entry records
        D       A system where separate accounts are kept for cost accounting and for financial accounting

4   A company carries out production in accordance with the special requirements of each customer.

Which costing method is MOST appropriate?

A   Batch costing
B   Job costing
C   Process costing
D   Service costing

5   Total costs incurred by a business may be expressed as:

$y = a + bx$

when   y represents the total costs
       a represents the total fixed costs
       b represents the variable costs per unit
       x represents the number of units of output

A company has variable costs of $12.20 per unit and total costs, for output of 7,400 units in a period, of $156,980.

Using the above formula and information, what are the total fixed costs in the period?

A   $42,540
B   $66,700
C   $90,280
D   $247,260

6   A company currently produces 6,000 units of its single product each period, incurring total variable costs of $60,000 and fixed costs of $42,000. Production will increase to 8,000 units per period if the company expands capacity resulting in changes both to the variable costs per unit and to the total fixed costs. For production of 8,000 units per period total variable costs would be $76,000 and fixed costs $50,000.

What is the reduction in total cost per unit comparing the costs for 8,000 units per period with the unit costs currently being incurred?

A   $0.50
B   $0.75
C   $1.25
D   $2.08

7   The following documents are used in accounting for raw materials:

(i)    Goods received note
(ii)   Materials returned note
(iii)  Materials requisition note
(iv)   Delivery note

Which of the documents may be used to record raw materials sent back to stores from production?

A   (i) and (ii)
B   (i) and (iv)
C   (ii) only
D   (ii) and (iii)

BPP
LEARNING MEDIA

8      Material M is used by a manufacturer. Inventory of Material M at 1 May was valued at a cost of $3,302 (260 kg at $12.70 per kg). 500 kg were purchased on 7 May for $6,500. 410 kg of Material M were used in production during the month. The LIFO method is applied at the end of each month.

What is the cost accounting entry for the issues of Material M during the month?

| | Debit | | Credit | |
|---|---|---|---|---|
| A | Material inventory | $5,252 | Work-in-progress | $5,252 |
| B | Work-in-progress | $5,252 | Material inventory | $5,252 |
| C | Material inventory | $5,330 | Work-in-progress | $5,330 |
| D | Work-in-progress | $5,330 | Material inventory | $5,330 |

9      How is the re-order level calculated if stock-outs are to be avoided?

A      Maximum usage × Maximum lead time
B      Maximum usage × Minimum lead time
C      Minimum usage × Maximum lead time
D      Minimum usage × Minimum lead time

10      The following information relates to a raw material inventory item:

Economic order quantity      800 units (established using the formula $\sqrt{\dfrac{2cd}{h}}$ )

Demand      12,000 units per annum
Cost of holding inventory      $1.50 per unit per annum

What is the cost of placing an order?

A      $27
B      $40
C      $71
D      $80

11      Which of the following labour records may be used to allocate costs to the various cost units in a factory?

(i)      Employee record card
(ii)      Attendance record card
(iii)      Time sheet
(iv)      Job card

A      (i) and (ii)
B      (i), (iii) and (iv)
C      (ii) and (iii)
D      (iii) and (iv)

12      How is the activity (production volume) ratio calculated?

A      Actual hours ÷ budgeted hours
B      Budgeted hours ÷ actual hours
C      Standard hours for actual output ÷ actual hours
D      Standard hours for actual output ÷ budgeted hours

13      Which of the following relates to capital expenditure?

A      Cost of acquiring or enhancing non-current assets
B      Expenditure on the manufacture of goods or the provision of services
C      Recorded as an asset in the income statement
D      Recorded as a liability in the balance sheet

14 Overheads in a factory are apportioned to four production cost centres (A, B, C and D). Direct labour hours are used to absorb overheads in A and B and machine hours are used in C and D. The following information is available:

|  | Production cost centre | | | |
|  | A | B | C | D |
| --- | --- | --- | --- | --- |
| Overhead expenditure ($) | 18,757 | 29,025 | 46,340 | 42,293 |
| Direct labour hours | 3,080 | 6,750 | 3,760 | 2,420 |
| Machine hours | 580 | 1,310 | 3,380 | 2,640 |

Which cost centre has the highest hourly overhead absorption rate?

A    Production Cost Centre A
B    Production Cost Centre B
C    Production Cost Centre C
D    Production Cost Centre D

15 A company sold 56,000 units of its single product in a period for a total revenue of $700,000. Finished inventory increased by 4,000 units in the period. Costs in the period were:

Variable production          $3.60 per unit
Fixed production             $258,000 (absorbed on the actual number of units produced)
Fixed non-production         $144,000

Using absorption costing, what was the profit for the period?

A    $82,000
B    $96,400
C    $113,600
D    $123,200

16 A company with a single product sells more units than it manufactures in a period.

Which of the following correctly describes the use of marginal costing in comparison with absorption costing in the above situation?

A    Both profit and inventory values will be higher
B    Both profit and inventory values will be lower
C    Profit will be higher; inventory values will be lower
D    Profit will be lower; inventory values will be higher

17 A product has the following unit costs:

Variable manufacturing          $7.60
Variable non-manufacturing      $1.40
Fixed manufacturing             $3.70
Fixed non-manufacturing         $2.70

The selling price of the product is $17.50 per unit

What is the contribution/sales ratio?

A    12.0%
B    48.6%
C    51.4%
D    56.6%

18    A company manufactures and sells four types of component. The labour hours available for manufacture are restricted but any quantities of the components can be brought-in from an outside supplier in order to satisfy sales demand. The following further information is provided:

|  | Component | | | |
|---|---|---|---|---|
|  | A | B | C | D |
|  | per unit | per unit | per unit | per unit |
| Selling price ($) | 12.00 | 15.00 | 18.00 | 20.00 |
| Variable manufacturing costs ($) | 6.00 | 8.0 | 9.00 | 11.50 |
| Bought-in price ($) | 11.00 | 11.50 | 13.00 | 16.00 |
| Labour (hours) | 0.8 | 0.8 | 0.8 | 0.8 |

Which is the best component to buy-in in order to maximise profit?

A    Component A
B    Component B
C    Component C
D    Component D

19    An investment project has net present values as follows:

At a discount rate of 5%        $69,700 positive
At a discount rate of 14%       $16,000 positive
At a discount rate of 20%       $10,500 negative

Using the above figures, what is the BEST approximation of the internal rate of return of the investment project?

A    17.6%
B    17.9%
C    18.0%
D    22.7%

20    A company has decided to lease a machine. Six annual payments of $8,000 will be made with the first payment on receipt of the machine. Below is an extract from an annuity table:

| Year | Annuity factor 10% |
|---|---|
| 1 | 0.909 |
| 2 | 1.736 |
| 3 | 2.487 |
| 4 | 3.170 |
| 5 | 3.791 |
| 6 | 4.355 |

What is the present value of the lease payments at an interest rate of 10%?

A    $30,328
B    $34,840
C    $38,328
D    $48,000

# 48 Mixed bank 2 (12/06)

1    Which of the following describes the control process?

    A     The action of monitoring something to keep it on course
    B     The choice between alternatives
    C     The development of strategies to achieve objectives
    D     The establishment of a plan for a future period

2    Consider the following statements in relation to management information:

    (i)     It should always be provided regardless of its cost
    (ii)    It is data that has been processed in such a way as to be meaningful to the person who receives it
    (iii)   It should not be provided until it is as detailed and accurate as possible

Which of the above statements is/are true of good management information?

    A     (i) only
    B     (ii) only
    C     (i) and (iii)
    D     (ii) and (iii)

3    Which of the following is a feature of cost accounting but not of financial accounting?

    A     Control accounts
    B     Cost classification
    C     Cost units
    D     Periodic stocktaking

4    Which of the following factors may affect the choice of computer output medium?

    (i)     Whether a hard copy of the output is required
    (ii)    Whether the output requires further computer processing
    (iii)   Whether a large volume of output is to be used for reference purposes

    A     (i) and (ii) only
    B     (i) and (iii) only
    C     (ii) and (iii) only
    D     All three factors

5    Production units and total costs relating to the last three periods have been:

|  | Period 1 | Period 2 | Period 3 |
|---|---|---|---|
| Production (units) | 129,440 | 117,620 | 126,310 |
| Total cost ($) | 198,968 | 187,739 | 195,376 |

Using the high-low method, what is the estimated variable cost per unit of production?

    A     $0.87
    B     $0.95
    C     $1.05
    D     $1.15

6    What is the first-in first-out (FIFO) method used for?

    A     Calculating normal/abnormal losses
    B     Estimating equivalent units
    C     Valuing raw material issues from inventory
    D     Valuing raw material receipts into inventory

7    Wastage of a raw material during a manufacturing process is 20% of input quantity.

What input quantity of raw material is required per kg of output?

A    0.8 kg
B    1.2 kg
C    1.25 kg
D    1.33 kg

8    In the context of inventory control what is the maximum stock control level?

A    The level below which inventory should not fall if usage is at the maximum expected
B    The level below which inventory should not fall if average usage occurs
C    The level that inventory should not exceed if usage is at the minimum expected
D    The level that inventory should not exceed if average usage occurs

9    Production labour costs may include:

(i)    cost centre supervisors' wages
(ii)   overtime hours of direct operatives at basic rate
(iii)  overtime costs of indirect operatives
(iv)   piecework payments to direct operatives

Which items will usually be included in production overheads?

A    (i) and (iii) only
B    (i) and (iv) only
C    (i), (ii) and (iii) only
D    (ii), (iii) and (iv) only

10   The following statements relate to the depreciation of a fixed (non-current) asset:

(i)    A higher expected disposal value at the end of the asset's useful life would result in a lower
       depreciation charge

(ii)   The use of the machine hour method may result in a different depreciation charge each period

(iii)  If the actual disposal value of the asset exceeds its net book value a further depreciation cost will
       arise

Which of the statements is/are true?

A    (i) only
B    (i) and (ii) only
C    (ii) and (iii) only
D    All three statements

11   The overheads of two service departments (SCC1 and SCC2) in a factory require reapportionment to the two
     production departments (PCC1 and PCC2):

|        | Total overhead | % to PCC1 | % to PCC2 |
|--------|----------------|-----------|-----------|
| SCC1   | $32,170        | 35        | 65        |
| SCC2   | $24,850        | 65        | 35        |

What is the total reapportionment to production department PCC2?

A    $19,957
B    $27,412
C    $29,608
D    $37,063

12 A company with a single product manufactured 10,200 units in a period in which 10,300 units were sold. Consider the following statements:

(i) The profit for the period would be higher using absorption costing (compared with marginal costing)

(ii) Inventory values would be higher using absorption costing (compared with marginal costing)

Are the statements true or false in relation to the situation described?

|  | Statement (i) | Statement (ii) |
|---|---|---|
| A | False | False |
| B | False | True |
| C | True | False |
| D | True | True |

13 A manufacturing business worked on four jobs during a period:

|  | Job 1 | Job 2 | Job 3 | Job 4 |
|---|---|---|---|---|
|  | $ | $ | $ | $ |
| Work-in-progress at the beginning of the period | 5,260 | 3,170 | 6,940 | - |
| Direct materials in the period | 1,120 | 4,650 | 6,010 | 3,360 |
| Direct labour in the period | 580 | 3,970 | 5,170 | 2,980 |

Production overheads totalled $11,430 in the period are absorbed into the cost of jobs as a percentage of direct labour cost. Jobs 1, 3 and 4 were all completed in the period.

What is the value of work-in-progress at the end of the period?

A $8,620
B $11,790
C $12,193
D $15,363

14 For which costing method is the concept of equivalent units relevant?

A Batch costing
B Job costing
C Process costing
D Service costing

15 Costs incurred in a process totalled $61,600 for a period. 22,000 units of finished product were manufactured, of which 440 units were rejected. This is the normal level of rejects for the process. Rejected units are sold for $1.80 per unit.

What was the cost per unit of good output (to the nearest cent)?

A $2.76
B $2.80
C $2.82
D $2.86

16 A process requires the input a of a single raw material at the start of the process. There are no process losses. 10,000 units of the material were input to the process in a period. At the end of the period, processing was only 75% complete on 800 units of the material. There was no work-in-progress at the beginning of the period.

What were the equivalent units of production?

|  | Raw material | Conversion costs |
|---|---|---|
| A | 9,400 | 9,400 |
| B | 9,800 | 9,800 |
| C | 10,000 | 9,400 |
| D | 10,000 | 9,800 |

17    Products X and Y are joint products. The joint process costs for a period, during which 10,000 units of X and 15,000 units of Y were manufactured, were $87,500.

The sales value method is used to apportion the joint process costs. Selling prices are $6.00 per unit for Product X and $8.00 per unit for Product Y.

What is Product X's share of the joint process costs?

A    $29,167
B    $35,000
C    $37,500
D    $43,750

18    A hotel has 60 available rooms. Room occupancy was 80% during a 90 day period during which total costs incurred were $104,976.

What was the cost per occupied room per night in the period?

A    $12.44
B    $15.55
C    $19.44
D    $24.30

19    A company has fixed costs per period as follows:

Manufacturing                $56,000
Non-manufacturing            $38,000

Variable costs of the company's single product are $4.20 per unit and the selling price is $7.00 per unit.

What sales revenue (to the nearest $'000) is required in a period to make a profit of $6,000?

A    $163,000
B    $167,000
C    $241,000
D    $250,000

20    A capital investment project requires a cash outflow of $81,000 at the start of the project. Annual cash inflows are forecast to be constant for four years (Years 1 to 4).

The net present value (NPV) of the project at a discount rate of 12% per annum is $8,683 (positive). The internal rate of return of the project is 17%. Annuity factors (Years 1 to 4) at 12% and 17% are 3.037 and 2.743 respectively.

What is the forecast annual cash inflow?

A    $23,810
B    $26,670
C    $29,530
D    $32,695

# 49 Mixed bank 3 (6/07)

1 Which of the following best describes a profit centre?

   A   Part of a business where management makes investment decisions
   B   Part of a business that provides a service to other parts of the business
   C   Part of a business where finished products are manufactured
   D   Part of a business where management is responsible for revenues and costs

2 In a large company, which of the following activities may be the responsibility of an accounting technician?

   A   Calculating cost variances
   B   Making capital investment decisions
   C   Approving budgets
   D   Allocating warehouse space

3 Which of the following are characteristics of management accounting information?

   (i)    Non-financial as well as financial
   (ii)   Used by all stakeholders
   (iii)  Concerned with cost control only
   (iv)   Not legally required

   A   (i) and (iv)
   B   (ii) and (iii)
   C   (i), (ii) and (iii)
   D   (ii), (iii) and (iv)

4 When production has been completed what double-entry would be made in a cost accounting system?

|   | Debit | Credit |
|---|-------|--------|
| A | Cost of sales | Finished goods |
| B | Finished goods | Work-in-progress |
| C | Finished goods | Cost of sales |
| D | Work-in-progress | Finished goods |

5 The following is an extract from the list of accounts of a motor vehicle manufacturer:

|   | Cost codes |
|---|-----------|
| Direct materials | 1000 – 1999 |
| Indirect materials | 2000 – 2999 |
| Direct labour | 3000 – 3999 |
| Indirect labour | 4000 – 4999 |

Which of the following is coded INCORRECTLY?

|   | Code | Description |
|---|------|-------------|
| A | 4262 | Wages of materials stores personnel |
| B | 4131 | Wages of canteen supervisor |
| C | 1008 | Metal for vehicle body |
| D | 1361 | Cleaning materials |

6 The following shows the cost per unit of an item of expense at different levels of activity:

| Activity (units) | Cost per unit ($) |
|------------------|-------------------|
| 1 | 10,000 |
| 50 | 200 |
| 100 | 120 |
| 150 | 80 |

What is the correct behavioural classification for the expense item?

- A    Fixed cost
- B    Semi-variable cost
- C    Stepped-fixed cost
- D    Variable cost

---

7    Which of the following would be classified as a fixed cost in the operation of a motor vehicle?

- A    Oil change every 10,000 kilometres
- B    Petrol
- C    Insurance
- D    Tyre replacement

---

8    A particular cost is classified as being semi-variable.

What is the effect on the cost per unit if activity increases by 10%?

- A    Decrease by 10%
- B    Decrease by less than 10%
- C    Increase by less than 10%
- D    Remain constant

---

9    The raw materials issued to a job were overestimated and the excess is being sent back to the materials store.

What document is required?

- A    Stores credit note
- B    Stores debit note
- C    Materials returned note
- D    Materials transfer note

---

10    Analysis of the gross wages in a factory reveals:

|  | Direct operatives ($) | Indirect operatives ($) |
| --- | --- | --- |
| Productive hours at basic rate | 41,200 | 17,600 |
| Overtime premium | 1,100 | 450 |
| Idle time | 760 |  |
| Group bonuses | 2,780 |  |
| Total gross pay | 45,840 | 18,050 |

What amount would NORMALLY be accounted for as production overhead?

- A    $18,050
- B    $18,810
- C    $21,590
- D    $22,690

---

11    Which of the following are aspects of payroll systems?

- (i)    Attendance records
- (ii)    Calculation of bonuses
- (iii)    Employee tax codes
- (iv)    Apportionment of wages to cost centres

- A    (i), (ii) and (iii) only
- B    (ii), (iii) and (iv) only
- C    (i), (ii) and (iv) only
- D    All four items

12    The direct labour capacity ratio for a period was 104%.

What could have caused this?

A    Actual hours worked being greater than budgeted hours
B    Actual hours worked being less than budgeted hours
C    Standard time for actual output being greater than budgeted hours
D    Standard time for actual output being less than budgeted hours

13    The following may occur depending upon how overhead absorption rates are set and used:

(i)     Delay in the establishment of job costs
(ii)    Change in unit costs reflecting seasonal activity
(iii)   Overhead over or under recovery

Which of the above may result from the use of predetermined rates set for a year rather than actual rates recalculated every three months?

A    (i) only
B    (ii) only
C    (iii) only
D    None

14    A company manufactures and sells 4,000 units of a product each month at a selling price of $22 per unit. The prime cost of the product is $11·60 per unit and the monthly overheads are:

|                                      | $      |
|--------------------------------------|--------|
| Variable production                  | 7,200  |
| Variable selling and administration  | 5,200  |
| Fixed production                     | 16,400 |
| Fixed selling and administration     | 6,800  |

What is the product's gross profit margin (to one decimal place)?

A    6.8%
B    20.5%
C    33.2%
D    59.5%

15    A product has the following costs:

|                          | $/unit |
|--------------------------|--------|
| Variable production costs | 4.80   |
| Total production costs    | 7.50   |
| Total variable costs      | 5.90   |
| Total costs               | 10.00  |

11,400 units of the product were manufactured in a period during which 11,200 units were sold.

What is the profit difference using absorption costing rather than marginal costing?

A    The profit for the period is $540 lower
B    The profit for the period is $540 higher
C    The profit for the period is $820 lower
D    The profit for the period is $820 higher

16    A job cost estimate includes 630 productive labour hours. In addition, it is anticipated that idle time will be 10% of the total hours paid for the job. The wage rate is $12 per hour.

What is the total estimated labour cost for the job?

A    $6,804
B    $7,560
C    $8,316
D    $8,400

17    Costs incurred in a process totalled $216,720 for a period. 24,000 units of finished product were
      manufactured including 1,200 units which were rejected on inspection and disposed of. The level of rejects
      in the period was normal. Rejects are sold for $2·00 per unit.

      What was the cost per unit for the process?

      A    $8.93
      B    $9.03
      C    $9.40
      D    $9.51

18    The following information relates to a production process for a period:

      Input costs                                    $194,860
      Completed output                               11,400 units
      Closing work-in-progress                       1,200 units (60% complete)
      There were no process losses or opening work-in-progress.

      What was the cost per unit for the process?

      A    $15.47
      B    $16.08
      C    $16.40
      D    $17.09

19    Are the following statements about joint product cost apportionment TRUE or FALSE?

      1    Using the sales value method of cost apportionment, and where there is no further processing, the
           gross profit margin of each product will be the same

      2    Using the units of output method of cost apportionment, the joint cost per unit will be the same for
           all joint products

           *Statement 1*                             *Statement 2*
      A    False                                     False
      B    False                                     True
      C    True                                      False
      D    True                                      True

20    In a 30 day period a restaurant was open for nine hours per day. Costs incurred in the period totalled
      $65,124. The following additional information is available:

      Number of tables available                    15
      Number of seats per table                      4
      Customer turnround                             1 hour
      Seating occupancy achieved                     60%

      What was the cost per customer?

      A    $4.02
      B    $6.70
      C    $16.08
      D    $26.80

# 50 Mixed bank 4 (12/07)

1    Sources of useful data may be:

    1    External
    2    Internal
    3    Financial
    4    Non-financial

Which of the above sources may be used by an accounting technician?

    A    1, 2 and 3 only
    B    2, 3 and 4 only
    C    2 and 3 only
    D    all four sources

2    Which of the following statements about cost and management accounting are true?

    1    Cost accounting cannot be used to provide inventory valuations for external financial reporting
    2    There is a legal requirement to prepare management accounts
    3    The format of management accounts may vary from one business to another
    4    Management accounting provides information to help management make business decisions

    A    1 and 2
    B    1 and 4
    C    2 and 3
    D    3 and 4

3    Which of the following are features of an efficient and effective cost coding system?

    1    Codes need to be complex to include all items
    2    Each code must have a combination of alphabetic and numeric characters
    3    Codes for a particular type of item should be consistent in length and structure

    A    1 only
    B    3 only
    C    1 and 2
    D    2 and 3

4    Four cost behaviour patterns are demonstrated on the chart below.

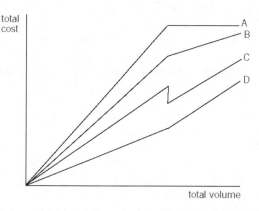

Which line on the chart represents the behaviour of total raw material costs where a volume discount applies to all purchases in a period once a required level is reached?

A   Line A
B   Line B
C   Line C
D   Line D

---

5   Production costs have been estimated at two levels of output

|  | 50,000 units | 55,000 units |
|---|---|---|
| Prime costs | $430,000 | $473,000 |
| Overheads | $330,000 | $339,000 |

What are the estimated production costs per unit at an output level of 54,000 units?

A   $14·76
B   $14·84
C   $15·20
D   $17·00

---

6   A particular cost is classified as 'semi-variable'. What effect would a 15% reduction in activity have on the unit cost?

A   Increase by less than 15%
B   Increase by 15%
C   Reduce by less than 15%
D   Remain constant total volume total cost

---

7   The inventory record of a raw material has the following details for a week:

| Day | Cost ($ per unit) | Receipts (units) | Issues (units) |
|---|---|---|---|
| 2 | 160 | 18 | |
| 3 | 270 | 12 | |
| 4 | | | 10 |
| 6 | | | 14 |

The first-in first-out (FIFO) method is used for pricing issues. There was no raw material at the start of Day 1.

Which was the value of the inventory on Day 5?

A   $5,200
B   $5,220
C   $5,320
D   $5,400

---

8   Average usage of a raw material is 200 kg per day, the average ordering lead time is five days, the reorder level is1,600 kg and the reorder quantity is 2,800 kg.

What is the average raw material inventory?

A      800 kg
B   1,400 kg
C   1,700 kg
D   2,000 kg

---

9   The costs associated with labour turnover can be classified as 'preventative' costs or 'replacement' costs. Which of the following is a preventative cost?

A   Provision of leisure facilities for employees
B   Lower productivity of new employees
C   Increased wastage of raw materials
D   Training costs for new employees

10 Consider the following statements, regarding the reapportionment of service cost centre overheads to production cost centres, where reciprocal services exist:

1. The direct method results in costs being reapportioned between service cost centres
2. If the direct method is used, the order in which the service cost centre overheads are reapportioned is irrelevant
3. The step down method results in costs being reapportioned between service cost centres
4. If the step down method is used, the order in which the service cost centre overheads are reapportioned is irrelevant

Which statement(s) is/are correct?

A 1, 2 and 4
B 1, 3 and 4
C 2 only
D 2 and 3

---

11 A firm uses job costing. Details of the three jobs worked on during a period are:

| | Job BA | Job DC | Job FE |
| --- | --- | --- | --- |
| | $ | $ | $ |
| Opening work-in-progress | 22,760 | 3,190 | – |
| Direct materials in the period | 4,620 | 11,660 | 14,335 |
| Direct labour in the period | 12,125 | 10,520 | 7,695 |

Overheads are absorbed at 40% of prime cost in each period. Jobs DC and FE remained incomplete at the end of the period. What is the value of the closing work-in-progress?

A $61,894
B $65,084
C $66,360
D $68,952

---

12 Costs totalling $4,250 were incurred in a process in a period. 80 units of output were rejected and destroyed in the period, 20 units more than allowed for as a normal loss, leaving 420 units of good production to be transferred to finished goods.

What is the amount written off as abnormal loss (to the nearest $)?

A $170
B $177
C $193
D $202

---

13 Consider the following statements relating to process costing:

Statement 1: normal losses are credited to the process account at the cost per unit incurred on normal production

Statement 2: abnormal gains are debited to the process account at the cost per unit incurred on normal production

Which statement(s) is/are true?

A Both statements are true
B Neither statement is true
C Statement 1 only is true
D Statement 2 only is true

14  Conversion costs incurred in a process totalled $71,628 in a period. There was no work-in-progress at the beginning of the period. 9,000 units of product were completed in the period, leaving 1,000 units, 40% complete as to conversion costs, still in-progress at the end of the period

What was the conversion cost per unit of production?

A  $7.16
B  $7.46
C  $7.62
D  $7.96

15  What is a by-product?

A  A product that has insignificant saleable value compared with the joint products
B  A product that has no saleable value
C  A product that can be further processed
D  A waste product that has to be disposed of at a cost

16  5,400 units of a company's single product were sold for a total revenue of $140,400. Fixed costs in the period were $39,420 and net profit was $11,880.

What was the contribution per unit?

A  $7.30
B  $9.50
C  $16.50
D  $18.70

17  A company manufactures and sells four products. Details are as follows:

|  | Product | | | |
|  | P | Q | R | S |
|  | $ | $ | $ | $ |
| Contribution per unit | 16.0 | 14.5 | 17.6 | 19.0 |
| Net profit per unit | 4.6 | 4.8 | 5.2 | 5.0 |
| Contribution per machine hour | 5.0 | 4.8 | 4.4 | 3.8 |
| Net profit per machine hour | 1.4 | 1.6 | 1.3 | 1.0 |

Machine hours available in the next period will not be sufficient to meet production requirements. There are no product-specific fixed costs.

What should be the order of priority for production in order to maximise profit?

A  Product P, Product Q, Product R, Product S
B  Product Q, Product P, Product R, Product S
C  Product R, Product S, Product Q, Product P
D  Product S, Product R, Product P, Product Q

18  A company has incurred development costs of $25,000 to date on a proposed new product. Further costs of $18,000would be required to complete the development of the product.

In deciding whether to continue with the new product development which of the following is correct regarding development costs?

|  | Sunk cost | Incremental cost |
| A | $0 | $43,000 |
| B | $18,000 | $25,000 |
| C | $25,000 | $18,000 |
| D | $43,000 | $0 |

19  A company is proposing to launch a new product. Incremental net cash inflows of $36,000 per annum for five years are expected, starting at Time 1.

An existing machine, with a net book value of $85,000, would be used to manufacture the new product. The machine could otherwise be sold now, Time 0, for $60,000. The machine, if used for the manufacture of the new product, would be depreciated on a straight-line basis over five years, starting at Time 1.

What are the relevant amounts that should be used, at Time 0 and Time 1, in the discounted cash flow appraisal of the project?

|   | Time 0 | Time 1 |
|---|--------|--------|
| A | $0 | $19,000 |
| B | $0 | $24,000 |
| C | ($60,000) | $36,000 |
| D | ($85,000) | $36,000 |

20  An investment project has net present values as follows:

Discount rate 11% per annum: net present value $35,170 positive
Discount rate 15% per annum: net present value $6,040 positive.

What is the best estimate of the internal rate of return?

A    14.5%
B    15.8%
C    19.5%
D    19.8%

# Answers

# 1 Objective test questions: Management information and information technology

1   C   Bank interest and charges would be included in the financial accounts but may be excluded from the cost accounts.

2   D   This is the correct definition of a management information system.

3   ✓   Internal managers of an organisation

4   D   Electronic point of sale (EPOS) devices act as both cash registers and as terminals connected to a main computer. Fully itemised, accurate and descriptive receipts can be produced for customers who will also benefit from faster moving queues at the checkout.

5   D   Laser printers print a whole page at a time, rather than line by line. They are more expensive than other types of printer and can print up to 500 pages per minute.

6   C   Marginal costing is a common feature of cost accounting but not financial accounting.

7   B   Management information should be clear to the user and relevant for its purpose.

8   A   Graphical user interfaces are the means by which humans communicate with machines and feature windows, icons, a mouse and pull-down menus.

9   C   Management information is used for planning, control and decision-making.

10  B   Management accounting data can be captured with bar codes and stored on disks and tape. Printers are used for the output of data.

# 2 Compulsory written question: Management information and information technology

(a)   **Financial accounts** detail the performance of an organisation over a defined period and the state of affairs at the end of that period. In contrast, **management accounts** are used to aid management in the recording, planning and control of an organisation's activities and also to help in the decision-making process.

Limited companies must, by law, prepare **financial accounts**, whereas there is no legal requirement for companies to prepare **management accounts.**

The **format** of published **financial accounts** is determined by law (mainly the Companies Acts), by Statements of Standard Accounting Practice and by Financial Reporting Standards. The format of **management accounts** is entirely at management discretion with each individual organisation devising its own management accounting system and format of reports.

**Financial accounts** concentrate on the business as a whole, aggregating revenues and costs from different operations. **Management accounts**, on the other hand, can focus on specific areas of an organisation's activities.

Most **financial accounting** information is of a monetary nature whereas **management accounts** also incorporate non-monetary measures.

**Financial accounts** present an essentially historical picture of past operations. **Management accounts** are both an historical record and a future planning tool.

(b)   (i)   **MICR**

**Magnetic Ink Character Recognition** (MICR) involves the recognition by a machine of special formatted characters printed in magnetic ink. The characters are read using a specialised reading device. The main advantage of MICR is its speed and accuracy, but MICR documents are expensive to produce. The main commercial application of MICR is in the banking industry – on cheques and deposit slips.

(ii)   **OMR**

**Optical Mark Reading** (OMR) involves the marking of a pre-printed form with a ballpoint pen or typed line or cross in an appropriate box. The card is then read by an OMR device which senses the mark in each box using an electronic current and translates it into machine code. Applications in which OMR is used include **Lotto** entry forms, and answer sheets for multiple choice questions.

(iii)   **EPOS**

**Electronic Point of Sale** (EPOS) devices include bar code readers. Bar codes are groups of marks which, by their spacing and thickness, indicate specific codes and values. EPOS applications include bar code readers in large retail stores eg supermarkets scan items and the cost of each item is included within the bar code.

# 3 Objective test questions: Cost classification and cost behaviour

1   C   In options A and B, the hour of operation and the unit of electricity are both examples of cost units for which costs have been ascertained.

Option D is an example of a particular cost unit which may be used for control purposes. It is not a definition of the term 'cost unit'.

2   C   Option A is the definition of a cost unit.

Option B describes the *cost* of an activity or cost centre.

Option D describes a budget centre. Although a budget centre may also be a cost centre at times, this is not always the case.

3   B   Prime cost is the total of direct material, direct labour and direct expenses. Therefore the correct answer is B.

Option A describes total production cost, including absorbed production overhead. Option C is only a part of prime cost. Option D is an overhead or indirect cost.

4   A   Option A is a part of the cost of direct materials.

Options B and D are production overheads. Option C is a selling and distribution expense.

5   A   Depreciation is an indirect cost because it does not relate directly to a specific cost unit produced.

Items (ii) and (iii) can be traced directly to specific cost units, therefore they are direct expenses.

6   | ✓ |   Direct expense

The royalty cost can be traced in full to units of the product, therefore it is a direct expense.

7   | ✓ |   Cheque received and processed

| ✓ |   Customer account

Telephone expense is a cost for the department, not a potential cost unit.

8   | ✓ |   A stores assistant in a factory store

The stores assistant's wages cannot be charged directly to a product, therefore the stores assistant is part of the indirect labour force.

9   A   The depicted cost has a basic fixed element which is payable even at zero activity. A variable element is then added at a constant rate as activity increases. Therefore the correct answer is A.

Graphs for the other options would look like this.

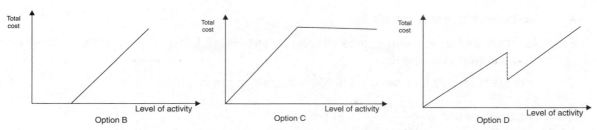

| | | | | |
|---|---|---|---|---|
| Total cost | | Total cost | | Total cost |
| Option B | | Option C | | Option D |
| Level of activity | | Level of activity | | Level of activity |

10  A   The cost described will increase in steps, remaining fixed at each step until another supervisor is required. Graph 1 depicts a step cost therefore the correct answer is A.

11  B   A variable cost will result in a constant cost per unit at each activity level. A semi-variable cost will result in a different cost per unit at each activity level, because of the spreading of fixed costs. A fixed cost is the same absolute amount of total cost for each activity level.

|  Cost type | Cost per unit for 100 units $ | Cost per unit for 140 units $ | Cost behaviour |
|---|---|---|---|
| W | 80.00 | 75.43 | Semi-variable |
| X | Constant cost for both activity levels | | Fixed |
| Y | 65.00 | 65.00 | Variable |
| Z | 67.00 | 61.29 | Semi-variable |

12  D   The salary is part fixed ($650 per month) and part variable (5 pence per unit). Therefore it is a semi-variable cost and answer D is correct.

If you chose options A or B you were considering only part of the cost.

Option C, a step cost, involves a cost which remains constant up to a certain level and then increases to a new, higher, constant fixed cost.

13  A   Variable cost for 340 guest-nights  = $570 – $400 = $170
Variable cost per guest-night      = $170/340 = $0.50

Therefore the correct answer is A

If you selected option B you have calculated the fixed cost per guest-night for the stated activity level ($400 ÷ 340).

If you selected option C you have calculated the average total cost per guest-night ($570 ÷ 340).

14  ✓   Graph 2

15  ✓   Graph 1

16  ✓   Graph 1

      ✓   Graph 3

      ✓   Graph 4

A semi-variable or mixed cost is a cost which contains both fixed and variable components and so is partly affected by changes in the level of activity.

17  ✓   Graph 1

18  B

| | Production costs $ | Output |
|---|---|---|
| Highest | 254,554 | 14,870 |
| Lowest | 230,485 | 12,610 |
| | 24,069 | 2,260 |

$$\text{Variable production costs per unit} = \frac{\$24,069}{2,260 \text{ units}}$$
$$= \$10.65 \text{ per unit}$$

| 19 | A | Increased storage requirements |
|----|---|---|

20 B As activity levels rise, the fixed production cost per unit will fall. This is the situation that is shown in the graph given in the question.

21 C Suppose fixed costs for a period = $10,000 and activity in period = 10,000 units.

Fixed cost per unit = $\dfrac{\$10,000}{10,000 \text{ units}}$ = $1 per unit

If the activity level in the period falls by 50%, ie to 5,000 units then:

Fixed cost per unit = $\dfrac{\$10,000}{5,000 \text{ units}}$ = $2 per unit

A reduction in activity of 50% therefore causes the fixed cost per unit to increase from $1 to $2, ie an increase in cost per unit of 100%.

22 B Storage costs are fixed at $60,000 at production levels of 50,100 and 150 units of Product X. At a production level of 200 units of Product X, total cost increases in a 'step' to $90,000. The correct answer is therefore B.

23 B (i) direct and (iv) production could be applied to the cost of raw materials used by a company in the manufacture of its range of products.

24 B A semi-variable cost is a cost which contains both fixed and variable components and is partly affected by changes in the level of activity. Therefore, if activity increases by 10%, total variable costs will increase by 10% and fixed costs will remain constant. The total costs will therefore increase, but **not** in proportion to the change in activity.

25 C

|  | Costs | Activity |
|--|-------|----------|
|  | $ |  |
| Highest | 29,764 | 12,880 |
| Lowest | 28,420 | 11,600 |
|  | 1,344 | 1,280 |

Variable costs per unit = $\dfrac{\$1,344}{1,280}$ = $1.05 per unit

# 4 Compulsory written question: Cost classification and cost behaviour

(a)

> **Helping hand**
>
> If you had trouble remembering these definitions, go back to your BPP Interactive Study Text to revise those definitions highlighted in the list of key terms.

A **cost centre** is a production or service location, function, activity or item of equipment whose costs may be attributed to cost units. A **cost unit** is a unit of product or service in relation to which costs are ascertained.

(b)

> **Helping hand**
>
> You will need to use the high-low method to analyse the two semi-variable costs into their fixed and variable elements. The unit cost for the variable costs can be found by simple division. The total fixed cost remains the same for every activity level.

*Initial working*

Analysis of semi-variable costs using high-low method.

| **Electricity cost** | Production | Cost |
|---|---|---|
| | Units | $ |
| High | 12,000 | 9,000 |
| Low | 10,000 | 8,000 |
| Difference | 2,000 | 1,000 |

Variable cost per unit = $1,000/2,000 = $0.50 per unit

| | $ |
|---|---|
| Substituting in high activity: | |
| variable cost of 12,000 units (× $0.50) = | 6,000 |
| total cost | 9,000 |
| ∴ fixed cost | 3,000 |

| **Inventory insurance cost** | Production | Cost |
|---|---|---|
| | Units | $ |
| High | 12,000 | 11,000 |
| Low | 10,000 | 9,500 |
| Difference | 2,000 | 1,500 |

Variable cost per unit = $1,500/2,000 = $0.75 per unit

| | $ |
|---|---|
| Substituting in high activity: | |
| variable cost of 12,000 units (× $0.75) = | 9,000 |
| total cost | 11,000 |
| ∴ fixed cost | 2,000 |

**Avocet Limited – Budgeted overheads for the year ended 31 December 20X2**

| Production units | | 15,000 |
|---|---|---|
| | $ | $ |
| Factory rent | | 5,000 |
| Machine depreciation | | 7,500 |
| Indirect labour ($20,000/10,000 = $2 per unit) | | 30,000 |
| Indirect materials ($12,000/10,000 = $1.20 per unit) | | 18,000 |
| Electricity: variable @ $0.50 per unit | 7,500 | |
| fixed | 3,000 | |
| | | 10,500 |
| Stock (inventory) insurance: variable @ $0.75 per unit | 11,250 | |
| fixed | 2,000 | |
| | | 13,250 |
| Total | | 84,250 |

# 5 Compulsory written question: Information and cost function

**Helping hand**

Only four features of useful information are needed but a complete list is provided for revision purposes.

**What the Examiner said**

Part (b) was often not well answered and cost behaviour is not well understood. Answers failed to appreciate that there was a mix of variable and fixed costs.

(a)    **Relevance**

Management information must be relevant to the purpose for which a manager wants to use it. In practice, far too many reports fail to 'keep to the point' and contain irrelevant paragraphs which only annoy the managers reading them.

**Completeness**

An information user should have all the information he needs to do his job properly. If he does not have a complete picture of the situation, he might well make bad decisions.

**Accuracy**

Management information should obviously be accurate because using incorrect information could have serious and damaging consequences. However, management information should only be accurate enough for its purpose and there is no need to go into unnecessary detail for pointless accuracy.

**Clarity**

Management information must be clear to the user. If the user does not understand it properly he cannot use it properly. Lack of clarity is one of the causes of a breakdown in communication. It is therefore important to choose the most appropriate presentation medium or channel of communication.

**Confidence**

Management information must be trusted by the managers who are expected to use it. However not all management information is certain. Some information has to be certain, especially operating information, for example, related to a production process. Strategic information, especially relating to the environment, is uncertain. However, if the assumptions underlying it are clearly stated, this might enhance the confidence with which the management information is perceived.

**Volume**

There are physical and mental limitations to what a person can read, absorb and understand properly before taking action. An enormous mountain of management information, even if it is all relevant, cannot be handled. Reports to management must therefore be clear and concise and in many systems, control action works basically on the 'exception' principle.

**Timing**

Management information which is not available until after a decision is made will be useful only for comparisons and longer-term control, and may serve no purpose even then. Management information prepared too frequently can be a serious disadvantage. If, for example, a decision is taken at a monthly meeting about a certain aspect of a company's operations, management information to make the decision is only required once a month, and weekly reports would be a time-consuming waste of effort.

**Channel of communication**

There are occasions when using one particular method of communication will be better than others. For example, job vacancies should be announced in a medium where they will be brought to the attention of the people most likely to be interested. The channel of communication might be the company's in-house journal, a national or local newspaper, a professional magazine, a job centre or school careers office. Some internal memoranda may be better sent by 'electronic mail'. Some information is best communicated informally by telephone or word-of-mouth, whereas other information ought to be formally communicated in writing or figures.

**Cost benefit**

Management information should have some value, otherwise it would not be worth the cost of collecting and filing it. The benefits obtainable from the management information must also exceed the costs of acquiring it, and whenever management is trying to decide whether or not to produce management information for a particular purpose (for example whether to computerise an operation or to build a financial planning model) a cost/benefit ought to be made.

(b)  (i)   y = $106,250
           a = $41,990
           x = 8,400 units
           b = ?

           106,250            = 41,990 + (b × 8,400)
           106,250 – 41,990   = b × 8,400
           64,260             = b × 8,400
           b                  = $\dfrac{64,260}{8,400}$
                              = $7.65

     (ii)  When x = 8,660 units

           y = 41,990 + (7.65 × 8,660)
             = 41,990 + 66,249
             = $108,239

     (iii) When x = 8,500 units

           y = 41,990 + (7.65 × 8,500)
             = 41,900 + 65,025
             = $107,015

           Cost per unit = $\dfrac{107,015}{8,500}$
                         = $12.59

|       |       |                        |      | Marks |
|-------|-------|------------------------|------|-------|
| (a)   |       | 1½ marks for each feature |   | 6     |
| (b)   | (i)   | variable cost per unit |      | 2     |
|       | (ii)  | variable cost          | 1½   |       |
|       |       | fixed cost             | ½    |       |
|       |       |                        |      | 2     |
|       | (iii) | cost per unit          |      | 2     |
|       |       |                        |      | 12    |

# 6 Objective test questions: Materials

1   C   The lead time, sometimes called the delivery period, is the time between sending a purchase order to the supplier and receiving the goods into stores. Therefore the correct answer is C. None of the other time periods described are in common use in the calculation of inventory control levels.

2   D   When inventory reaches the predetermined reorder level a replenishment order should be placed with the supplier.

        Option A describes the reorder quantity which should be ordered when inventory reaches the reorder level. Option B is the maximum level and option C is the minimum level.

3   B   Average inventory   = safety inventory + ½ reorder quantity
                            = 280 + (0.5 × 1,200)
                            = 880

        If you selected one of the other options you were trying various combinations of the data provided, but you had obviously forgotten the formula for average inventory!

4     The economic order quantity is $\boxed{300}$ units.

The formula for the economic order quantity (EOQ) is

$$EOQ = \sqrt{\frac{2cd}{h}}$$

with    c = \$10
        d = 5,400 ÷ 12 = 450 per month
        h = \$0.10

$$EOQ = \sqrt{\frac{2 \times \$10 \times 450}{£0.10}}$$

$$= \sqrt{90,000}$$

$$= 300 \text{ units}$$

5   C    Maximum inventory control level             =   reorder level + reorder quantity –
                                                             (minimum usage × minimum lead time)

∴ Maximum inventory control level         =   1,600 + 1,400 – (600 × 1)
                                                      =   3,000 – 600
                                                      =   2,400 kg

6   C    Minimum inventory control level    = reorder level – (average usage × average lead time)

∴ Minimum inventory control level   = 1,600 – (700 × 1.5)
                                                 = 1,600 – 1,050
                                                 = 550 kg

7   A    Buffer inventory is the inventory that is kept in reserve to cope with fluctuations in demand and with suppliers who cannot be relied upon to deliver the right quality and quantity of materials at the right time. The introduction of buffer inventory would result in the increase of average inventory levels. The introduction of buffer inventory would not have an effect on holding costs, ordering costs nor the EOQ.

8     Using the weighted average price method of inventory valuation, the total value of the components remaining in inventory on 23 March was \$ $\boxed{20,790}$

Average price of inventory on 23 March:

| Units | | \$ |
|---|---|---|
| 2,400 | × \$6 | 14,400 |
| 4,000 | × \$6.20 | 24,800 |
| 2,000 | × \$6.86 | 13,720 |
| 8,400 | | 52,920 |

Average price per component         = \$52,920/8,400 = \$6.30
Value of inventory on 23 March      = (8,400 – 5,100) × \$6.30
                                                    = \$20,790

9   ✓    Product costs are understated and profits overstated

FIFO uses the price of the oldest items in inventory. When prices are rising this will be the items with the lowest prices. Consequently costs are lower and profits are higher.

10     Using the FIFO method of inventory valuation, the total value of the components issued on 23 March was \$ $\boxed{31,140}$

The FIFO method uses the price of the oldest batches first:

| Units | | $ |
|---|---|---|
| 2,400 | × $6 | 14,400 |
| 2,700 | × $6.20 | 16,740 |
| 5,100 | | 31,140 |

11    Using the FIFO method, the total value of the issues on 30 April is $ [ 2,765 ]

| Date | Receipts units | Issues units | Balance units | $ |
|---|---|---|---|---|
| 1 April | | | 275 @ $3.20 | 880 |
| 8 April | 600 | | 600 @ $3.00 | 1,800 |
| 15 April | 400 | | 400 @ $3.40 | 1,360 |
| | | | | 4,040 |

| | | | | $ |
|---|---|---|---|---|
| 30 April | | 275 @ $3.20 = | | 880 |
| | | 600 @ $3.00 = | | 1,800 |
| | | 25 @ $3.40 = | | 85 |
| | | 900 | | 2,765 |

12    The maximum level of inventory is [ 3,400 ]

Reorder level   = maximum usage × maximum lead time
= 600 × 4 = 2,400 units

Maximum level = reorder level + reorder quantity − (min. usage × min. lead time)
= 2,400 + 1,900 − (300 × 3)
= 3,400 units

13    D    The FIFO method prices issues of raw materials in the order that they were received into inventory. The prices paid for the oldest material in inventory are therefore used to price issues of raw material to production. Option B describes the LIFO method of inventory valuation. Option C describes what is likely to be physically happening (any good storekeeper will issue goods in the order that they were received) but this does not have any effect on the cost accounting procedures adopted. It is unlikely that the situation described in option A would happen. If the last material received were the first issued to production then there would be a greater risk of the oldest items left in inventory becoming obsolete.

14    D    The stock (inventory) count revealed 21 fewer units of Z99 and the **same number** more units of Z100 than expected. Since the two types of bracket are very similar, the most likely explanation of the difference is that some brackets were mistakenly put in the incorrect storage racks.

15    B    When material prices are falling, FIFO will give rise to **higher production costs** than LIFO. If production costs are higher, then the cost of sales will be higher also. If the cost of sales is higher, then the **profits will be lower.**

16    D    The economic order quantity is calculated as follows.

$$Q = \sqrt{\frac{2cd}{h}}$$

where  h   = the cost of holding one unit of inventory for one year
       c   = the cost of ordering a consignment
       d   = the annual demand
       Q   = the economic order quantity

Holding costs (h) include the cost of storing materials (1), the cost of interest (2) and the cost of insuring materials (4). The cost of ordering materials (3) relates to (c) in the EOQ equation. Therefore items 1, 2, 3 and 4 would be needed in order to calculate the economic order quantity.

**17**     $ | 16,264 |

*Working*

**LIFO**

| Issue date | Units | | Value $ |
|---|---|---|---|
| 03 May 20X2 | 430 | 430 @ $10.50 | 4,515 |
| 17 Sept 20X2 | 550 | 350 @ $11.00 = $3,850 | |
| | | 170 @ $10.50 = $1,785 | |
| | | 30 @ $10.00 = $300 | 5,935 |
| 11 Nov 20X2 | 510 | 510 @ $11.40 | 5,814 |
| | | | 16,264 |

**18**     $ | 16,166 |

*Working*

**FIFO**

| Issue date | Units | | Value $ |
|---|---|---|---|
| 03 May 20X2 | 430 | 100 @ $10.00 = $1,000 | |
| | | 330 @ $10.50 = $3,465 | 4,465 |
| 17 Sept 20X2 | 550 | 270 @ $10.50 = $2,835 | |
| | | 280 @ $11.00 = $3,080 | 5,915 |
| 11 Nov 20X2 | 510 | 70 @ $11.00 = $770 | |
| | | 440 @ $11.40 = $5,016 | 5,786 |
| | | | 16,166 |

**19**     If materials already issued but not required for one job can be used for another job in progress, there is no point in returning the materials to the warehouse, so instead a **materials transfer** note can be raised. This prevents one job being charged with too many materials and another with too little.

**20**   A   Statement 1 is true but statements 2 and 3 are false.

If prices are rising then the LIFO method will charge the more recent, higher prices to production costs. Therefore statement 1 is true, and statement 2 is false because higher production costs will result in lower profits with LIFO. Inventory valuations with FIFO use the most recent, higher prices therefore statement 3 is false.

**21**   B

| | $ |
|---|---|
| 60 units @ $5.00 | 300 |
| 10 units @ $5.50 | 55 |
| Value of issue on Day 7 | 355 |

**22**   C

| | $ |
|---|---|
| 50 units @ $6 | 300 |
| 20 units @ $5.50 | 110 |
| Value of issue on Day 7 | 410 |

**23**   A   Average inventory held

$$= \frac{\text{Order quantity}}{2}$$

$$= \frac{250 \text{ units}}{2}$$

$$= 125 \text{ units}$$

Inventory holding cost   = $3 per unit per annum
= $3 × 125 units
= $375

24  B  The formula for the economic order quantity is as follows.

$$Q = \sqrt{\frac{2cd}{h}}$$

Where   h = inventory holding cost
        c = ordering cost
        d = demand (usage)

The purchase price is therefore not relevant to the calculation of the economic order quantity of a raw material.

25  C  Average inventory held        = safety inventory + (order quantity ÷ 2)
                                     = 1,200 + 1,000
                                     = 2,200 kg

Total annual stock holding cost    = average inventory held × inventory holding cost per kg
                                     = 2,200 kg × $1.20
                                     = $2,640

# 7 Compulsory written question: Materials I

**Helping hand**

In order to answer this question, you need to remember the following formula:

Reorder level = Average usage × lead time

However, in this situation, we are also told that there is a inventory level. We must therefore adjust the reorder level formula as follows;

Reorder level = Safety inventory + (average usage × lead time)

(Note that if information concerning the maximum usage and maximum lead time are available, then these figures can be used to calculate the reorder level also.)

**What the Examiner said**

This was the best answered question on this paper but some candidates did not read the question carefully enough and/or made careless calculation errors.

(a)   We are given the following information.

EOQ                =  1,000 kg
Average usage      =  400 kg per week
Safety inventory   =  500 kg
Lead time          =  2 weeks

**Reorder level**      =  safety inventory + (average usage × lead time)
                       =  500 kg + (400 kg × 2 weeks)
                       =  500 kg + 800 kg
                       =  1,300 kg

(b)

| Date | | Receipts | | Issues | | | Balance | | Balance |
|------|------|------|------|------|------|------|------|------|------|
| | | Kg | $ | Kg | Cost/kg | $ | Kg | Cost/kg | $ |
| Bal b/fwd | | | | | | | 900 | 12.00 | 10,800 |
| Wk 1: | Day 3 | | | 400 | 12.00 | 4,800 | 500 | 12.00 | 6,000 |
| | Day 5 | 1,000 | 12.60 | | | | 1,500 | 12.40 | 18,600 |
| Wk 2: | Day 2 | | | 260 | 12.40 | 3,224 | 1,240 | 12.40 | 15,376 |
| | Day 4 | | | 170 | 12.40 | 2,108 | 1,070 | 12.40 | 13,268 |
| Wk 3: | Day 3 | | | 370 | 12.40 | 4,588 | 700 | 12.40 | 8,680 |

(c)     Inventory remaining at the end of three-week period = 700 kg (from part (b)).

Total issues in weeks 2 and 3  = (260 + 170 + 370) kg
                                              = 800 kg

Using LIFO, these issues would be valued at the cost of the receipt at Week 1: (Day 5) = $12.60. There would therefore be 200 kg (1,000 kg – 800 kg) of closing inventory valued at $12.60 = 200 × $12.60 = $2,520.

The remaining inventory units (500) would be valued at $10.80 (the cost of the inventory b/fwd on Week 1: Day 1) = 500 kg × $12 = $6,000.

∴ Total inventory value (using FIFO)       = $(2,520 + 6,000)
                                                          = $8,520

## Marking scheme

|     |                                          | Marks |     |
|-----|------------------------------------------|-------|-----|
| (a) | Safety inventory                         | 1     |     |
|     | Average usage × average lead time        | 1     |     |
|     | Re-order level                           | 1     |     |
|     |                                          |       | 3   |
| (b) | Weighted av prices – opening balance     | 0.5   |     |
|     | After receipt                            | 2     |     |
|     | Application opening balance              | 0.5   |     |
|     | After receipt                            | 2     |     |
|     |                                          |       | 5   |
| (c) | 500 kg                                   | 2     |     |
|     | 200 kg                                   | 2     |     |
|     |                                          |       | 4   |
|     |                                          |       | 12  |

# 8 Compulsory written question: Materials II

**What the Examiner said**

This question was quite well answered overall. In part (b) the term 'stockout costs' was clearly not widely understood. In part (c) many candidates were unable to apply the formula correctly.

(a)     Three examples of holding costs from:

- Costs of storage and stores operations
- Interest charges
- Insurance costs
- Risk of obsolescence
- Deterioration
- Theft

(b)     Two examples of stockout costs from:

- Lost contribution from lost sales
- Loss of future sales due to disgruntled customers
- Loss of customer goodwill
- Cost of production stoppages
- Labour frustration over stoppages
- Extra costs of urgent, small quantity, replenishment orders

(c)

> **Helping hand**
>
> $Q = \sqrt{\dfrac{2cd}{h}}$ Economic order quantity, or EOQ
>
> Where  h  is the cost of holding one unit of inventory for one year
> c  is the cost of ordering a consignment
> d  is the annual demand
> Q  is the 'economic order quantity' (EOQ), that is, the best amount to order

Holding cost (h) = $2.50 × 15% = $0.375 per kg

Ordering cost (c) = $60

Annual demand (d) = 20,000 kg

$$\text{EOQ} = \sqrt{\dfrac{(2 \times \$60 \times 20{,}000)}{\$0.375}}$$

$$= 2{,}530 \text{ kg}$$

(d)   Average inventory = $\dfrac{3{,}000}{2}$ + 1000 = 2,500 kg

Holding costs = 2,500 kg × $0.375 = $937.50

## Marking scheme

|     |     |     | Marks |
| --- | --- | --- | --- |
| (a) | 1 mark for each | | 3 |
| (b) | 1 mark for each | | 2 |
| (c) | Formula | 1 | |
|     | Holding costs per kg | 1 | |
|     | Solution | 3 | |
|     | | | 5 |
| (d) | Average inventory | 3 | |
|     | Holding costs per kg | 1 | |
|     | Solution | 1 | |
|     | | | 5 |
|     | | | 15 |

# 9 Compulsory written question: Materials III

> **Helping hand**
>
> This question tests the subject of raw material inventory management.
>
> In part (a) when calculating the quantity of material purchases make sure you:
>
> - multiply by 0.72 kg per unit
> - include the loss as $\dfrac{1}{0.9}$
> - deduct the change in inventory
>
> In part (b) (i) on the calculation of EOQ make sure you do not put the square root sign over the numerator only.
>
> In part (b) (ii) make sure you do not forget to add the safety inventory.

(a)    Purchase quantity of Material X

Usage = $(0.72 \div 0.9) \times 26,000$
= 20,800 kilograms

Purchase = 20,800 − 1,000
= 19,800 kilograms

(b)    (i)    Economic order quantity of Material Y

= $\sqrt{[(2 \times 45 \times 120,000) \div 0.3]}$

= 6,000 litres

(ii)    Reorder level of Material Y

= $[(120,000 \div 50) \times 1.5] + 2,500$
= 6,100 litres

(iii)    Annual ordering cost of Material Y

= $(120,000 \div 6,000) \times 45$
= $900

(iv)    Annual holding cost of Material Y

$[(6,000 \div 2) + 2,500] \times 0.3$
= $1,650

## Marking scheme

|  |  |  |  | Marks |
|---|---|---|---|---|
| (a) | Wastage | | 2 | |
| | Demand | | 1 | |
| | Inventory adjustment | | 1 | 4 |
| (b) | (i) | EOQ | | 4 |
| | (ii) | Weekly demand | 1½ | |
| | | Lead time | 1 | |
| | | Safety inventory | 1 ½ | 4 |
| | (iii) | Orders | 2 | |
| | | Value | 1 | 3 |
| | (iv) | Av inventory (excl safety) | 1 | |
| | | Safety inventory | 1 | |
| | | Value | 1 | 3 |
| | | | | 18 |

# 10 Objective test questions: Labour

**1    B**    The only direct costs are the wages paid to direct workers for ordinary time, plus the basic pay for overtime.

$25,185 + $5,440 = $30,625.

If you selected option A you forgot to include the basic pay for overtime of direct workers, which is always classified as a direct labour cost.

If you selected option C you have included overtime premium and shift allowances, which are usually treated as indirect costs. However, if overtime and shiftwork are incurred specifically for a particular cost unit, then they are classified as direct costs of that cost unit. There is no mention of such a situation here.

Option D includes sick pay, which is classified as an indirect labour cost.

**2    C**    The maintenance assistant is not working directly on the organisation's output but is performing an indirect task. All the other three options describe tasks that involve working directly on the output.

**3    D**    The personnel manager's salary would be incurred regardless of the level of labour turnover.

Options A, B and C are all costs which would be incurred as a result of employees leaving and being replaced.

**4    C**    Group bonus schemes are useful to reward performance when production is integrated so that all members of the group must work harder to increase output, for example in production line manufacture. Statement (i) is therefore true.

Group bonus schemes are not effective in linking the reward to a particular individual's performance. Even if one individual makes a supreme effort, this can be negated by poor performance from other members of the group. Therefore statement (ii) is not true.

Non-production employees can be included in a group incentive scheme, for example when all employees in a management accounting department must work harder to produce prompt budgetary control reports. Statement (iii) is therefore true, and the correct option is C.

**5    B**    **Efficiency ratio** $= \dfrac{(54,000 \times 8)\,\text{hours}}{480,000} \times 100\% = 90\%$

**Capacity ratio** $= \dfrac{480,000\,\text{hours}}{400,000\,\text{hours}} \times 100\% = 120\%$

The correct answer is therefore B.

If you selected option A, you calculated the efficiency ratio correctly but calculated the capacity ratio as 400,000 hours/480,000 hours instead of the other way round.

If you selected option C, you calculated both ratios incorrectly because you mixed up the numerators and denominators.

If you selected option D, you calculated the capacity ratio correctly but calculated the efficiency ratio as 480,000 hours/(54,000 × 8 hours) instead of the other way round.

**6    ✓**    Production overheads

Overtime premium is always classed as production overheads unless it is: worked at the specific request of a customer to get his order completed; or worked regularly by a production department in the normal course of operations, in which case it is usually incorporated into the direct labour hourly rate.

**7**    The employee's pay for the week is (to 2 decimal places) $ 416.00

| | |
|---|---:|
| Product X (6 × 2 hours) | 12 hours |
| Product Z (10 × 4 hours) | 40 hours |
| | 52 hours |

Therefore, employee's pay = 52 hours × $8 = $416 for the week.

8    C

| Day | Units produced | Piecework earnings @ \$0.20 per unit | Guaranteed minimum earnings | Total daily earnings |
|-----|----------------|-------------------------------------|-----------------------------|---------------------|
| | | \$ | \$ | \$ |
| Monday | 90 | 18 | – | 18 |
| Tuesday | 70 | 14 | 15 | 15 |
| Wednesday | 75 | 15 | – | 15 |
| Thursday | 60 | 12 | 15 | 15 |
| Friday | 90 | 18 | – | 18 |
| | | | | 81 |

9    D    Idle time may arise for many reasons. Sometimes it may be due to **uncontrollable external factors**, such as a world shortage of material supply. Therefore **options B and C** are incorrect. However idle time can also arise due to **controllable internal factors** such as inefficient production scheduling or inadequate machine maintenance leading to machine breakdowns. Therefore **option A** is incorrect.

10    C    $\text{Efficiency ratio} = \dfrac{\text{expected hours to make output}}{\text{active hours worked}} \times 100\%$

$= \dfrac{380 \text{ units} \times 2 \text{ hours}}{800 - 20} \times 100\%$

$= \dfrac{760}{780} \times 100\%$

$= 97.44\%$

11    C    Activity ratio = capacity ratio × efficiency ratio

∴ 1.035 = capacity ratio × 0.9

∴ Capacity ratio = $\dfrac{1.035}{0.9}$ = 1.15, or 115%

12    A

| | Basic pay | Overtime premium | Total |
|---|-----------|------------------|-------|
| | \$ | \$ | \$ |
| Direct labour | | 300 (W1) | 300 |
| Indirect labour | 2,200 (W2) | 150 (W3) | 2,350 |
| | 2,200 | 450 | 2,650 |

*Workings*

1    **Overtime premium – direct labour**

20 × 6 hours × \$2.50 per hour            = \$300

2    **Basic pay – indirect labour**

10 × 44 hours × \$5 per hour            = \$2,200

3    **Overtime premium – indirect labour**

10 × 6 hours × \$2.50 per hour            = \$150

13    B    $\text{Efficiency ratio} = \dfrac{\text{Expected hours to make output}}{\text{Actual hours taken}} \times 100\%$

$= \dfrac{351 \text{ hours}}{357 \text{ hours}} \times 100\%$

= 98.32% (to 2 decimal places)

*Workings*

| | |
|---|---|
| Standard time to produce 5,200 units | = 325 hours |
| | = 325 hours × 60 minutes |
| | = 19,500 minutes |

∴ Standard time to produce 1 unit $= \dfrac{325}{5,200}$

= 0.0625 hours per unit

∴ Standard time to produce 5,616 units = 5,616 units × 0.0625 hours

= 351 hours

**14  B   Direct wages**                                                                 $

| | |
|---|---:|
| 36 hours @ $3.60 | 129.60 |
| 2 hours @ $3.60 (special job basic) | 7.20 |
| 2 hours @ $1.80 (special job overtime) | 3.60 |
| Total direct wages | 140.40 |

**15  B**   1,065 units should take (× 2.4 minutes) = 2,556 minutes

$= \dfrac{2,556}{60}$

= $42.6 hours

| | |
|---|---|
| ∴ Productivity bonus | = (42.6 – 37.5) hours × ($8.50) ÷ 3) |
| | = 5.1 hours × $2.8333 |
| | = $14.45 |
| Basic salary | = 37.5 hours × ($8.50 ÷ 3) |
| | = $318.75 |
| ∴ Total earnings | = basic salary + productivity bonus |
| | = $318.75 + $14.45 |
| | = $333.20 |

**16  B**   Training of direct operatives and normal idle time in the factory only

**17  A**

| | | $ |
|---|---|---:|
| 620 units @ a basic rate of $0.50 per unit | = | 310 |
| 100 units @ $0.05 per unit premium | = | 5 |
| 20 units @ $0.10 per unit premium | = | 2 |
| | | 317 |

**18  B**   A direct cost is a cost that can be traced in full to saleable cost units that are being costed.

# 11 Compulsory written question: Labour I

> **Helping hand**
>
> We have given more than one advantage and one disadvantage of piecework schemes, so that you can use them for revision purposes. Do not waste valuable time doing this in the examination. Furthermore, you may have thought of other, equally valid, advantages or disadvantages.

(a)   **Earnings for the week ending 31 October 20X1**

| | A | B | C |
|---|---:|---:|---:|
| Output units | 520 | 600 | 480 |
| Reject units | 19 | 62 | 10 |
| Units qualifying for payment | 501 | 538 | 470 |

| | A | B | C |
|---|---|---|---|
| Paid as follows: | $ | $ | $ |
| First 100 units @ $0.40 | 40.00 | 40.00 | 40.00 |
| Next 100 units @ $0.48 | 48.00 | 48.00 | 48.00 |
| Next 100 units @ $0.56 | 56.00 | 56.00 | 56.00 |
| Remaining units @ $0.64 | | | |
| 201 × $0.64 | 128.64 | | |
| 238 × $0.64 | | 152.32 | |
| 170 × $0.64 | | | 108.80 |
| Weekly earnings | 272.64 | 296.32 | 252.80 |

(b) Advantages to an employer of using a piecework scheme include the following.

- Only **good output** is paid for (in this scheme)

- Employees are **encouraged to increase output**, particularly with a **differential scheme** such as that in use here

- Labour costs per unit can be **easily controlled**

(c) Disadvantages to an employer of using a piecework scheme include the following.

- **Total labour costs increase with output.** The employer does not benefit from a reduced unit cost for labour as output increases

- Employees may be encouraged to **increase quantity** at the **expense of quality**

# 12 Compulsory written question: Labour II

**Helping hand**

This question demonstrates the importance of being able to remember the formulae (by heart!) of the following ratios.

- Rate of labour turnover
- Efficiency ratio
- Capacity ratio
- Production volume ratio

You must make sure that you commit the above ratios to memory before your exam.

**What the Examiner said**

In part (a) some candidates failed to read the question carefully and listed costs that did not relate specifically to labour turnover. Very few candidates were able in part (b) to demonstrate they knew the ratio formulae and were able to apply them.

(a) **Replacement costs** are the costs incurred as a result of **hiring new employees** and they include the following.

- Cost of selection and placement
- Inefficiency of new employees
- Training costs of new employees
- Increased wastage due to lack of expertise among new staff

(b) **Preventative costs** are incurred in order to **prevent employees leaving** and they include the following.

- Cost of personnel administration (for maintaining good relationships)
- Cost of medical services
- Cost of welfare services (sports facilities, canteens)
- Cost of pension schemes

$$\text{Rate of labour turnover} = \frac{\text{Number of employees leaving/ being recruited in period}}{\text{Average number of employees in period}} \times 100\%$$

$$\text{Expected hours to make actual output} = \frac{16{,}390}{25 \text{ units per hour}}$$

$$= 655.6 \text{ hours}$$

(i) **Efficiency ratio** $= \dfrac{\text{Expected hours to make actual output}}{\text{Actual hours taken}}$

$$= \frac{655.6}{640} \times 100\%$$

$$= 102.4\% \text{ (to 1 decimal place)}$$

(ii) **Capacity ratio** $= \dfrac{\text{Actual hours worked}}{\text{Hours budgeted}} \times 100\%$

$$= \frac{640}{660} \times 100\%$$

$$= 97.0\% \text{ (to 1 decimal place)}$$

(iii) Production volume ratio $= \dfrac{\text{Expected hours to make actual output}}{\text{Budgeted hours}} \times 100$

$$= \frac{655.6}{660} \times 100\%$$

$$= 99.3\% \text{ (to 1 decimal place)}$$

## Marking scheme

|  |  |  | Marks |
|---|---|---|---|
| (a) | Replacement costs | 2 | |
|  | Preventative costs | 2 | |
|  | Labour turnover formula | 2 | |
|  |  |  | 6 |
| (b) | Efficiency ratio | 4 | |
|  | Capacity ratio | 3 | |
|  | Production volume ratio | 3 | |
|  |  |  | 10 |
|  |  |  | 16 |

# 13 Compulsory written question: Labour III

**Helping hand**

In parts (a) and (b) show your workings. This will ensure you still earn good marks even if you make an arithmetic error.

In part (a) (ii) make sure you calculate the percentage correctly. When working out a percentage divide by the original value (not the new or revised value).

Part (b) (i) was as easy as it looked – make certain that you get all the marks by showing all your workings.

Part (b) (ii) was perhaps the most difficult part of this question. If you are unable to calculate a particular value make and state any assumptions you need. Then go on and do as much of the question as you can. Remember the majority of the marks are for the workings and not the 'answer'.

(a)     **Time rate payment system**

  (i)     Labour cost per week = 6 operatives × 40 hours × $8.00 per hour = $1,920

          Labour cost per unit = $1,920 / 2,500 units = $0.768

  (ii)    Labour cost per unit for 2,750 units per week = $1,920 / 2,750 units = $0.698 per unit

          $$\text{Reduction in unit cost} = \frac{\$(0.768-0.698)}{\$0.768} \times 100\% = 9.1\%$$

(b)     **Incentive scheme**

  (i)     **Labour cost per unit (output 3,080 units per week)**

| | $ | $ |
|---|---|---|
| Basic: | | |
| 6 operatives x 40 hours at $4.00 per hour | | 960.00 |
| Differential piecework: | | |
| 2,500 units at $0.375 per unit | 937.50 | |
| 500 units at $0.45 per unit | 225.00 | |
| 80 units at $0.60 per unit | 48.00 | |
| | | 1,210.50 |
| | | 2,170.50 |

          $2,170.50 / 3,080 units = $0.705 per unit

  (ii)    **Level of output for common total labour cost**

| | $ | |
|---|---|---|
| Current system cost | 1,920.00 | |
| Less: Incentive scheme basic | 960.00 | |
| Piecework payments | 960.00 | |
| Less: Incentive scheme initial piecework | 937.50 | (for 2,500 units) |
| Additional piecework payments | 22.50 | |

          $22.50 / $0.45 per unit = 50 units (in excess of previous level)

          Level of output = 2,500 + 50 = 2,550 units

| | | | | Marks |
|---|---|---|---|---|
| (a) | (i) | Weekly total cost | 1 | |
| | | Cost per unit | 1 | |
| | | | | 2 |
| | (ii) | Revised cost unit | 1 | |
| | | % reduction | 1 | |
| | | | | 2 |
| (b) | (i) | Basic pay | 1 | |
| | | Initial piecework | 1 | |
| | | Differential piecework | 3 | |
| | | Cost per unit | 1 | |
| | | | | 6 |

(ii)   Differential piecework payments required                    2
       Extra units                                                 2
       Level of output                                             <u>1</u>
                                                                   <u>5</u>
                                                                   <u>15</u>

---

# 14 Objective test questions: Expenses

1   A   The purchase of a building and the extension to a building are both examples of **capital expenditure**. The correct answer is therefore A.

        Costs associated with fixing broken windows and replacing missing roof tiles are examples of **revenue expenditure**.

2   B
| | $ |
|---|---|
| Cost of new machinery | 40,000 |
| Cost of extension | 20,000 |
| Capital expenditure | 60,000 |

        If you selected option A, you forgot to include the cost of the extension as capital expenditure.

        If you selected option C, you incorrectly included maintenance costs of $4,000 as capital expenditure.

        If you selected option D, you incorrectly included both machinery maintenance costs and office repainting costs as capital expenditure. These are examples of revenue expenditure.

3   A   Using the straight line method, annual depreciation charge = $20,000/4 years = $5,000.

        After three years, depreciation charge = $5,000 × 3 = $15,000

        ∴ Net book value of asset = $20,000 − $15,000 = $5,000

4   C
| | $ |
|---|---|
| Purchase cost | 60,000 |
| Year 1 depreciation | (12,000) |
| NBV end year 1 | 48,000 |
| Year 2 depreciation | (9,600) |
| NBV end year 2 | 38,400 |
| Year 3 depreciation | (7,680) |
| NBV end year 3 | 30,720 |
| Year 4 depreciation | (6,144) |
| NBV end year 4 | 24,576 |

        If you selected option A, you calculated the net book value of the asset using the straight line method instead of the reducing balance method.

        If you selected option B, you calculated the net book value of the asset at the end of year 5 instead of year 4.

        If you selected option D, you calculated the net book value of the asset at the end of year 3 instead of year 4.

5   A   **Allocation** is the process by which whole cost items are charged direct to a cost unit or cost centre.

6   ✓   False

        Capital expenditure is **not** charged to the profit and loss account (income statement) as an expense. A **depreciation charge** is instead charged to the profit and loss account (income statement) in order to write off the capital expenditure over a period of time.

**7**

| ✓ | Administration expenses |
|---|---|
| ✓ | Plant maintenance costs |

The purchase of a building (new factory) or a vehicle (even if it is second-hand) are both items of capital expenditure.

**8**  Obsolescence

**9**  $ 14,250

$$\text{Machine-hour rate} = \frac{\text{Cost} - \text{residual value}}{\text{Useful life}}$$

$$= \frac{\$200,000 - \$10,000}{40,000 \text{ hours}}$$

$$= \frac{\$190,000}{40,000 \text{ hours}}$$

$$= \$4.75 \text{ per machine hour}$$

$$\text{Depreciation charge (year 1)} = 3,000 \text{ hours} \times \$4.75$$

$$= \$14,250$$

**10**

| | $ | Code |
|---|---|---|
| Supervisors' wages Department X | 2,000 | 400 |
| Supervisors' wages Department Y | 3,000 | 410 |
| Rent of premises shared by Departments X and Y | 1,500 | 880 |

The question asks for the **initial** coding of costs. This means that the total rent for the shared premises is firstly allocated to cost centre 880 and then $750 is re-allocated to Department X and $750 to Department Y.

**11**  C  Suppose the machine cost $10,000

$$\text{Straight-line depreciation} = \frac{\$10,000}{5 \text{ years}}$$

$$= \$2,000 \text{ per annum}$$

Reducing balance depreciation is as follows.

| | $ |
|---|---|
| | 10,000 |
| 25% – year 1 | 2,500 |
| | 7,500 |
| 25% – year 2 | (1,875) |
| | 5,625 |
| 25% – year 3 | (1,406) |
| | 4,219 |
| 25% – year 4 | (1,055) |
| | 3,164 |
| 25% – year 5 | (791) |
| | 2,373 |

Therefore, depreciation would be greater in year 1 but less in year 5 if the reducing balance method, rather than the straight-line method, was used.

**12**  D  Chart D shows the unit cost behaviour of straight-line depreciation costs.

| 13 | B | If the asset's initial value is $1000, depreciation each year would be: |

| Year | Straight line | 20% Reducing balance | 25% Reducing balance | 15% Reducing balance | 18% Reducing balance |
|------|---------------|----------------------|----------------------|----------------------|----------------------|
| 1 | 100 | 200 | 250 | 150 | 180 |
| 2 | 100 | 160 | 188 | 128 | 148 |
| 3 | 100 | 128 | 141 | 108 | 121 |

Using 20% reducing balance, depreciation will eventually be lower than the straight line method.
Depreciation is not lower in each year using 15% reducing balance.
Depreciation is not lower in year 2 using 18% reducing balance.

| 14 | A | Using the reducing balance method, depreciation will fall each year so, if output stays the same, unit costs will fall. |

Using the straight-line method, depreciation stays the same each year, so if output increases, costs per unit will decline.

# 15 Objective test questions: Overheads and absorption costing

| 1 | B | Overhead absorption (option A) is the final process of absorbing the total cost centre overheads into product costs. Overhead allocation (option C) is the allotment of whole items of overhead costs to a particular cost centre or cost unit. Overhead analysis (option D) is the general term used to describe all of the tasks of processing overhead cost data. |

| 2 | D | Number of employees in packing department = 2 direct + 1 indirect = 3 |

Number of employees in all production departments = 15 direct + 6 indirect
= 21

**Packing department overhead**

Canteen cost apportioned to packing department $= \dfrac{\$8,400}{21} \times 3$

$= \$1,200$

Original overhead allocated and apportioned $\quad = \underline{\$8,960}$

Total overhead after apportionment of canteen costs $\quad = \underline{\$10,160}$

If you selected option A you forgot to include the original overhead allocated and apportioned to the packing department. If you selected option B you included the four canteen employees in your calculation, but the question states that the basis for apportionment is the number of employees in each **production** cost centre.

If you selected option C you based your calculations on the direct employees only.

| 3 | B | From the four options available, a basis relating to space occupied would seem to be most appropriate. This eliminates options C and D. Since heating is required to warm the whole of the space occupied, from floor to ceiling, the volume of space is most appropriate. Therefore the correct answer is B. |

| 4 | A | Description B could lead to under-absorbed overheads if actual overheads far exceeded both budgeted overheads and the overhead absorbed. Description C could lead to under-absorbed overheads if overhead absorbed does not increase in line with actual overhead incurred. Description D could also lead to under absorption if actual overhead does not decrease in line with absorbed overheads. |

**5**   **B**

|  | $ |
|---|---|
| Actual overheads | 295,000 |
| Under-absorbed overheads | 9,400 |
| Overheads absorbed for 70,000 hours at budgeted absorption rate (x) | 285,600 |

70,000x = $285,600

x       = $285,600/70,000

         = $4.08

Option A is incorrect because it is based on the budgeted overhead and the actual machine hours. Option C is incorrect because it is the actual overhead rate per machine hour.

If you selected option D you added the under-absorbed overhead by mistake, at the beginning of the calculation.

**6**   ✓   Spread common costs over cost centres

Overhead apportionment involves sharing overhead costs as fairly as possible over a number of cost centres. Apportionment is used when it is not possible to allocate the whole cost to a single cost centre.

**7**   The budgeted overhead absorption rate per hour was $ | 14 |

|  | $ |
|---|---|
| Actual overheads | 640,150 |
| Over-absorbed overheads | 35,000 |
| Overheads absorbed for 48,225 hours at budgeted overhead absorption rate (x) | 675,150 |

48,225 x  =  675,150

$$x = \frac{675,150}{48,225}$$

x       =  $14

**8**   The number of machine hours (to the nearest hour) budgeted to be worked were | 14,850 | hours.

$$\text{Budgeted hours} = \frac{\text{Budgeted overheads}}{\text{Budgeted overhead absorption rate}}$$

$$= \frac{\$475,200}{£32}$$

$$= 14,850$$

**9**   ✓   Charge overheads to products

**10**  **C**   The number of machine hours budgeted for the cutting department is much higher than the budgeted number of labour hours. Therefore the activity is **machine intensive** and the type of overhead incurred is likely to be **machine related,** for example power costs, maintenance and depreciation. The most appropriate absorption rate in the cutting department is therefore one based on **machine hours.**

In the finishing department the budgeted number of labour hours is much higher than the budgeted number of machine hours. Therefore the most appropriate absorption rate in the finishing department is one based on **labour hours.**

**11**  **D**   Under or over absorbed overhead

**= actual overhead incurred – overhead absorbed**

**= actual overhead incurred – (actual hrs worked × machine hr rate)**

Therefore the calculation of the under or over absorbed overhead requires three pieces of information:

- Actual overhead incurred
- Actual hours worked
- Pre-determined machine hour rate

12   C     All of the methods are acceptable bases for absorbing production overheads. However the percentage of prime cost has **serious limitations** and the rate per unit can only be used if all cost units are **identical.**

13        $ | 55,000

*Workings*

|  | Production 1 $ | Production 2 $ | Service 1 $ | Service 2 $ |
|---|---|---|---|---|
| Apportioned overheads | 45,000 | 60,000 | 9,000 | 8,000 |
| Apportion service 1 costs (20:10) | 6,000 | 3,000 | (9,000) | – |
|  | 51,000 | 63,000 |  | 8,000 |
| Apportion service 2 costs (4:4) | 4,000 | 4,000 | – | (8,000) |
|  | 55,000 | 67,000 | – | – |

14        $ | 67,375

*Workings*

|  | Production 1 $ | Production 2 $ | Service 1 $ | Service 2 $ |
|---|---|---|---|---|
| Apportioned overheads | 45,000 | 60,000 | 9,000 | 8,000 |
| Apportion service 1 costs (20:10:10) | 4,500 | 2,250 | (9,000) | 2,250 |
|  | 49,500 | 62,250 |  | 10,250 |
| Apportion service 2 costs (4:4) | 5,125 | 5,125 | – | (10,250) |
|  | 54,625 | 67,375 | – | – |

15   A     It is necessary to have data available relating to the budgeted and actual activity levels (machine hours or direct labour hours). Without such data it is not possible to determine the overhead over/under absorption.

16   D     Under/over absorption = Actual overheads – absorbed overheads
                                    = \$126,740 – \$125,200
                                      = \$1,540

Under absorption has occurred because actual overheads incurred were greater than the overheads absorbed.

17   C     Total reapportionment to Cost Centre Y

|  | $ |
|---|---|
| 60% × \$42,000 | 25,200 |
| 45% × \$57,600 | 25,920 |
|  | 51,120 |

18   A

|  | $ |
|---|---|
| Actual overheads | 158,000 |
| Absorbed overheads (9,800 hrs × \$16.40) | 160,720 |
| Over-absorbed overheads | 2,720 |

$$\text{Overhead absorption rate per hour} = \frac{\text{Budgeted overheads}}{\text{Budgeted labour hours}}$$

$$= \frac{\$164,000}{10,000 \text{ hours}}$$

$$= \$16.40 \text{ per hour}$$

19   A     From the information given, it cannot be determined whether statements 1 and 2 are true or false.

20   D     Number of employees is the most appropriate basis for reapportioning the cost of personnel services.

21  B

|  |  | $ |
|---|---|---|
| Overhead absorbed 2,180 hours @ $12.00 | = | 26,160 |
| Actual overhead expenditure | = | 25,470 |
| Over absorbed | = | 690 |

22  D  Total overhead = $13,122 + $7,920 + $2,988 = $24,030

Number of machine hours = 216,000/120 = 1,800

Overhead absorption rate per machine hour = $24,030/1,800 = $13.35

# 16 Compulsory written question: Overheads and absorption costing I

**Helping hand**

Don't waste time calculating unnecessary absorption rates. Read the question carefully for which rate to apply to which cost centre.

**What the Examiner said**

A serious lack of understanding of absorption costing was demonstrated by many candidates.

(a)  (i)  Factory rent could be apportioned on the basis of floor area occupied by each cost centre.

(ii)  Staff canteen costs could be apportioned on the basis of the number of employees in each cost centre.

(b)  (i)  Production Cost Centre X:

$$\text{Overhead absorption rate per machine hour} = \frac{\$161,820}{8,700}$$

$$= \$18.60$$

Production Cost Centre Y:

$$\text{Overhead absorption rate per labour hour} = \frac{\$97,110}{8,300}$$

$$= \$11.70$$

(ii)  Production Cost Centre X:

Production overheads absorbed  = 8,960 × $18.60
= $166,656

Production Cost Centre Y:

Production overheads absorbed  = 7,870 × $11.70
= $92,079

(iii)  Production Cost Centre X:

|  | $ |
|---|---|
| Actual overhead | 163,190 |
| Overhead absorbed | 166,656 |
| Over-absorption | 3,466 |

Production Cost Centre Y:

|  | $ |
|---|---|
| Actual overhead | 96,330 |
| Overhead absorbed | 92,079 |
| Under-absorption | 4,251 |

|     |       |                                                          | Marks |
|-----|-------|----------------------------------------------------------|-------|
| (a) |       | 2 marks for each                                         | 4     |
| (b) | (i)   | 1 ½ marks for each                                       | 3     |
|     | (ii)  | 1 ½ marks for each                                       | 3     |
|     | (iii) | 1 mark for each figure <br> 1 mark for 'over', 'under'   | 2 <br> 2 |
|     |       |                                                          | 4     |
|     |       |                                                          | 14    |

# 17 Compulsory written question: Overheads and absorption costing II

**Helping hand**

This was perhaps the hardest of all the Section B questions. There are, however, some easy marks. Part (c) asks for general causes of overhead under absorption, although the rest of the question may help as a memory aid, this can be answered independently of the rest of the question. A recommended exam tactic is to attempt this before the numerical parts. Remember to leave lots of space for your answers to (a) and (b)!

In part (a) the examiner only gave information for machine hours or labour hours. You were, therefore, given no choice when calculating an appropriate OAR.

Part (b) was perhaps the most difficult part of this question. If you are unable to calculate an OAR in (a) then make up and state one for part (b). Then go on and do as much of the question as you can. Remember the majority of the marks are for the workings and not the 'answer'.

**What the Examiner said**

Candidates generally answered parts (a) and (b) well. The narrative in part (c) was poorly answered indicating a lack of a deeper understanding of the topic.

The few candidates who successfully calculated the over/under absorbed overheads in the answer to part (b) were all able to demonstrate that they understood what causes under absorption.

(a) **Predetermined production overhead absorption rates**

Department X – $51,240 / 4,200 machine hours = $12.20 per machine hour
Department Y – $87,120 / 5,280 machine hours = $16.50 per machine hour
Department Z – $66,816 / 11,520 direct labour hours = $5.80 per direct labour hour

(b) **Over/under absorption of overhead (Month 1)**

|              | Overhead incurred | Overhead absorbed |                    | Over/(under) absorption |
|--------------|-------------------|-------------------|--------------------|-------------------------|
|              | $                 | $                 |                    | $                       |
| Department X | 4,410             | 4,148             | (340 × 12.20)      | (262)                   |
| Department Y | 7,190             | 7,029             | (426 × 16.50)      | (161)                   |
| Department Z | 5,610             | 5,713             | (985 × 5.80)       | 103                     |
|              | 17,210            | 16,890            |                    | (320)                   |

(c) Two causes of overhead under absorption could be where actual overhead expenditure is greater than budget or where actual machine hours worked are less than budget.

<table>
<tr><td></td><td></td><td></td><td align="right">Marks</td></tr>
</table>

|       |                                        |       |
|-------|----------------------------------------|-------|
| (a)   | Dept X                                 | 2     |
|       | Depts Y and Z (1 for each)             | 2     |
|       |                                        | **4** |
| (b)   | Overhead absorbed (1 for each)         | 3     |
|       | Over/(under) absorption (1½ for each)  | 4½    |
|       | Net under absorption                   | 1½    |
|       |                                        | **9** |
| (c)   | 1½ for each reason                     | 3     |
|       |                                        | **16** |

# 18 Compulsory written question: Overheads and absorption costing III

**Helping hand**

Make sure you calculate overhead absorbed correctly as the number of machine or labour hours by the predetermined rates.

(a)     Overhead over/under absorption

|                          | **Cost centre X** |                                   |
|--------------------------|-------------------|-----------------------------------|
| Overhead absorbed        | $29,146           | (1,235 machine hours at $23.60)   |
| Overhead incurred        | $29,609           |                                   |
| Overhead under absorbed  | $463              |                                   |

|                          | **Cost centre Y** |                                   |
|--------------------------|-------------------|-----------------------------------|
| Overhead absorbed        | $53,718           | (6,395 machine hours at $8.40)    |
| Overhead incurred        | $52,567           |                                   |
| Overhead over absorbed   | $1,151            |                                   |

(b)     Predetermined, as opposed to actual, overhead absorption rates

Advantages:

−     enable overheads to be absorbed immediately after production
−     easier to estimate product/job costs
−     even out fluctuations that would otherwise occur in unit costs if production is uneven

|       |                          |       |
|-------|--------------------------|-------|
|       |                          | **Marks** |
| (a)   | Cost centre X – figure   | 2     |
|       | Cost centre Y – figure   | 2     |
|       | Cost centre X – 'under'  | 1     |
|       | Cost centre Y – 'over'   | 1     |
|       |                          | **6** |
| (b)   | Advantages – 2 for each  | 4     |
|       |                          | **10** |

# 19 Compulsory written question: Coding systems and overhead apportionment

(a)  (i)  Once costs have been classified, a coding system can be applied to make it easier to manage the cost data, both in manual systems and in computerised systems.

A code is 'a system of symbols designed to be applied to a classified set of items to give a brief, accurate reference, facilitating entry, collection and analysis'. (CIMA *Official Terminology*)

(ii)  Note only **two** features need to be listed

- The code must be **easy to use and communicate**.

- Each item should have a **unique code**.

- The coding system must **allow for expansion**.

- The code should be **flexible** so that small changes in a cost's classification can be incorporated without major changes to the coding system itself.

- The coding system should provide a **comprehensive** system, whereby every recorded item can be suitably coded.

- The coding system should be **brief**, to save clerical time in writing out codes and to save storage space in computer memory and on computer files. At the same time codes must be **long enough** to allow for the suitable coding of all items.

- The likelihood of **errors** going undetected should be minimised.

- Code numbers should be **issued from a single central point**. Different people should not be allowed to add new codes to the existing list independently.

- Codes should be **uniform** (that is, have the same length and the same structure) to assist in the detection of missing characters and to facilitate processing.

- The coding system should **avoid problems** such as confusion between I and 1, O and 0 (zero), S and 5 and so on.

- The coding system should, if possible, be **significant** (in other words, the actual code should signify something about the item being coded).

- If the code consists of alphabetic characters, it should be derived from the item's description or name (that is, **mnemonics** should be used).

(b)  (i)  Allocated and apportioned factory overhead costs for each cost centre:

| | Total $ | P1 $ | P2 $ | Materials store $ | Employee facilities $ | Basis of apportionment |
|---|---|---|---|---|---|---|
| Overheads allocated | 348,000 | 107,000 | 89,000 | 68,000 | 84,000 | Actual |
| Buildings dep'n and insurance | 42,000 | 15,960 | 19,740 | 2,520 | 3,780 | Floor area |
| Management salaries | 27,000 | 9,000 | 12,000 | 3,000 | 3,000 | No of employees |
| Power to operate machinery | 12,600 | 6,510 | 6,090 | | | Machine hours |
| Other utilities | 9,400 | 3,290 | 4,230 | 940 | 940 | % share |
| Totals | 439,000 | 141,760 | 131,060 | 74,460 | 91,720 | |

(ii)  Re-apportioned service cost centre overheads:

| | | P1 | P2 | Materials store | Employee facilities | Basis |
|---|---|---|---|---|---|---|
| Employee facilities | | 34,395 | 45,860 | 11,465 | (91,720) | No of employees |
| Materials store overheads | | 34,370 | 51,555 | (85,925) | | % share |
| | | 210,525 | 228,475 | | | |

# 20 Objective test questions: Marginal costing and absorption costing

1  C  Difference in profit = change in stock (inventory) level × fixed overhead per unit
   = (200 – 250) × ($2.50 × 3)
   = $375

The absorption costing profit will be greater than the marginal costing profit because inventory has increased.

If you selected option A you calculated the correct profit difference but the absorption costing profit would be greater because fixed overheads are carried forward in the increasing inventory levels.

If you selected option B you multiplied the inventory difference by the direct labour – hour rate instead of by the total overhead cost per **unit**, which takes three hours.

If you selected option D you based the profit difference on the closing inventory only (250 units × $2.50 × 3).

2  B  Sales volume exceeded production volume by 500 units, therefore inventory reduced. The absorption costing profit will be lower than the marginal costing profit because fixed overheads were 'released' from inventory.

| Profit difference | = inventory reduction in units × fixed overhead per unit |
|---|---|
| | = 500 × $5 = $2,500 |
| Absorption costing profit | = $60,000 – $2,500 = $57,500 |

If you selected option A you based your calculation of the profit difference on the closing inventory of 2,500 units. Option C is calculated as $7 profit per unit × 8,500 units sold, however, this takes no account of the actual level of fixed overhead cost.

If you selected option D you calculated the correct profit difference but you added it to the marginal costing profit instead of subtracting it.

| 3 | D | Decrease in inventory levels | = 48,500 − 45,500 = 3,000 units |
| | | Difference in profits | = $315,250 − $288,250 = $27,000 |
| | | Fixed overhead per unit | $= \dfrac{\$27,000}{3,000} = \$9$ per unit |

If you selected one of the other options you attempted various divisions of all the data available in the question!

4   C   Argument (i) is correct. SSAP 9 requires closing inventory values to include a share of fixed production overhead. Argument (ii) is not correct. Opponents of absorption costing argue that under and over absorption are one of the biggest problems with the use of the method. Argument (iii) is correct. Absorption costing carries fixed overheads forward in inventory to be matched against sales as they arise.

Therefore the correct answer is C.

5   D   Under marginal costing, closing inventory will be valued **lower** than under absorption costing. If production is greater than sales the inventory level has increased during the month. Absorption costing would therefore produce a higher profit than marginal costing.

6   The fixed overhead absorption rate per unit (to the nearest penny) was $ 3.20

| Change in inventory | = | 33,480 units − 25,920 units | = 7,560 units |
| Difference in profit | = | $228,123 − $203,931 = $24,192 | |

$\therefore$ Fixed overhead absorption rate $= \dfrac{\text{Difference in profit}}{\text{Change in inventory}}$

$= \dfrac{24,192}{7,560 \text{ units}}$

$= $3.20 per unit

7   The profit using absorption costing would be $ 23,900

| | Litres |
| --- | --- |
| Opening inventory | 8,500 |
| Closing inventory | 6,750 |
| Change in inventory | 1,750 |
| × overhead absorption rate | $2 |
| Profit difference | 3,500 |

Since inventory reduced during the period the absorption costing profit would be lower than the marginal costing profit. Absorption costing profit = $27,400 − $3,500 = $23,900.

8   The profit using marginal costing would be $ 118,000

| Marginal cost profit | = | Absorption cost profit + ((opening inventory − closing inventory) × fixed overhead absorption rate) |
| | = | $130,000 + ((5,000 − 8,000) × $4) |
| | = | $118,000 |

9   ✓   If inventory levels reduce, absorption costing will report a lower profit than marginal costing.

✓   If production and sales volumes are equal, marginal costing and absorption costing will report the same profit figure.

If inventory reduce, fixed overheads are 'released' from inventory using absorption costing, and the absorption costing profit will be lower than the marginal costing profit.

A difference in reported profits arises only when inventory volumes change, therefore the third statement is correct.

10   A   Opening inventory          = nil

Closing inventory          = (97,000 – 96,000) units
                           = 1,000 units

∴ Profit difference        = 1,000 units × $1.40 per unit
                           = $1,400

During the period, inventory levels have increased, and therefore marginal costing profits will be less than absorption costing profits.

Therefore, the correct answer is: '$1,400 less using marginal costing'.

11   D   Statement 1 is true

Inventory value at the end of the period would be higher than at the beginning of the period because 2,000 more units were manufactured than sold. These 'extra' units will give rise to an increase in inventory volume, and hence inventory value, during the period.

Statement 2 is true

Inventory values both at the beginning and at the end of the period would be higher using absorption rather than marginal costing. Absorption costing inventory valuations include a share of fixed production costs, whereas marginal costing inventory valuations do not. Absorption costing inventory valuations will be higher, therefore, than marginal costing inventory valuations.

12   C   Inventory valuation using absorption costing includes a share of all production costs.

13   A   In absorption costing, closing inventory valuation is higher, so profits are higher than if marginal costing is used. Only production overheads are absorbed into the cost of the product.

# 21 Compulsory written question: Marginal costing and absorption costing I

(a)

> **Helping hand**
>
> Remember that under marginal costing principles fixed costs are treated as a period cost and are not included in the production costs (unlike absorption costing where fixed costs are included in the production costs).

PROFIT STATEMENT – MARGINAL COSTING

|  | Month 1 | | Month 2 | |
|---|---|---|---|---|
|  | $ | $ | $ | $ |
| Sales |  | 98,000 |  | 106,400 |
| Variable cost of sales: |  |  |  |  |
| Opening inventory |  |  | 6,450 |  |
| Variable production cost (W1) | 51,600 |  | 46,440 |  |
| Closing inventory (W2) | (6,450) |  | (3,870) |  |
| Variable cost of production | 45,150 |  | 49,020 |  |
| Variable administration cost (W3) | 4,900 |  | 5,320 |  |
|  |  | 50,050 |  | 54,340 |
| Contribution |  | 47,950 |  | 52,060 |
| Fixed production overheads |  | 30,000 |  | 30,000 |
| Fixed administration overheads |  | 13,000 |  | 13,000 |
| Profit |  | 4,950 |  | 9,060 |

*Workings*

1    *Cost of production*

| | $ per unit |
|---|---|
| Direct material | 6.10 |
| Direct labour | 5.20 |
| Variable overhead | 1.60 |
| | 12.90 |

Variable cost of production – Month 1  = 4,000 × $12.90
= $51,600

Variable cost of production – Month 2  = 3,600 × $12.90
= $46,440

2    *Closing inventory*

| | |
|---|---|
| Opening inventory + production – sales | = closing inventory |
| 0 + 4,000 – 3,500 | = 500 units |
| Month 1 closing inventory | = 500 units @ $12.90 |
| | = $6,450 |
| ∴ Month 2 closing inventory | = 500 + 3,600 – 3,800 = 300 units |
| | = 300 units @ $12.90 |
| | = $3,870 |

3    *Variable administration cost*

| | |
|---|---|
| Month 1 – $98,000 × 5% | = $4,900 |
| Month 2 – $106,400 × 5% | = $5,320 |

(b)

|  | Month 2<br>$ |
|---|---|
| Marginal costing profit | 9,060 |
| Adjust for fixed production overhead in inventory: | |
| Fixed overhead in opening inventory $\left(\dfrac{500}{4,000} \times \$30,000\right)$ | (3,750) |
| Fixed production overhead in closing inventory $\left(\dfrac{300}{3,600} \times \$30,000\right)$ | 2,500 |
| Absorption costing profit | 7,810 |

## Marking scheme

|  |  |  | Marks |
|---|---|---|---|
| (a) | Sales | | 1 |
| | Variable production cost | | 3 |
| | Variable administration cost | | 2 |
| | Contribution | | 2 |
| | Fixed production cost | | 1 |
| | Fixed administration cost | | 1 |
| | | | 10 |
| (b) | Inventory differences – calculation and reconciliation | | 3 |
| | Fixed overhead in inventory (absorption) | | 1 |
| | Fixed overhead in period cost (marginal) | | 1 |
| | Inventory change | | 2 |
| | | | 7 |
| | | | 17 |

# 22 Compulsory written question: Marginal costing and absorption costing II

(a)     Profit Statement using absorption costing

|  | $ | $ | Calculation |
|---|---|---|---|
| Sales |  | 547,200 | 45,600 litres × $12 |
| Production cost of sales |  |  |  |
| Prime costs | 239,200 |  | 46,000 litres × $5.20 |
| Production overhead | 128,800 |  | 46,000 litres × $2.80 |
| Cost of production | 368,000 |  | 46,000 litres × $8 |
| Less Closing inventory | 3,200 |  | (46,000 – 45,600) × $8 |
| Production cost of sales |  | 364,800 | 45,600 litres × $8 |
| Gross profit |  | 182,400 | 45,600 litres × ($12 – $8) |
| Non-production overheads: |  |  |  |
| Variable | 29,640 |  | 45.600 litres × $0.65 |
| Fixed | 78,200 |  | 46,000 litres × $1.70 |
|  |  | 107,840 |  |
| Net profit |  | 74,560 |  |

(b)     Marginal costing is an alternative method of costing to absorption costing. In marginal costing, only variable costs are charged as a cost of sale. Fixed costs are charged in full to profits in the year in which they are incurred. In absorption costing, fixed costs are absorbed into the cost of units and carried forward in inventory. This means that, using absorption costing, closing inventory will be valued higher and so profits will be higher.

The amount of fixed cost is $2.80 per unit, so the difference in profit is:

400 units at $2.80 = $1,120

## Marking scheme

|  |  |  | Marks |
|---|---|---|---|
| (a) | Sales |  | 1 |
|  | Production sales cost |  | 3 |
|  | Gross profit (term & figure) |  | 1 |
|  | Non-production overheads – variable |  | 1.5 |
|  |  – fixed |  | 1.5 |
|  |  |  | 8 |
| (b) | Inventory valuation |  | 2 |
|  | Fixed production overhead |  | 2 |
|  | Reconciliation |  | 2 |
|  |  |  | 6 |
|  |  |  | 14 |

# 23 Objective test questions: Cost bookkeeping

**1**    **B**    The question describes interlocking accounts, where the cost accounts are distinct from the financial accounts.

With integrated accounts, option D, a single set of accounting records provides both financial and cost accounts.

**2**    **C**    The reconciliation statement will contain all the items which result in a difference between the cost accounting profit and the financial accounting profit.

Item (i) would cause a profit difference therefore it **would appear** in the reconciliation statement.

Item (ii) would be included in both sets of accounts therefore it would **not** appear in the reconciliation account. Occasionally a **notional rent** charge may be included in the cost accounts but not in the financial accounts, and this **would** be included in the reconciliation statement. However we are told that this amount is for rent **paid** so it would not be included.

Item (iii) would appear in the financial accounts but not in the cost accounts therefore it **would be included** in the reconciliation statement.

Therefore the correct answer is C.

**3**    **C**    Statement (i) is correct because **only one set of accounts is kept in an integrated system.** Statement (ii) is incorrect because in a system of integrated accounts the financial and cost accounts are **combined** in one set of accounts. Statement (iii) is correct because **profit differences do not arise with an integrated system.**

**4**    **B**    The credit balance on the wages control account indicates that the amount of wages incurred and analysed between direct wages and indirect wages was **higher** than the wages paid through the bank. Therefore there was a $12,000 balance of **wages owing** at the end of February and statement B is not correct. Therefore the correct option is B.

Statement A is correct. $128,400 of wages was paid from the bank account.

Statement C is correct. $79,400 of direct wages was transferred to the work in progress control account.

Statement D is correct. $61,000 of indirect wages was transferred to the production overhead control account.

**5**    **C**    Statement (i) is not correct. A debit to stores with a corresponding credit to work in progress (WIP) indicates that **direct materials returned** from production were $18,000.

Statement (ii) is correct. **Direct costs of production** are 'collected' in the WIP account.

Statement (iii) is correct. **Indirect costs of production or overhead** are 'collected' in the overhead control account.

Statement (iv) is correct. The purchases of materials on credit are credited to the creditors account and debited to the material stores control account.

Therefore the correct answer is C.

**6**

| | Debit $ | Credit $ | No entry in this a/c $ |
|---|---|---|---|
| Work in progress | | | ✓ |
| Materials inventory | ✓ | | |
| Cost of sales | | | ✓ |
| Cash | | | ✓ |
| Creditors | | ✓ | |

7  [✓]  Production overhead control account

8

|  | Debit $ | Credit $ | No entry in this a/c $ |
|---|---|---|---|
| Overhead control account | ✓ | | |
| Work in progress account | | | ✓ |
| Income statement | | ✓ | |

Over-absorbed overhead means that the overhead charged to production was too high therefore there must be a credit to the income statement.

9  [✓]  DR  Overhead control  CR  Wages control

Indirect wages are 'collected' in the overhead control account, for subsequent absorption into work in progress.

10  An interlocking system features two ledgers.

(a)  The [financial] ledger contains asset, liability, revenue, expense and appropriation accounts.

(b)  The [cost] ledger is where cost information is analysed in more detail.

11  D  Items appearing in the cost accounts but not in the financial accounts are infrequent, but usually relate to notional costs.

12  C  Indirect materials are treated as a production overhead. Therefore, when indirect materials are issued, the material inventory account is credited and the production overhead account is debited with the value of the indirect materials.

13  D  **Debit** Work in Progress Account **Credit** Production Overhead Account

14  D  Direct labour costs are debited to the work-in-progress account and credited to wages control.

# 24 Compulsory written question: Cost bookkeeping

The company operates a marginal costing system and hence production overhead is not included in the value of WIP or finished goods but is treated as a period cost and written off directly to the profit and loss account (income statement) (income statement).

(a)  COST LEDGER CONTROL ACCOUNT (CLC)

| | $ | | $ |
|---|---|---|---|
| Sales account (h) | 88,000 | Opening balance b/f | 75,100 |
| Income statement) (j) | 2,170 | Stores ledger control (b) | 28,700 |
| Closing balance c/f | 85,000 | Factory wages control (c) | 58,900 |
| | | Production overhead control (d) | 1,970 |
| | | Selling overheads control (g) | 10,500 |
| | 175,170 | | 175,170 |
| | | Opening balance b/f | 85,000 |

(b) **STORES LEDGER CONTROL ACCOUNT**

| | $ | | $ |
|---|---|---|---|
| Opening balance b/f | 36,400 | WIP control (e) | 21,300 |
| Purchases – CLC (a) | 28,700 | Production overhead control (d) | 4,200 |
| | | Income statement (inventory written off) (j) | 1,200 |
| | | Closing balance c/f | 38,400 |
| | 65,100 | | 65,100 |
| Balance b/f | 38,400 | | |

(c) **FACTORY WAGES CONTROL ACCOUNT**

| | $ | | $ |
|---|---|---|---|
| Gross wages – CLC (a) | 58,900 | WIP control (balancing figure) (e) | 39,400 |
| | | Production overhead control (d) | 19,500 |
| | 58,900 | | 58,900 |

(d) **PRODUCTION OVERHEAD CONTROL ACCOUNT**

| | $ | | $ |
|---|---|---|---|
| Stores ledger control (b) | 4,200 | Income statement (balancing figure)(j) | 25,670 |
| Factory wages control (c) | 19,500 | | |
| Other costs – CLC (a) | 1,970 | | |
| | 25,670 | | 25,670 |

(e) **WORK IN PROGRESS (WIP) CONTROL ACCOUNT**

| | $ | | $ |
|---|---|---|---|
| Opening balance b/f | 23,000 | Finished goods control (f) (balancing figure) | 53,060 |
| Stores ledger control (b) | 21,300 | | |
| Factory wages control (c) | 39,400 | Closing balance c/f (23,000 + 7,640) | 30,640 |
| | 83,700 | | 83,700 |
| Balance b/f | 30,640 | | |

(f) **FINISHED GOODS CONTROL ACCOUNT**

| | $ | | $ |
|---|---|---|---|
| Opening balance b/f | 15,700 | Cost of sales (i) | 52,800 |
| WIP control (e) | 53,060 | Closing balance c/f | 15,960 |
| | 68,760 | | 68,760 |
| Balance b/f | 15,960 | | |

(g) **SELLING OVERHEAD CONTROL ACCOUNT**

| | $ | | $ |
|---|---|---|---|
| CLC (a) | 10,500 | Cost of sales a/c (i) | 10,500 |

(h) **SALES ACCOUNT**

| | $ | | $ |
|---|---|---|---|
| Income statement (j) | 88,000 | CLC – sales (a) | 88,000 |

(i) **COST OF SALES ACCOUNT**

| | $ | | $ |
|---|---|---|---|
| Finished goods control (f) | 52,800 | Income statement (j) | 63,300 |
| Selling overhead control (g) | 10,500 | | |
| | 63,300 | | 63,300 |

## (j) COSTING INCOME STATEMENT

| | $ | | $ |
|---|---|---|---|
| Cost of sales account (i) | 63,300 | Sales account (h) | 88,000 |
| Production overhead (d) | 25,670 | Loss (balance) CLC (a) | 2,170 |
| Stores ledger control – | | | |
| Inventory written off (b) | 1,200 | | |
| | 90,170 | | 90,170 |

## TRIAL BALANCE AS AT 28 FEBRUARY 20X1
(not required by the question)

| | $ | $ |
|---|---|---|
| Cost ledger control account | | 85,000 |
| Stores ledger control account | 38,400 | |
| Work in progress control account | 30,640 | |
| Finished goods control account | 15,960 | |
| | 85,000 | 85,000 |

# 25 Objective test questions: Job, batch and service costing

1  A  Job costing is a costing method applied where work is **undertaken to customers' special requirements.** Option B describes process costing, C describes service costing and D describes absorption costing.

2  C  *Workings*

Total labour cost incurred during period = $(12,500 + 23,000 + 4,500)
= $40,000

∴ Overhead absorption rate = ($140,000/$40,000) × 100%
= 350% of labour cost

| | $ |
|---|---|
| Opening WIP | 46,000 |
| Labour for period | 4,500 |
| Overhead absorbed ($4,500 × 350%) | 15,750 |
| Total production cost | 66,250 |
| 50% mark up | 33,125 |
| Sales value of job 3 | 99,375 |
| | |
| Selling price per circuit board = $99,375 ÷ 2,400 | $41.41 |

Option B is the selling price without the inclusion of any overhead absorbed. If you selected option D you calculated a 50 per cent margin based on the selling price, instead of a 50% mark up on cost.

3  C  Since wages are paid on a piecework basis they are a variable cost which will increase in line with the number of binders. The machine set-up cost and design costs are fixed costs for each batch which will not be affected by the number of binders in the batch.

For a batch of 300 binders:

| | $ |
|---|---|
| Direct materials (30 × 3) | 90.00 |
| Direct wages (10 × 3) | 30.00 |
| Machine set up | 3.00 |
| Design and artwork | 15.00 |
| Production overhead (30 × 20%) | 6.00 |
| Total production cost | 144.00 |
| Selling, distribution and administration overhead (+ 5%) | 7.20 |
| Total cost | 151.20 |
| Profit (25% margin = 33$\frac{1}{3}$% of cost) | 50.40 |
| Selling price for a batch of 300 | 201.60 |

If you selected option A you calculated the cost correctly, but added a profit mark up of 25% of cost, instead of a margin of 25% of selling price.

If you selected option B you failed to absorb the appropriate amount of fixed overhead. If you selected option D you treated all of the costs as variable costs.

4     The price to be quoted for job B124 is $ | 124.50 |

Production overhead absorption rate = $240,000/30,000 = $8 per labour hour

Other overhead absorption rate = ($150,000/$750,000) × 100% = 20% of total production cost

| **Job B124** | $ |
| --- | --- |
| Direct materials (3 kgs × $5) | 15.00 |
| Direct labour (4 hours × $9) | 36.00 |
| Production overhead (4 hours × $8) | 32.00 |
| Total production cost | 83.00 |
| Other overhead (20% × $83) | 16.60 |
| Total cost | 99.60 |
| Profit margin: 20% of sales (× $^{20}/_{80}$) | 24.90 |
| Price to be quoted | 124.50 |

5    ✓    Production of the product can be completed in a single accounting period

      ✓    Production relates to a single special order

Job costing is appropriate where each cost unit is **separately identifiable** and is of relatively **short duration**.

6    B    In service costing it is difficult to identify many attributable direct costs. Many costs must be **shared over several cost units**, therefore characteristic (i) does apply. Composite cost units such as tonne-mile or room-night are often used, therefore characteristic (ii) does apply. Equivalent units are more often used in **costing for tangible products**, therefore characteristic (iii) does not apply, and the correct answer is B.

7    C    Cost per tonne-kilometre (i) is appropriate for cost control purposes because it **combines** the distance travelled and the load carried, **both of which affect cost.**

The fixed cost per kilometre (ii) is not particularly useful for control purposes because it varies with the number of kilometres travelled.

The maintenance cost of each vehicle per kilometre (iii) can be useful for control purposes because it focuses on a particular aspect of the cost of operating each vehicle. Therefore the correct answer is C.

8    D    All of the activities identified would use service costing, except the light engineering company which will be providing **products not services**.

9    B    The most appropriate cost unit is the **tonne-mile**. Therefore the cost per unit =

$$\frac{\$562,800}{375,200} = \$1.50$$

Option A is the cost per mile travelled. This is not as useful as the cost per tonne-mile, which **combines** the distance travelled and the load carried, **both of which affect cost**.

Option C is the cost per hour worked by drivers and D is the cost per driver employed. Costs are more likely to be incurred in relation to the distance travelled and the load carried.

10    A    | Total costs for period |

      B    | Number of service units in the period |

11

| Service | Cost unit |
|---------|-----------|
| Hotels | D |
| Education | C |
| Hospitals | B |
| Catering organisations | A |

12    1 = Intangibility
      2 = Simultaneity
      3 = Perishability
      4 = Heterogeneity

13    D    The cost of the tools is a **direct cost** of the job because it can be specifically identified with the job.

14    66,325

*Working*

**Calculation of tonne-km**

| Journey | Tonnes | Km | Tonne-km |
|---------|--------|-----|----------|
| 1 | 34 | 180 | 6,120 |
| 2 | 28 | 265 | 7,420 |
| 3 | 40 | 390 | 15,600 |
| 4 | 32 | 115 | 3,680 |
| 5 | 26 | 220 | 5,720 |
| 6 | 40 | 480 | 19,200 |
| 7 | 29 | 90 | 2,610 |
| 8 | 26 | 100 | 2,600 |
| 9 | 25 | 135 | 3,375 |
|   | 280 | 1,975 | 66,325 |

15    $  0.16    per tonne-kilometre (to the nearest penny).

*Working*

$$\text{Average cost per tonne-kilometre} = \frac{\text{Total cost}}{\text{Total tonne - kilometres}}$$

$$= \frac{\$10,390}{66,325}$$

$$= \$0.16 \text{ per tonne-kilometre (to the nearest penny)}$$

16    B    Production cost of $3,633 is 70% of selling price

$3,633 = 0.7 × selling price

Selling price    = $3,633/0.7
                 = $5,190

17    C    Manufacturing overhead is absorbed at a predetermined rate.

# 26 Compulsory written question: Job costing I

(a)

|  |  | Job X124 | Job X125 | Job X126 |
|---|---|---|---|---|
|  | **Direct material** | $ | $ | $ |
|  | Month 6 | 7,220 |  |  |
|  | Month 7 – issues | 6,978 | 18,994 | 12,221 |
|  | Month 7 – returns |  | (700) | (2,170) |
|  | Month 7 – transfers | – | 860 | (860) |
| (i) | Total direct material | 14,198 | 19,154 | 9,191 |
|  | **Direct labour** |  |  |  |
|  | Month 6 | 6,076 | – | – |
|  | Month 7 (@ $7 per hour) | 5,460 (780 hrs) | 16,548 (2,364 hrs) | 10,570 (1,510 hrs) |
| (ii) | Total direct labour | 11,536 | 16,548 | 10,570 |
|  | **Production overhead** |  |  |  |
|  | Month 6 | 10,416 |  |  |
|  | Month 7 (@ $12 per dir. labour hour) | 9,360 (780 hrs) | 28,368 (2,364 hrs) | 18,120 (1,510 hrs) |
| (iii) | Total production overhead | 19,776 | 28,368 | 18,120 |

(b)

|  | Job X124 | Job X125 |
|---|---|---|
| Invoiced to customers | 60,000 | 79,000 |
| Total production cost ((i)+(ii)+(iii)) | (45,510) | (64,070) |
| 20% total production cost | (9,102) | (12,814) |
| Total cost | (54,612) | (76,884) |
| Profit on job | 5,388 | 2,116 |

# 27 Compulsory written question: Job costing II

**Helping hand**

Set your workings out clearly and be careful with the net profit margin.

**What the Examiner said**

The labour bonus, production overhead and sales margin calculations proved especially problematic among those candidates who had difficulty with the question.

(a) **Estimated production cost of the job**

|  | $ | $ |
|---|---|---|
| Direct materials |  | 2,893 |
| Direct labour: |  |  |
| Basic (210 hours × $8) | 1,680 |  |
| Bonus ((4,000 – 3,400)/4,000 × $8 × 210 | 252 |  |
|  |  | 1,932 |
| Prime cost |  | 4,825 |
| Production overhead: |  |  |
| 20% of prime cost (20% × 4,825) | 965 |  |
| $9 per direct labour hour ($9 × 210) | 1,890 |  |
|  |  | 2,855 |
| Total production cost |  | 7,680 |

(b)    **Price that should be quoted for the job**

|  |  | $ |
|---|---|---:|
| Total production cost |  | 7,680 |
| Non-production overheads (25% × 7,680) |  | 1,920 |
| Total cost |  | 9,600 |
| Profit (9,600 × 20/80) |  | 2,400 |
| Selling price |  | 12,000 |

# 28 Compulsory written question: Service costing

> **Helping hand**
>
> In a question such as this, where your costing schedule includes calculated figures, make sure that you set out your workings clearly so that the examiner can see exactly where each figure has come from.
>
> **What the Examiner said**
>
> Part (a) was very poorly answered with a lack of description of costing implications for services compared to manufactured products. Answers to part (b) frequently demonstrated a failure to follow instructions.

(a)    Service costing is a method of accounting for services provided to internal customers, for example, canteens, maintenance and personnel and/or external customers (hospitals and schools). These may be referred to as service centres, service departments or service organisations.

Service organisations do not make or sell tangible goods. Profit-seeking service organisations include accountancy firms, law firms, transport companies, banks and hotels. Almost all not-for-profit organisations – hospitals, schools, libraries and so on – are also service organisations.

Service costing differs from other costing methods in the following ways.

(i)    In general, with service costing, the cost of direct materials consumed will be relatively small compared to the labour, direct expenses and overhead costs.

(ii)    Indirect costs tend to represent a higher proportion of total cost compared with product costing.

(iii)    The output of most service organisations is often intangible and it is therefore difficult to establish a measurable unit cost.

(iv)    Services cannot be stored and therefore the requirement to value work-in-progress/finished goods stock (inventory) does not arise.

**(b)** **Vehicle operating costs per kilometre**

|  | *Cost per vehicle per annum* |
|---|---|
|  | $ |
| Depreciation (W1) | 10,500 |
| Road fund licence and insurance | 2,290 |
| Tyres (W2) | 3,360 |
| Servicing (W3) | 3,250 |
| Fuel (W4) | 20,000 |
| Driver | 18,000 |
| Total vehicle operating costs | 57,400 |

Total vehicle operating costs per kilometre = $\dfrac{\$57,400}{80,000 \text{ km}}$ = $0.7175 per km

*Workings*

1 **Depreciation**

|  | $ |
|---|---|
| Cost per vehicle | 46,000 |
| Disposal value | (4,000) |
|  | 42,000 |

Depreciation(straight line basis) $= \dfrac{\$42,000}{4 \text{ years}}$

$= \$10,500$ per annum

2 **Tyres**

$= \dfrac{80,000 \text{ km per vehicle}}{40,000 \text{ km}} \times 8$ new tyres @ $210 per tyre

= $3,360 per vehicle per annum

3 **Servicing**

$\dfrac{80,000 \text{ km}}{16,000 \text{ km}} \times \$650$ per vehicle service = $3,250

4 **Fuel**

$\dfrac{80,000 \text{ km}}{3.2 \text{ km}} \times \$0.8 = \$20,000$

**Marking scheme**

|  |  |  | **Marks** |
|---|---|---|---|
| (a) | Up to 2 for each | max | 6 |
| (b) | Depreciation | 2½ |  |
|  | Licence and insurance | ½ |  |
|  | Tyres | 1½ |  |
|  | Servicing | 1½ |  |
|  | Fuel | 2 |  |
|  | Driver | ½ |  |
|  | Cost per km | 1½ |  |
|  |  |  | 10 |
|  |  |  | 16 |

# 29 Objective test questions: Process costing

**1**   **B**   This is the correct definition of an equivalent unit.

**2**   **C**   **Step 1.**   **Determine output**

| Input Units | Output | Total Units | Materials Units | % | Labour and overhead Units | % |
|---|---|---|---|---|---|---|
| | Finished units (balance) | 400 | 400 | 100 | 400 | 100 |
| 500 | Closing stock (inventory) | 100 | 100 | 100 | 80 | 80 |
| 500 | | 500 | 500 | | 480 | |

*Equivalent units* (spanning Materials and Labour and overhead columns)

**Step 2.**   **Calculate the cost per equivalent unit**

| Input | Cost $ | Equivalent production in units | Cost per unit $ |
|---|---|---|---|
| Materials | 9,000 | 500 | 18 |
| Labour and overhead | 11,520 | 480 | 24 |
| | | | 42 |

**Step 3.**   **Calculate total cost of output**

Cost of completed units = $42 × 400 units = $16,800

If you selected option A you omitted the absorption of overhead at the rate of 200 per cent of direct wages. If you selected option B you did not allow for the fact that the work in progress was incomplete. Option D is the total process cost for the period, some of which must be allocated to the work in progress.

**3**   **B**   Using the data from answer 2 above, extend **step 3** to calculate the value of the work in progress.

| | Cost element | Number of equivalent units | Cost per equivalent unit $ | Total $ |
|---|---|---|---|---|
| **Work in progress:** | Materials | 100 | 18 | 1,800 |
| | Labour and overhead | 80 | 24 | 1,920 |
| | | | | 3,720 |

If you selected option A you omitted the absorption of overhead into the process costs. If you selected option C you did not allow for the fact that the work in progress was incomplete. Option D is the total process cost for the period, some of which must be allocated to the completed output.

**4**   **B**   Joint products are two or more products produced by the same process and separated in processing, each having a sufficiently high saleable value to merit recognition as a main product.

A joint product may be subject to further processing, as implied in option A, but this is not the case for all joint products.

**5**   **D**   A by-product is output of some value produced in manufacturing something else (the main product).

Option A is incorrect because a by-product has some value.

Option B is incorrect because this description could also apply to a joint product.

Option C is incorrect because the value of the product described could be relatively high, even though the output volume is relatively low.

**6**   **D**   The abnormal loss units are valued at their **full production cost** and **credited** to the process account, so that their occurrence does not affect the cost of good production. Therefore the correct answer is D.

Options A and C are incorrect because the scrap value of the abnormal loss is debited to the **scrap account** and credited to the **abnormal loss account**, it has no impact on the process account.

**7** The value credited to the process account for the scrap value of the normal loss for the period will be

$ | 100 |

Normal loss = 10% × input
= 10% × 5,000 kg
= 500 kg

When scrap has a value, normal loss is valued at the value of the scrap ie 20c per kg.

Normal loss = $0.20 × 500 kg
= $100

**8** The value of the abnormal loss for the period is $ | 300 |

| | kg |
|---|---|
| Input | 5,000 |
| Normal loss (10% × 5,000 kg) | (500) |
| Abnormal loss | (300) |
| Output | 4,200 |

$$\text{Cost per kg} = \frac{\text{Input costs} - \text{scrap value of normal loss}}{\text{Expected output}}$$

$$= \frac{\$4,600^* - \$100}{5,000 - 500}$$

$$= \frac{\$4,500}{4,500} = \$1.00$$

Value of abnormal loss = 300 × $1.00 = $300

| | $ |
|---|---|
| *Materials (5,000 kg × 0.5) | 2,500 |
| Labour | 700 |
| Production overhead | 1,400 |
| | 4,600 |

**9** The value of the closing work in progress for the period was $ | 4,698 |

STATEMENT OF EQUIVALENT UNITS

| | Total units | Materials | | Labour and overhead | units |
|---|---|---|---|---|---|
| Completed output | 8,000 | (100%) | 8,000 | (100%) | 8,000 |
| Normal loss | 1,000 | (0%) | | (0%) | - |
| Abnormal loss | 100 | (100%) | 100 | (100%) | 100 |
| Closing WIP | 900 | (100%) | 900 | (75%) | 675 |
| | 10,000 | | 9,000 | | 8,775 |

STATEMENT OF COST PER EQUIVALENT UNIT

| | Materials | Labour and overhead |
|---|---|---|
| Total costs | *$40,500 | $8,424 |
| Equivalent units | 9,000 | 8,775 |
| Cost per equivalent unit | $4.50 | $0.96 |

* $40,800 less scrap value normal loss $300 = $40,500

**Value of work in progress:**

| | $ |
|---|---|
| Materials 900 equivalent units × $4.50 | 4,050 |
| Labour and overhead 675 equivalent units × $0.96 | 648 |
| | 4,698 |

**10**  Material [ 30 ] equivalent litres

Conversion costs [ 15 ] equivalent litres

**Closing work in progress**

|  | Litres |
|---|---|
| Input | 300 |
| Normal loss (300 × 5%) | (15) |
| Abnormal loss | (5) |
| Transfer to finished goods | (250) |
| Closing work in progress | 30 |

|  | Material | | Conversion costs | |
|---|---|---|---|---|
|  | % | Equiv. litres | % | Equiv. litres |
| 30 litres in progress | 100 | 30 | 50 | 15 |

**11**  The value of the output for the period is $ [ 4,200 ]

| Output | = 4,200 kg |
|---|---|
| Cost per kg | = $1 (from solution 9) |
| ∴ Output value | = 4,200 × $1 |
|  | = $4,200 |

**12  C**  The **point of separation,** also referred to as the split-off point, is the point in a process where **joint products** become separately identifiable. Costs incurred prior to this point are common or **joint costs**.

**13  A**  Abnormal loss units are valued at the same cost per unit as completed output. The cost per unit of output and the cost per unit of abnormal loss are based on expected output.

**14  ✓**  Production costs excluding direct materials

**15  D**

| Let | x | = material input to process |
|---|---|---|
|  | 0.1x | = normal loss |
|  | 0.05x | = abnormal loss |

| ∴ Output | = x − 0.1x − 0.05x |
|---|---|
| 340 litres | = x − 0.15x |
| 340 litres | = 0.85x |

$$x = \frac{340 \text{ litres}}{0.85}$$

= 400 litres

**16  D**

**17  C**

|  | Total Litres | Materials Litres | Conversion costs Litres |
|---|---|---|---|
| Output | 250 | 250 (100%) | 250 (100%) |
| WIP | 50 | 50 (100%) | 25 (50%) |
|  | 300 | 300 | 275 |

**18  D**  Debited at a cost per unit based on total production cost divided by normal output.

**19  D**  $30,000 \times \dfrac{(4,000 \times 18)}{(4,000 \times 18) + (2,000 \times 12)} = \$22,500$

|  | Product | | |
|---|---|---|---|
|  | A | B | Total |
|  | $ | $ | $ |
| Total sales value | (2,000 × $12) 24,000 | (4,000 × $18) | 96,000 |

$$\text{Joint process costs – product B} = \frac{72,000}{96,000} \times \$30,000$$
$$= \$22,500$$

20 C **Statement 1 is true**

If the net realisable value of normal losses increases, the actual process costs are reduced by these amounts. If total process costs are reduced, the cost per unit of normal output is also reduced (or lowered).

21 B Raw materials per unit = $12,800/(3,600 + 400) = $3.20

Conversion costs per unit = $18,430/((3,600 + (70% × 400)) = $4.75

Total production cost per unit = $3.20 + $4.75 = $7.95

22 B If the percentage completion of WIP is understated, when corrected, it will have to be increased, increasing the total value of WIP. Costs will be shared between more units so cost per unit will decrease.

23 C Realisable value of product A = 12,000 × $6.00 = $72,000

Realisable value of product B = 22,000 × $4.00 = $88,000

Total realisable value = $160,000

$$\text{Joint costs apportioned to product B} = \$202,000 \times \frac{88,000}{160,000} = \$56,100$$

24 A Normal loss = 10% × 12,000 kg
= 1,200 kg

Actual loss = 12,000 kg – 10,920 kg
= 1,080 kg

Abnormal gain = Actual loss – normal loss
= 1,080 – 1,200
= 120 kg

25 C Equivalent units are notional whole units which represent incomplete work.

# 30 Compulsory written question: Process costing I

(a) **Joint process costs**

|  | $ |
| --- | --- |
| Direct materials | 24,000 |
| Direct labour | 48,000 |
|  | 72,000 |
| Factory overhead (120% × $72,000) | 86,400 |
|  | 158,400 |
| Scrap proceeds * | (5,120) |
| Joint process costs | 153,280 |

* Scrap = 10% × 3,200 litres
= 320 litres @ $16 per litre
= $5,120

(b) **Total sales value**

|  | Chemical X | Chemical Y | Chemical Z |
| --- | --- | --- | --- |
| Output | 1,440 litres | 864 litres | 576 litres |
| Selling price | × $100 | × $80 | × $60 |
| Sales value of output | $144,000 | $69,120 | $34,560 |

Total sales value = $(144,000 + 69,120 + 34,560)
= $247,680

(c)     **Total output**                                                    =   (1,440 + 864 + 576) litres

                                                                             =   2,880 litres

        Total joint process costs                                           =   $153,280

        ∴ Share of joint process costs charged to chemical X

                                                                             =   $\dfrac{1,440}{2,880} \times \$153,280 = \$76,640$

(d)     **Total sales value**                                               =   $247,680

        Total joint process costs                                           =   $153,280

        ∴ Share of joint process costs charged to chemical Y

                                                                             =   $\dfrac{69,120}{247,680} \times \$153,280$

                                                                             =   $42,776 (to the nearest $)

## Marking scheme

|       |                    |      | Marks |
|-------|--------------------|------|-------|
| (a)   | Direct costs       | 0.5  |       |
|       | Overhead           | 1.5  |       |
|       | Scrap              | 2.0  |       |
|       |                    |      | 4     |
| (b)   | Chemical X, Y & Z  | 1.0  |       |
|       | Total              | 1.0  |       |
|       |                    |      | 2     |
| (c)   | Share              |      | 3     |
| (d)   | Share              |      | 3     |
|       |                    |      | 12    |

# 31 Compulsory written question: Process costing II

**What the Examiner said**

Answers to part (b) the examples provided were frequently acceptable although some were not specific enough. In part (b) candidates displayed the common difficulties of dealing with equivalent units.

(a)     (i)     **Job costing** may be applied by a building business for example.

                In job costing, production is usually carried out in accordance with the **special requirements of each customer**. It is usual, therefore, for each job to differ in one or more respects from every other job, which means that a separate record must be maintained to show the details of a particular job.

                The work relating to a job is of **comparatively short duration** and is usually carried out within a factory or workshop and moves through processes and operations as a **continuously identifiable unit**.

        (ii)    **Process costing** is a costing method used where it is not possible to identify separate units of production, usually because of the continuous nature of the production processes involved. It is common to identify process costing with **continuous production** such as the following.

                - Oil refining
                - The manufacture of soap
                - Paint manufacture
                - Food and drink manufacture

Other features of process costing include the following:

- There is often a loss in process due to spoilage, wastage, evaporation and so on.
- The output of one process becomes the input of the next until the finished product is made in the final process.
- Output from production may be a single product, but there may also be one or more **by-products** and/or **joint products**.

(b)

> **Helping hand**
>
> Remember that process costing situations involving closing work in progress will usually require you to calculate **equivalent units of production**.
>
> **Equivalent units** are notional whole units which represent incomplete work, and which are used to apportion costs between work in process and completed output.

(i) **Cost per equivalent unit calculations**

| | Total Units | Process I costs Units | | Materials added Units | | Conversion costs Units |
|---|---|---|---|---|---|---|
| Finished goods | 1,950 | 1,950 | | 1,950 | | 1,950 |
| Closing work in progress | 210 | 210 | (80%) | 168 | (40%) | 84 |
| Equivalent units | 2,160 | 2,160 | | 2,118 | | 2,034 |
| Costs | | $22,032 | | $5,295 | | $8,136 |
| Cost per equivalent unit | $16.70 | $10.20 | | $2.50 | | $4.00 |

(ii) **Value of transfer to finished goods warehouse**

1,950 units were transferred to the finished goods warehouse. Each unit cost $16.70 to manufacture (as calculated above in part (i)).

∴ Total value of transfers = 1,950 units × $16.70
= $32,565

(iii) **Value of closing work in progress**

From part (i), closing work in progress may be analysed as follows.

| | Equivalent Units | Cost per equivalent unit $ | Total Cost $ |
|---|---|---|---|
| Process I costs | 210 | 10.20 | 2,142 |
| Materials added | 168 | 2.50 | 420 |
| Conversion costs | 84 | 4.00 | 336 |
| Value of closing WIP | | | 2,898 |

| | | | Marks |
|---|---|---|---|
| (a) | (i) | Example 1; features 3 | 4 |
| | (ii) | Example 1; features 3 | 4 |
| (b) | (i) | Units transferred | 1½ |
| | | Closing WIP | 2½ |
| | | Cost per unit | 2 |
| | | | 6 |
| | (ii) | Transfer value | 2 |
| | (iii) | Closing WIP value: | |
| | | Process 1 | ½ |
| | | Material added | 1 |
| | | Conversion costs | 1 |
| | | Total | ½ |
| | | | 3 |
| | | | 19 |

# 32 Compulsory written question: Process costing III

> **Helping hand**
>
> You need to work out the output figures and then the total costs, before being able to work out the cost per tonne. Make sure you show your workings clearly.
>
> **What the Examiner said**
>
> This question was frequently well answered but answers were not always well presented.

(a)  Output:

| | Tonnes | |
|---|---|---|
| Input | 600 | |
| Normal loss | 72 | (600 tonnes × 12%) |
| Normal output | 528 | |
| Actual output | 521 | |
| Abnormal loss | 7 | |

Costs:

| | $ | |
|---|---|---|
| Materials | 430,032 | |
| Conversion | 119,328 | |
| Sales value of normal loss | (18,720) | (72 tonnes × $260) |
| Total net cost | 530,640 | |

$$\text{Cost per tonne} = \frac{\text{Total net cost}}{\text{Normal output}}$$

$$= \frac{\$530,640}{528}$$

$$= \$1,005$$

(b)  *Working*

Cost of finished goods = 521 tonnes × $1,005 = $523,605
Cost of abnormal loss = 7 tonnes × $1,005 = $7,035

Process Account:

| | Tonnes | $ | | Tonnes | $ |
|---|---|---|---|---|---|
| Materials | 600 | 430,032 | Finished goods | 521 | 523,605 |
| Conversion costs | | 119,328 | Normal loss | 72 | 18,720 |
| | | | Abnormal loss | 7 | 7,035 |
| | 600 | 549,360 | | 600 | 549,360 |

# 33 Compulsory written question: Process costing IV

**Helping hand**

In part (a) the tricky part is the apportionment of joint costs. Part (b) tests your understanding of the further processing decision.

**What the Examiner said**

The answers to both parts (a) and (b) were in many cases disappointing. In part (a), many candidates, having calculated the sales value for each product and in total, were unable to provide any apportionment of the joint costs. The answers to both parts of (b) were often very similar and generally failed to address the specific statements made in the question.

(a) **Gross profit statement**

| | Product Y | | Product X | |
|---|---|---|---|---|
| | $ | | $ | |
| Sales revenue | 24,000 | (2,000 × $12) | 56,000 | (3,500 × $16) |
| Joint costs | 15,600 | (24/80 × $52,000) | 36,400 | (56/80 × $52,000) |
| Gross profit | 8,400 | | 19,600 | |
| Per unit | 4.20 | | 5.60 | |

(b)  (i)  Joint costs are not separately identifiable until the split off point is reached, so they are apportioned, in this case, on the basis of weight of output. The issue is whether the joint process as a whole is profitable, not if each joint product is covering its apportioned cost. The decision as to whether or not to process the products further should be taken based on whether the incremental revenue is greater than the incremental cost.

(ii)  This is the correct test as to whether or not Product A should be processed further.

| | $ |
|---|---|
| Incremental revenue from further processing (11.50 – 9.00) | 2.50 |
| Incremental cost | 2.10 |
| Benefit from further processing | 0.40 |

Each kg of Product AA will generate extra profit of $0.40 so Product A should be processed further.

| | | | Marks |
|---|---|---|---|
| (a) | | Sales value | 2 |
| | | Joint cost apportionment | 3 |
| | | Statement | 4 |
| | | | 9 |
| (b) | (i) | Correct justification – up to 2 marks | |
| | | Irrelevance of cost share – up to 2 marks | max 3 |
| | (ii) | Correct basis | 1 |
| | | Correct conclusion | 1 |
| | | Justification | 2 |
| | | | 4 |
| | | | 16 |

# 34 Compulsory written question: Process costing V

**Helping hand**

Make sure that you use an appropriate method to apportion joint costs in part (a) and clearly state the method used. Note that in part (b) you need to justify your comments on whether products should be further processed or discontinued.

(a)     Joint costs

220 kg x $12·00 per kg = $2,640

Weight of output is the method used to apportion the joint costs

(b)     Comments

(i)     The loss on an individual joint product is irrelevant to any decision concerning the joint process because the apportionment of the joint costs is arbitrary. The key is whether the process as a whole is profitable. On the basis of the information available, the process is profitable overall and thus should be continued i.e.

| | $ |
|---|---|
| Product JP1 (100 kg × $8.00 kg) | 800 |
| Product JP2 (120 kg× ($2.00) per kg) | (240) |
| Net | 560 |

(ii)     Product JP1 should be further processed to form Product FP1 because the further processing operation results in an incremental profit i.e.

| | $ per kg |
|---|---|
| Incremental revenue ($25·00 – $20·00) | 5.00 |
| Incremental costs | 3.50 |
| Incremental profit | 1.50 |

Marks

| (a) | | Joint costs | 1½ | |
|---|---|---|---|---|
| | | Method | 1½ | |
| | | | | 3 |
| (b) | (i) | Narrative | 2 | |
| | | Calculation | 2 | |
| | | | | 4 |
| | (ii) | Narrative | 2 | |
| | | Calculation | 2 | |
| | | | | 4 |
| | | | | 11 |

# 35 Objective test questions: Cost-volume-profit (CVP) analysis

**1  B**   $\text{Breakeven point} = \dfrac{\text{Fixed costs}}{\text{Contribution per unit}} = \dfrac{\$30,000}{\$(15-5)} = 3,000 \text{ units}$

If you selected option A you divided the fixed cost by the selling price, but remember that the selling price also has to cover the variable cost. Option C is the margin of safety, and if you selected option D you seem to have divided the fixed cost by the variable cost per unit.

**2  B**   The margin of the safety is the difference in units between the expected sales volume and breakeven sales volume and it is sometimes expressed as a percentage of the expected sales volume.

**3  D**   $\text{Breakeven point} = \dfrac{\text{Fixed costs}}{\text{Contribution per unit}}$

$= \dfrac{10,000 \times (\$4.00 + 0.80)}{(\$6.00 - (\$1.20 + \$0.40))} = \dfrac{\$48,000}{\$4.40} = 10,909 \text{ units}$

If you selected option A you divided the fixed cost by the selling price, but the **selling price also has to cover the variable cost.** Option B ignores the selling costs, but these are costs that **must be covered before the breakeven point is reached.** Option C is the budgeted sales volume, which happens to be below the breakeven point.

**4  D**

| Contribution required for target profit | = | fixed costs + profit |
|---|---|---|
| | = | $48,000 + $11,000 |
| | = | $59,000 |
| ÷ Contribution per unit (from qu 3) | = | $4.40 |
| ∴ Sales units required | = | 13,409 units |

If you selected option A you divided the required profit by the contribution per unit, but the fixed costs must be covered before any profit can be earned. If you selected option B you identified correctly the contribution required for the target profit, but you then divided by the selling price per unit instead of the contribution per unit. Option C ignores the selling costs, which must be covered before a profit can be earned.

**5**   The contribution/sales ratio for product E is ⎡ 50 ⎤ % (to the nearest whole percent).

The contribution/sales ratio (C/S ratio) is another term used to describe the profit/volume ratio (P/V ratio).

$$\text{C/S ratio} = \frac{\text{contribution per unit}}{\text{selling price per unit}}$$

$$= \frac{\$(50 - 7 - 8 - 8 - 2)}{£50} \times 100\%$$

$$= 50\%$$

6    The required annual sales to achieve a profit of $7,800 is $\boxed{13,000}$ units.

$$\text{Required sales} = \frac{\text{fixed costs} + \text{required profit}}{\text{contribution per unit}}$$

$$= \frac{(12,000 \times (\$13.00 + \$2.60) + \$7,800}{\$19.50 - \$(3.90 + 0.60)}$$

$$= \frac{\$195,000}{£15}$$

$$= 13,000 \text{ units}$$

7    The contribution at level of activity R can be read as $\boxed{D}$ less $\boxed{B}$

The contribution is the difference between the sales value and the variable cost incurred at activity level R.

8    A    Breakeven point $= \dfrac{\$48,000}{0.4} = \$120,000$ sales value

Margin of safety $= \$140,000 - \$120,000 = \$20,000$ sales value

$(\div \$10) = 2,000$ units

Option B is the breakeven point and option C is the actual sales in units. If you selected option D you calculated the margin of safety correctly as 20,000 but you misinterpreted the result as the sales **volume** instead of the sales **value**.

9    D    Breakeven quantity $= \dfrac{\text{Fixed costs}}{\text{Contribution per unit}}$

Since we do not know the contribution per unit, and we cannot determine it from the information available, it is not possible to calculate the breakeven point in terms of units. Therefore the correct answer is D.

We can determine the **value** of breakeven sales as $90,000/0.4 = $225,000, but this does not tell us the number of units required to break even. If you selected option C you probably performed this calculation.

10    A    Breakeven point $= \dfrac{\text{Fixed costs}}{\text{C/S ratio}} = \dfrac{\$76,800}{0.40}$        $=$        $192,000

| | | |
|---|---|---|
| Actual sales | $=$ | $224,000 |
| Margin of safety in terms of sales value | | $32,000 |
| $\div$ selling price per unit | | $\div \$16 |
| Margin of safety in units | | 2,000 |

If you selected option B you calculated the breakeven point in units, but forgot to take the next step to calculate the margin of safety. Option C is the actual sales in units and D is the margin of safety in terms of sales value.

11    C    Contribution per unit $= \$90 - \$40 = \$50$. The sale of 6,000 units just covers the annual fixed costs, therefore the fixed costs must be $50 \times 6,000 = $300,000.

If you selected option A you calculated the correct contribution of $50 per unit, but you then divided the 6,000 by $50 instead of multiplying. Option B is the total annual variable cost and option D is the annual revenue.

**12** ☑    Fixed cost

The profit line on a profit/volume chart cuts the y-axis at the point representing **the loss incurred at zero activity.** This is the fixed cost which must be paid **even if no units are sold.**

**13** ☑    Profit/volume chart

The chart shows a single line depicting **the profit for a range of levels of activity.** Therefore it is a profit volume chart.

All of the other options would depict cost lines rather than profit lines, and the first two options would also include a sales revenue line.

**14**    The contribution/sales ratio for product Q is  | 25 |  % (to the nearest percent)

The contribution/sales ratio (C/S ratio) is another term used to describe the profit/volume ratio (P/V ratio).

$$C/S \text{ ratio} = \frac{\text{Contribution per unit}}{\text{Selling price per unit}}$$

$$= \frac{\$(60-14-12-19)}{\$60} \times 100\%$$

$$= 25\%$$

**15**    B    $C/S \text{ ratio} = \dfrac{\text{Contribution per unit}}{\text{Selling price per unit}}$

$$= \frac{\$(20-4-3-2-1)}{\$20} \times 100\% = 50\%$$

If you selected option A you calculated profit per unit as a percentage of the selling price per unit. Option C excludes the variable selling costs from the calculation of contribution per unit and option D excludes the variable production overhead cost, but **all variable costs must be deducted from the selling price to determine the contribution.**

**16**    C

| | $ |
|---|---:|
| Target profit | 6,000 |
| Fixed costs (5,000 × $2) | 10,000 |
| Target contribution | 16,000 |
| | |
| Contribution per unit ($10 – $6) | $4 |
| Units required to achieve target profit | 4,000 |

If you selected option A you divided $6,000 target profit by the $4 contribution per unit, but **the fixed costs must be covered before any profit can be earned.** If you selected option B you divided by the selling price, but the variable costs must also be taken into account. If you selected option D you divided by the profit per unit instead of the contribution per unit, but the fixed costs are taken into account in the calculation of the target contribution.

**17**    B

| | |
|---|---:|
| Fixed costs ($10,000 × 120%) | $12,000 |
| Units required now to break even (÷ $4 contribution) | 3,000 |
| Budgeted units of sales | 5,000 |
| Margin of safety (units) | 2,000 |

In percentage terms, margin of safety $= \dfrac{2,000}{5,000} \times 100\% = 40\%$

Option A increases the **variable** cost by 20% and option C increases the **activity** by 20%. If you selected option D you calculated the margin of safety as a percentage of the breakeven volume, but it is **usually expressed as a percentage of budgeted sales.**

| | | $ |
|---|---|---|
| **18 B** Total cost of 150,000 units (× $41.50) | | 6,225,000 |
| Total cost of 100,000 units (× $47.50) | | 4,750,000 |
| Variable cost of 50,000 units | | 1,475,000 |
| Variable cost per unit | | $29.50 |

| | $ |
|---|---|
| *Substituting:* | |
| Total cost of 100,000 units | 4,750,000 |
| Variable cost of 100,000 units (× $29.50) | 2,950,000 |
| Fixed costs | 1,800,000 |

$$\therefore \text{ Breakeven point} = \frac{\$1,800,000}{\$(49.50 - 29.50)} = 90,000 \text{ units}$$

If you selected option A you divided the fixed cost by the unit selling price, but the variable costs must also be taken into account. If you selected option C you assumed that the production overheads and the marketing and administration costs were wholly fixed. In fact the marketing costs are the only wholly fixed costs. You can test this by multiplying the unit rate by the output volume at each level of activity. If you selected option D you divided the fixed cost by the profit per unit instead of the contribution per unit.

**19 C** Contribution at level of activity x = sales value less variable costs, which is indicated by distance C. Distance A indicates the profit at activity x, B indicates the fixed costs and D indicates the margin of safety in terms of sales value.

**20** The direct wages cost for the period was $ | 64,224 |

| Contribution earned for the period | = | $48,000 + $5,520 |
|---|---|---|
| | = | $53,520 |
| ∴ Sales value = $53,520/0.2 | = | $267,600 |
| Variable cost = $(267,600 − 53,520) | = | $214,080 |
| Direct wages cost = $214,080 × 0.3 | = | $64,224 |

| **21 C** Required contribution | = | fixed costs + target profit |
|---|---|---|
| | = | $210,000 + $65,000 |
| | = | $275,000 |

$$\text{Required sales} = \frac{\text{Required contribution}}{\text{Contribution per unit}}$$

$$= \frac{\$275,000}{\$2\,*}$$

= 137,500 units

$$*\text{ Contribution per unit} = \frac{\text{Sales revenue} - \text{variable costs}}{\text{Sales units}}$$

$$= \frac{\$640,000 - \$384,000}{128,000 \text{ units}}$$

= $2 per unit

| Selling price per unit | = | $5 ($640,000 ÷ $128,000) |
|---|---|---|
| ∴ Sales revenue required | = | 137,500 × $5 |
| | = | $687,500 |

22    C    Required contribution    = fixed costs + target profit
                                     = $210,000 + $52,000
                                     = $262,000

      Required sales    $$= \frac{\$262,000}{\text{Contribution per unit}}$$

                        $$= \frac{\$262,000}{\$2\ *}$$

                        = 131,000 units

      * Contribution per unit    $$= \frac{\text{Sales revenue} - \text{variable costs}}{\text{Sales units}}$$

                        $$= \frac{\$640,000 - \$384,000}{128,000 \text{ units}}$$

                        = $2 per unit

23    B    Year    Cash inflow        Cumulative cash inflow
                      $                         $
            1       30,000                   30,000
            2       30,000                   60,000
            3       30,000                   90,000
            4       30,000                  120,000

      Payback: $3 + (\frac{(100,000 - 90,000)}{(120,000 - 90,000)} \times 12 \text{ months}) = 3.3$ years.

      The $15,000 already incurred is not a relevant cost.

# 36 Compulsory written question: Cost-volume-profit (CVP) analysis I

**Helping hand**

Be careful not to confuse units and $s.

**What the Examiner said**

Candidates regularly failed to read the question properly.

(a)    *Workings*

       Selling price to bookshops = $15 × 80% = $12

       Variable costs = (15% × $12) + $3.20 = $5

       Contribution per unit    = Selling price − Variable costs
                                = $12 − $5
                                = $7

       Fixed costs = $25,000 + $80,000 = $105,000

       (i)    Breakeven number of copies    $$= \frac{\text{Fixed costs}}{\text{Contribution per unit}}$$

                        $$= \frac{\$105,000}{\$7}$$

                        = 15,000

(ii)    Required number of copies to be sold to make a profit of $35,000

$$= \frac{(\text{fixed cost} + \text{required profit})}{\text{contribution per unit}}$$

$$= \frac{\$105,000 + \$35,000}{\$7}$$

$$= 20,000 \text{ copies}$$

(b)

> **Helping hand**
>
> You can pick up easy marks in an examination for drawing graphs neatly and accurately. Always use a ruler, label your axes and use an appropriate scale.

Profit/volume chart for book publication:

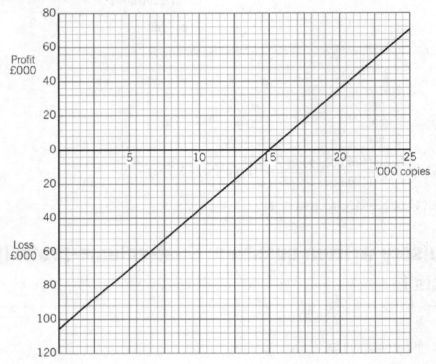

BPP
LEARNING MEDIA

# 37 Compulsory written question: Cost-volume-profit (CVP) analysis II

| Helping hand |
| --- |
| You can pick up easy marks in an examination for drawing graphs neatly and accurately. Always use a ruler, label your axes and use an appropriate scale.<br><br>**What the Examiner said**<br><br>Presentation, scaling and labelling of the charts was frequently inadequate. In part (b), for 6 marks candidates should appreciate the basis for their listing. |

(a)   Profit/volume chart for Company A

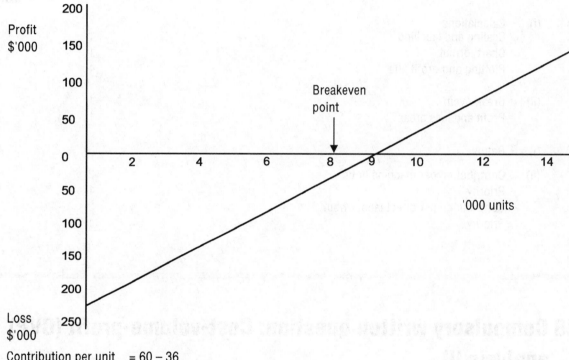

Contribution per unit   = 60 – 36
                        = $24

Loss at zero            = fixed costs
                        = $216,000

Breakeven               = $\dfrac{\text{Fixed costs}}{\text{Contribution}}$
                        = 216,000/24
                        = 9,000 units

Profit at 14,000 units  = (14,000 × 24) – 216,000
                        = $120,000

(b)   (i)

|  | Product A | Product B | Product C |
| --- | --- | --- | --- |
|  | $ | $ | $ |
| Selling price per unit | 10.00 | 12.50 | 18.70 |
| Variable costs per unit | 5.20 | 7.50 | 9.35 |
| Contribution per unit | 4.80 | 5.00 | 9.35 |
| C/S Ratio | 48% | 40% | 50% |

(ii)

| | Product A | Product B | Product C |
|---|---|---|---|
| Machine hours | 0.6 | 0.5 | 1 |
| Contribution per machine hour | $8.00 | $10.00 | $9.35 |
| Ranking | 3 | 1 | 2 |

(iii)

| | Product A | Product B | Product C |
|---|---|---|---|
| Labour hours | 1 | 1.2 | 2.5 |
| Contribution per labour hour | $4.80 | $4.17 | $3.74 |
| Ranking | 1 | 2 | 3 |

## Marking scheme

| | | | Marks | |
|---|---|---|---|---|
| (a) | (i) | Calculations | 2 | |
| | | Scaling and labelling | 1 | |
| | | Chart format | 1 | |
| | | Plotting and profit line | 4 | |
| | | | | 8 |
| | (ii) | Break-even | 1 | |
| | | Profit and loss areas | 1 | |
| | | | | 2 |
| (b) | (i) | Ratios | | 2 |
| | (ii) | Contribution per machine hour | 2 | |
| | | Priority | 1 | |
| | | Contribution per direct labour hour | 2 | |
| | | Priority | 1 | |
| | | | | 6 |
| | | | | 18 |

# 38 Compulsory written question: Cost-volume-profit (CVP) analysis III

**Helping hand**

This question tests your **understanding** of a P/V chart and you need to know how to calculate a contribution/sales ratio.

**What the Examiner said**

The question was poorly answered or not attempted at all. Candidates were in general unable to identify required values from a chart. Some even attempted to redraw the chart.

(a) (i) The break-even sales revenue is where the Company A profit line crosses the sales revenue horizontal axis at $400,000.

(ii) The total fixed costs is given by the loss where there is zero activity for Company A, where the profit line hits the vertical axis at $180,000.

(iii) The gradient of the profit line is the contribution per unit. Company A has a steeper profit line than Company B so Company A has a higher contribution/sales ratio.

(iv) The sales at the point where the two companies' profit lines cross are $480,000.

(b)     Breakeven sales = $\dfrac{\text{Contribution required to break even}}{\text{C/S ratio}}$

C/S ratio = $\dfrac{180,000}{400,000}$ = 0.45 or 45%

The breakeven point identified = $400,000 = $180,000/0.45

|  |  |  |  | Marks |
|---|---|---|---|---|
| (a) | (i) | Breakeven | | 2 |
| | (ii) | Fixed costs | | 2 |
| | (iii) | Higher C/S ratio | | 3 |
| | (iv) | Common level of sales | | 2 |
| (b) | | C/S ratio | 3 | |
| | | Breakeven | 1 | |
| | | | | 4 |
| | | | | 13 |

# 39 Compulsory written question: Cost-volume-profit (CVP) analysis IV

**Helping hand**

This question requires the understating and application of the cost – volume – profit relationships.

In part (a) (i) make sure you deduct all the variable costs in calculating the contribution, including the variable non-production costs.

It is important to appreciate that contribution is sales revenue minus all variable costs including production and non-production.

Make sure you read the question carefully and note that parts (a) and (b) were different scenarios and that the fixed costs had changed.

**What the Examiner said**

The Examiner noted that in part (a) (i) some candidates incorrectly reversed the c/s ratio.

A number of candidates incorrectly stated their final answer in currency rather than percentage.

(a)     (i)     Contribution/sales ratio

Contribution per unit = 200 – (120 + 16)
                                    = $64

Contribution sales ratio = (64 ÷ 200) x 100%
                                        = 32%

        (ii)    Total fixed costs

Fixed costs = contribution at break-even point

Therefore $120,000 x 0·32= $38,400

(b)     Contribution per unit = fixed costs ÷ break-even sales units
                                    = $39,000 ÷ 500 units
                                    = $78 per unit

| | | | | Marks |
|---|---|---|---|---|
| (a) | (i) | Contribution per unit | 1 | |
| | | Ratio | 2 | |
| | | | | 3 |
| | (ii) | Fixed costs | | 3 |
| (b) | | Formula | 1 | |
| | | Application | 3 | |
| | | | | 4 |
| | | | | 10 |

# 40 Objective test questions: Decision making

1  C  A decision is about the future, therefore relevant costs are future costs (i). If a cost is unavoidable then any decision taken about the future will not affect the cost, therefore unavoidable costs are not relevant costs (ii). Incremental costs are extra costs which will be incurred in the future therefore relevant costs are incremental costs (iii). Differential costs are the difference in total costs between alternatives and they are therefore affected by a decision taken now and they are associated with relevant costs (iv).

2  B  Only future costs that will be affected by the decision are relevant for decision making.

Committed costs **cannot be altered by a decision** taken now therefore they are not relevant and the correct answer is B.

Differential cost (option A) is the difference in total costs between alternatives and is therefore **affected by a decision** and is a relevant cost.

An out-of-pocket cost (option C) is a **cash cost** to be incurred in the future and is therefore relevant. Incremental costs (option D) are **extra costs which will be incurred in the future** and they are therefore relevant costs.

3  D  An opportunity cost is 'the value of the benefit sacrificed when one course of action is chosen, in preference to an alternative' (CIMA *Official Terminology*).

A sunk cost (option A) is a **past cost** which is not relevant to the decision. An incremental cost (option B) is an **extra cost** to be incurred in the future as the result of a decision taken now. The salary cost forgone is certainly relevant to the decision therefore option C is not correct.

4  B  $5,000 has been spent on market research already and is therefore a sunk cost and irrelevant to the decision. The further $2,000 will only be spent if Sue continues with the project, therefore it is an incremental (relevant) cost of the decision to go ahead.

The cost is not an opportunity cost (option D) because Sue has not forgone an alternative use for the resources.

5  The relevant cost of using the material for a special job is $ | 12,500 |

The original cost of $45,000 is a non-relevant sunk or past cost. The material would not be reworked, since its value would increase by only $5,000 ($17,500 – $12,500) for a cost of $7,500.

The relevant cost of using the material for the special job is therefore the opportunity cost of the $12,500 scrap sale forgone.

6  ✓  A notional cost

The use of a charge for notional rent enables a more meaningful comparison of the cost of different factories.

**7**

| ✓ | A cost which is irrelevant for decision making |

| ✓ | A cost that has already been incurred |

A cost that is unaffected by future fluctuations in the level of activity has not necessarily been irreversibly incurred and so is not a sunk cost.

**8  C**  The **material is in regular use** and so 1,000 kgs will be purchased. 500 kgs of this will replace the 500 kgs in inventory that is used, 100 kgs will be purchased and used and the remaining 400 kgs will be kept in inventory until needed. The relevant cost is therefore 600 × $3.25 = $1,950.

If you selected option A you valued the inventory items at their resale price. However, the items are in regular use therefore they would not be resold.

Option B values the inventory items at their original purchase price, but this is a sunk or past cost. Option D is the cost of the 1,000 kg that must be purchased, but since the material is in regular use the excess can be kept in inventory until needed.

**9  C**  **Relevant cost of material K**

|  |  | $ |
|---|---|---|
| 500 kg in inventory: | If not used on this order, would be sold ($1.50 × 500) | 750 |
| 300 kg extra required: | Need to be purchased at current price ($5 × 300) | 1,500 |
|  |  | 2,250 |

The 300 extra kg which must be purchased represent an extra or incremental cost. If the 500 kg were not used on this job they would be sold, therefore the revenue forgone is an **opportunity cost** of $750. Therefore the correct answer is C.

Although the original $2,000 paid for the 500 kg in inventory is a **sunk cost**, in this situation there is an **alternative use for the material**, therefore the opportunity cost becomes relevant and options A and B are not correct.

Option D is not correct because there is no need to incur an incremental cost of $4,000 since some of the material required is in inventory.

**10  C**  The relevant cost of Material X in this situation is the current replacement cost because Material X is used regularly by the company in its normal business, and is available from inventory.

**11**  Most profitable product | S |

Least profitable product | M |

|  | Product M | Product F | Product S |
|---|---|---|---|
| Contribution per unit | $57 | $73 | $69 |
| Hours required per unit | 5 | 6 | 4 |
| Contribution per hour of labour | $11.40 | $12.17 | $17.25 |
| Ranking | 3rd | 2nd | 1st |

**12**  The limiting factor next period will be:

| ✓ | Material |

|  | Quantity per unit | Quantity required | Quantity available |
|---|---|---|---|
| Material ($72 ÷ $8) | 9 litres (× 2,000) | 18,000 litres | 16,000 litres |
| Labour ($49 ÷ $7) | 7 hours (× 2,000) | 14,000 hours | 15,000 hours |

**13**  The relevant cost of labour to be used in making one unit of the new product would be $ | 70 | (to the nearest $)

The rate of $10 per hour currently paid to the skilled employee is not relevant because it would be paid anyway. The relevant hourly rate is the incremental cost of $9 per hour.

BPP
LEARNING MEDIA

|  | $ per unit |
|---|---|
| Skilled labour 5 hours × $9 | 45 |
| Semi-skilled labour 5 hours × $5 | 25 |
|  | 70 |

**14**

First: product **K**

Second: product **L**

Third: product **J**

|  | Product J | Product K | Product L |
|---|---|---|---|
|  | $ per unit | $ per unit | $ per unit |
| Selling price | 140 | 122 | 134 |
| Variable cost | 106 | 86 | 77 |
| Contribution | 34 | 36 | 57 |
| Kg of material | 11 | 7 | 13 |
| Contribution per kg | $3.09 | $5.14 | $4.39 |
| Ranking | 3 | 1 | 2 |

**15   A**

|  | Quantity per unit |  | Quantity required | Quantity available |
|---|---|---|---|---|
| Material ($8 ÷ $2) | 4 kg | (× 6,000) | 24,000 kg | 22,000 kg |
| Labour ($18 ÷ $6) | 3 hrs | (× 6,000) | 18,000 hrs | 19,000 hrs |

Sales demand is not a limiting factor because there is not sufficient material to satisfy the demand of 6,000 units.

Options B and C are incorrect because there is sufficient labour to satisfy the demand of 6,000 units.

**16   B**

|  | Product P | Product Q | Product R |
|---|---|---|---|
| Contribution per unit | $82 | $108 | $100 |
| Kgs required per unit | 4 | 2 | 6 |
| Contribution per kg of material | $20.5 | $54 | $16.67 |
| Ranking | 2 | 1 | 3 |

Therefore Q is the most profitable and R is the least profitable.

If you selected option A you ranked the products according to their profit per unit, but this takes no account of the **limiting factor** and is distorted by the fixed costs. Option C ranks according to the contribution per unit, but this takes no account of the **limiting factor.**

**17   C**

|  | Z1 | Z2 | Z3 |
|---|---|---|---|
|  | $ | $ | $ |
| Selling price per unit | 15 | 18 | 17.00 |
| Variable costs per unit | 7 | 11 | 12.70 |
| Contribution per unit | 8 | 7 | 4.30 |

|  | Z1 | Z2 | Z3 |
|---|---|---|---|
| Labour cost per unit | $2 | $4 | $1.80 |
| Contribution per $ of labour cost | $4 | $1.75 | $2.39 |
| Rank order of production | 1 | 3 | 2 |

If you selected option A you ranked the products according to their selling price, but this takes no account of their relative cost structure or resource utilisation. Option B ranks products according to their profit per unit sold, but this is distorted by the unit fixed costs and takes no account of the amount of **limiting factor** consumed. Option D ranks products in reverse order of their labour cost per unit, but takes no account of their selling prices or of other variable cost incurred.

18  B   We begin by calculating the contribution per unit of limiting factor.

<table>
<tr><td></td><td></td><td></td><td>Priority ranking</td></tr>
<tr><td>Scratch</td><td>= $6/2</td><td>= $3 per labour hour</td><td>1</td></tr>
<tr><td>Purr</td><td>= $7/3</td><td>= $2.33 per labour hour</td><td>3</td></tr>
<tr><td>Buzz</td><td>= $8/3</td><td>= $2.67 per labour hour</td><td>2</td></tr>
<tr><td></td><td></td><td></td><td>Hours</td></tr>
<tr><td>*Production priorities:*</td><td colspan="2">1st Scratch (700 units × 2 hours)</td><td>1,400</td></tr>
<tr><td></td><td colspan="2">2nd Buzz (400 units × 3 hours)</td><td>1,200</td></tr>
<tr><td></td><td></td><td></td><td>2,600</td></tr>
<tr><td>*Production mix (units)*</td><td colspan="2">700 Scratch, 400 Buzz, 0 Purr</td><td></td></tr>
</table>

If you selected option A you allocated the available hours according to the contribution earned per unit of product. However, this does not take account of the **limiting factor**. Option C is the maximum demand for each product, but there are insufficient labour hours available to manufacture this volume of output. Option D allocates all the available hours to Scratch, the product which earns the highest contribution per hour. However, the maximum demand for Scratch is 700 units. Once that demand has been met the remainder of the available hours must be allocated to Buzz, the next product in the priority ranking.

19  B

| | | $ |
|---|---|---|
| Contribution | : Scratch (700 × $6) | 4,200 |
| | : Buzz (400 × $8) | 3,200 |
| | | 7,400 |
| Less: fixed costs | | 1,700 |
| | | 5,700 |

If you selected one of the incorrect options you calculated the profit for the incorrect product mix that you selected in question 18.

20  The relevant cost of using the component currently held in inventory for this contract is

$ [ 50 ]

The net book value is not relevant; it is a **sunk cost**. The company would not purchase a new component because it would be cheaper to modify the existing component in inventory incurring an incremental cost of $50.

21  D

| | Product A<br>$2.80/1.4 | Product B<br>$2.60/1.2 | Product C<br>$1.90/0.9 | Product D<br>$2.40/1.0 |
|---|---|---|---|---|
| Contribution per skilled labour hour | $2.00 | $2.17 | $2.11 | $2.40 |
| Order | 4th | 2nd | 3rd | 1st |

The correct answer is therefore D.

22  D   Opportunity cost is the benefit sacrificed when one course of action is chosen in preference to an alternative.

# 41 Compulsory written question: Decision making I

> **Helping hand**
>
> It is assumed in limiting factor analysis that management wishes to maximise profit and that profit will be maximised when contribution is maximised.
>
> Remember that contribution will be maximised by earning the biggest possible contribution from each unit of limiting factor.
>
> **What the Examiner said**
>
> A large number of candidates gained no marks on this question. Many treated it as a requirement to calculate the total net profit of each product which was especially time consuming. Many candidates demonstrated confusion between labour costs and labour hours.

(a)

|  | Product A | Product B | Product C | Total |
|---|---|---|---|---|
| Direct labour hours per unit (W1) | 0.3 | 0.3 | 0.4 |  |
| Sales demand (units) | 6,200 | 8,000 | 11,500 |  |
| Direct labour hours required | 1,860 | 2,400 | 4,600 | 8,860 |
| Direct labour hours available |  |  |  | 8,500 |
| Shortfall of direct labour hours |  |  |  | 360 |

There is a shortfall of 360 direct labour hours and therefore the availability of the direct labour will be a limiting factor in the next period.

*Working*

**Direct labour hours per unit**

Product A $= \dfrac{\$2.40}{\$8.00} = 0.30$ direct labour hours

Product B $= \dfrac{\$2.40}{\$8.00} = 0.30$ direct labour hours

Product C $= \dfrac{\$3.20}{\$8.00} = 0.40$ direct labour hours

(b)

|  | Product A per unit | Product B per unit | Product C per unit |
|---|---|---|---|
| Selling price | $9.70 | $11.10 | $13.80 |
| *Variable costs* |  |  |  |
| Direct materials | $2.80 | $3.90 | $4.92 |
| Direct labour | $2.40 | $2.40 | $3.20 |
| Variable overheads | $0.90 | $0.90 | $1.20 |
| Contribution per unit | $3.60 | $3.90 | $4.48 |
| Direct labour hours per unit | 0.30 | 0.30 | 0.40 |
| Contribution per direct labour hour | $12.00 | $13.00 | $11.20 |
| Ranking | 2nd | 1st | 3rd |

*Direct labour hours used*

| | |
|---|---|
| Product B – maximum | 2,400 |
| Product A – maximum | 1,860 |
| Product C – balance (8,500 – 2,400 – 1,860) | 4,240 |
| Total direct labour hours | 8,500 |

*Production schedule*

| | Product A | Product B | Product C |
|---|---|---|---|
| Units of Product A = 2,400 hours ÷ 0.3 hours per unit | 8,000 | | |
| Units of Product B = 1,860 hours ÷ 0.3 hours per unit | | 6,200 | |
| Units of Product C = 4,240 hours ÷ 0.4 hours per unit | | | 10,600 |

## Marking scheme

| | | | Marks |
|---|---|---|---|
| (a) | Direct labour hours required | 3 | |
| | | 1 | |
| | | | 4 |
| (b) | Contribution/unit | 3 | |
| | Contribution/direct labour hour | 3 | |
| | Priority | 1 | |
| | Production schedule | 3 | |
| | | | 10 |
| | | | 14 |

# 42 Compulsory written question: Decision making II

**Helping hand**

Follow a methodical approach and clearly label your workings as there is a great deal of data to work through.

Transport company

(a) Total cost per coach on each route

| | Route A | | Route B | |
|---|---|---|---|---|
| | $ | | $ | |
| Drivers' wages | 34,320 | (W1) | 34,320 | |
| Fuel and maintenance | 46,818 | (W2) | 52,949 | (W3) |
| Fixed costs: | | | | |
| Vehicle tax & insurance | 3,870 | | 3,870 | |
| Apportioned costs | 10,880 | (W4) | 10,880 | |
| | $95,888 | | $102,019 | |

(b) Cost per kilometre on each route

| | Route A | | Route B | |
|---|---|---|---|---|
| Total cost | $95,888 | | $102,019 | |
| ÷ total kilometres | 52,416 | (W5) | 59,280 | (W6) |
| Cost per kilometres | $1.8294 | | $1.7210 | |

(c)    Profit per kilometre on each route

|  | Route A<br>$ per km |  | Route B<br>$ per km |  |
|---|---|---|---|---|
| Revenue | 2.0986 | (W7) | 1.6211 | (W8) |
| Costs | 1.8294 |  | 1.7210 |  |
| Profit/(loss) | $0.2695 | per km | $(0.0999) | per km |

*Workings*

W1    $110/coach x 6 days/week x 52 weeks/year

W2    $0·8932/km x 12 journeys/day x 14 km/journey x 6 days/week x 52 weeks/year

W3    $0·8932/km x 10 journeys/day x 19 km/journey x 6 days/week x 52 weeks/year

W4    $21,760/route ÷ 2 coaches/route

W5    12 journeys/day x 14 km/journey x 6 days/week x 52 weeks/year

W6    10 journeys/day x 19 km/journey x 6 days/week x 52 weeks/year

W7    13 passengers/journey x $2·26/passenger ÷ 14 km/journey

W8    11 passengers/journey x $2·80/passenger ÷ 19 km/journey

## Marking scheme

|  |  |  | Marks |
|---|---|---|---|
| (a) | Driver's wages | 2 |  |
|  | Fuel | 5 |  |
|  | Fixed costs | 3 |  |
|  |  |  | 10 |
| (b) | Total km | 3 |  |
|  | Cost per km | 2 |  |
|  |  |  | 5 |
| (c) | Revenue per km | 3 |  |
|  | Cost & profit per kilometre | 2 |  |
|  |  |  | 5 |
|  |  |  | 20 |

# 43 Objective test questions: Capital investment appraisal

1    B    Current rate is 6% pa payable monthly

∴ Effective rate is 6/12% = ½% compound every month

∴ In the six months from January to June, interest earned =

($1,000 × [1.005]$^6$) − $1,000 = $30.38

Option A is incorrect since it is simply 6% × $1,000 = $60 in one year, then divided by 2 to give $30 in six months.

Option C represents the annual interest payable (6% × $1,000 = $60 pa).

Option D is also wrong since this has been calculated (incorrectly) as follows.

0.05 × $1,000     = $50 per month
Over six months  = $50 × 6
                        = $300 in six months

| 2 | B | $2,070 = 115% of the original investment |

∴ Original investment $= \dfrac{100}{115} \times \$2,070$

$\qquad\qquad\qquad\quad = \$1,800$

∴ Interest $\qquad\qquad = \$2,070 - \$1,800$

$\qquad\qquad\qquad\quad = \$270$

Option D is calculated (incorrectly) as follows.

$\dfrac{x}{\$2,070} = 15\%$

∴ $x = 0.15 \times \$2,070$

$\qquad = \$310.50$

Make sure that you always tackle this type of question by establishing what the original investment was first.

| 3 | C | We need to calculate the effective rate of interest. |

8% per annum (nominal) is 2% per quarter. The effective annual rate of interest is $[1.02^4 - 1] = 0.08243 = 8.243\%$.

Now we can use $S = X(1 + r)^n$

$\qquad\qquad\qquad S = 12,000\,(1.08243)^3$

$\qquad\qquad\qquad S = \$15,218.81$

∴ The principal will have grown to approximately $15,219.

Option A is incorrect because this represents $\$12,000 \times (1.08)^3 = \$15,117$. You forgot to calculate the effective annual rate of interest of 8.243%.

Option B represents the present value of $12,000 at the end of three years, ie $\$12,000 \times 0.794$ (from present value tables) at an interest rate of 8%.

Option D represents the cumulative present value of $12,000 for each of the next three years at an interest rate of 8%.

| 4 | D | | | $ |
|---|---|---|---|---|
| | | PV of $1,200 in one year | $= \$1,200 \times 0.926 =$ | 1,111.20 |
| | | PV of $1,400 in two years | $= \$1,400 \times 0.857 =$ | 1,199.80 |
| | | PV of $1,600 in three years | $= \$1,600 \times 0.794 =$ | 1,270.40 |
| | | PV of $1,800 in four years | $= \$1,800 \times 0.735 =$ | 1,323.00 |

| 5 | D | Effective quarterly rate | $= 1\% \ (4\% \div 4)$ |
|---|---|---|---|
| | | Effective annual rate | $= [(1.01)^4 - 1]$ |
| | | | $= 0.0406 = 4.06\% \ pa$ |

You should have been able to eliminate options A and B immediately. 1% is simply 4% ÷ 4 = 1%. 4% is the nominal rate and is therefore not the effective annual rate of interest.

| 6 | B | The formula to calculate the IRR is $a\% + \left[\dfrac{A}{A-B} \times (b-a)\right]\%$ |

where　a = one interest rate

$\qquad\quad$ b = other interest rate

$\qquad\quad$ A = NPV at rate a

$\qquad\quad$ B = NPV at rate b

IRR $\quad = 9\% + \left[\dfrac{22}{22+4} \times 1\right]\%$

$\qquad\quad = 9 + 0.85 = 9.85\%$

If you selected option A you took A to be 'the other interest rate', and you subtracted the 0.85 instead of adding it.

You should have spotted that Options C and D were invalid because if the NPV is positive at one rate and negative at another rate, the IRR will be somewhere between the two rates, ie between 9% and 10%.

7    B    The discount factor for 10 years at 7% is 0.508.

∴ Original amount invested    = $2,000 × 0.508
                                          = $1,016

If you selected Option A, you mixed up the rate and the period in the present value tables and therefore found the discount factor for 7 years at 10%.

If you selected option C, you divided $2,000 by the discount factor instead of multiplying it.

If you selected option D, you used the cumulative present value tables instead of the simple present value tables. Always check your answers for common sense – an investment **growing** at 7% per annum is unlikely to fall in value!

8    B    If house prices rise at 2% per calendar month, this is equivalent to

$(1.02)^{12} = 1.268$ or 26.8% per annum

If you selected option A, you forgot to take the effect of compounding into account, ie 12 × 2% = 24%.

If you chose answer C, you correctly calculated that $(1.02)^{12} = 1.268$ but then incorrectly translated this into 12.68% instead of 26.8%.

If you selected option D, you forgot to raise 1.02 to the power 12, and instead you multiplied it by 12.

9    D    Annuity                   = $700
          Annuity factor        = 1 + 6.247 (cumulative factor for 9 years, first payment is **now**)
                                       = 7.247

$$\text{Annuity} = \frac{\text{PV of annuity}}{\text{Annuity factor}}$$

$$\$700 = \frac{\text{PV of annuity}}{7.247}$$

$700 × 7.247    = PV of annuity
PV of annuity    = $5,073 (to the nearest $)

If you selected option A, you have calculated the present value of an annuity from years 1-10 instead of from time 0-9.

If you selected option B, you have used the present value tables instead of the cumulative present value tables, ie $700 × (1 + 0.5) = $1,050.

If you selected option C, you appear to have mixed up the interest rate and periods and obtained an annuity factor for years 0-8 at 10% = $4,435.

10

| 267.65 |

$200 × (1.06)^5    = $267.65

11

| 9 |

$$\text{Annuity} = \frac{\text{Present value of annuity}}{\text{Annuity factor}}$$

$$\text{Annuity factor} = \frac{86,400}{19,260} = 4.486$$

From tables, this annuity factor corresponds to an interest rate of 9% over six years.

**12**   $ | 12,656.25 |

Using the compound interest formula, $V = X(1 + r)^n$, we have $X = \$40,000, r = -0.25, n = 4$

∴ $V = 40,000 (1 - 0.25)^4 = 12,656.25$
∴ Written down value $= \$12,656.25$

**13**   $ | 480,000 |

The present value of a perpetuity is:

$$PV = \frac{a}{r}$$

where   $a$ = annuity = $24,000

$r$ = cost of capital as a proportion = 5% = 0.05

∴ $PV = \dfrac{24,000}{0.05}$

$= \$480,000$

**14**   %  | 18 |

The internal rate of return (IRR) of the investment can be calculated using the following formula.

$$IRR = a\% + \left( \frac{A}{A - B} \times (b - a) \right)\%$$

where   a = first interest rate = 12%
b = second interest rate = 20%
A = first NPV = $24,000
B = second NPV = $(8,000)

$IRR = 12\% + \left( \dfrac{24,000}{24,000 + 8,000} \times (20 - 12) \right)\%$

$= 12\% + 6\%$

$= 18\%$

**15**   The non-discounted payback period of Project Beta = | 2 | years and | 6 | months.

*Workings*

**Project Beta**

| Year | Cash inflow | Cumulative cash inflow |
|------|-------------|------------------------|
|      | $           | $                      |
| 1    | 250,000     | 250,000                |
| 2    | 350,000     | 600,000                |
| 3    | 400,000     | 1,000,000              |
| 4    | 200,000     | 1,200,000              |
| 5    | 150,000     | 1,350,000              |
| 6    | 150,000     | 1,500,000              |

Project Beta has a payback period of between 2 and 3 years.

Payback period = 2 years + $\left[ \dfrac{\$200,000}{\$400,000} \times 12\,\text{months} \right]$

= 2 years + 6 months

**16**

The discounted payback period of Project Alpha is between ⎡ 3 ⎤ and ⎡ 4 ⎤ years.

*Workings*

**Project Alpha**

| Year | Cash flow | Discount factor | PV | Cum. PV |
|------|-----------|-----------------|-----|---------|
| | $ | 10% | $ | $ |
| 0 | (800,000) | 1.000 | (800,000) | (800,000) |
| 1 | 250,000 | 0.909 | 227,250 | (572,750) |
| 2 | 250,000 | 0.826 | 206,500 | (366,250) |
| 3 | 400,000 | 0.751 | 300,400 | (65,850) |
| 4 | 300,000 | 0.683 | 204,900 | 139,050 |
| 5 | 200,000 | 0.621 | 124,200 | 263,250 |
| 6 | 50,000 | 0.564 | 28,200 | 291,450 |

The discounted payback period is therefore between three and four years.

**17**  B  The payback period is the time that is required for the total of the cash inflows of a capital investment project to equal the total of the cash outflows, ie initial investment ÷ annual net cash inflow.

**18**  B

| | $ |
|---|---|
| Investment | (60,000) |
| PV of cash inflow | 64,600 |
| NPV @ 10% | 4,600 |

| | $ |
|---|---|
| Investment | (60,000) |
| PV of cash inflow | 58,200 |
| NPV @ 15% | (1,800) |

The IRR of the machine investment is therefore between 10% and 15% because the NPV falls from $4,600 at 10% to –$1,800 at 15%. Therefore at some point between 10% and 15% the NPV = 0. When the NPV = 0, the internal rate of return is reached.

**19**  A  Let x = investment at start of project.

| Year | Cash flow | Discount factor | Present value |
|------|-----------|-----------------|---------------|
| | $ | 10% | $ |
| 0 | x | 1.000 | (x) |
| 1 – 5 | 18,000 | 3.791 | 68,238 |
| | | | 7,222 |

∴ –x + $68,238 = $7,222

x = $68,238 – $7,222

x = $61,016

**20**  D  Statements 2 and 4 are true.

**21**  B  IRR is the discount rate at which the net present value of the cash flows from an investment is zero.

**22**  C  At the end of year 3, $74,600 has been 'paid back'. The remaining $15,400 for payback will be received during year 4.

**23**  C  $(1.021)^4 - 1 = 0.0867 = 8.67\%$

# 44 Compulsory written question: Compound interest formula and NPV

> **Helping hand**
>
> Set your calculations out clearly and neatly and show all your workings, so the examiner can see exactly what you've done.
>
> **What the Examiner said**
>
> Candidates seem to understand the formulae but frequently cannot apply them.

(a)  (i)  P is the original sum invested.
          r is the interest rate, expressed as a decimal.
          n is the number of periods, normally years.

   (ii)  $P = \$5,000$
         $r = 0.08$
         $n = 4$

         $S = P(1 + r)^n$
         $= \$5,000 \times (1.08)^4$
         $= \$6,802$

(b)  (i)  Depreciation per annum is $\dfrac{\$175,000}{5} = \$35,000$

          This needs to be added back to the profit figures in order to calculate the cash flow from the project.

| Year | Profit/losses $ | Depreciation $ | Cash flow $ | Discount factor @ 10% | Present value $ |
|------|------|------|------|------|------|
| 0 |  |  | (175,000) | 1 | (175,000) |
| 1 | (11,000) | 35,000 | 24,000 | 0.909 | 21,816 |
| 2 | 3,000 | 35,000 | 38,000 | 0.826 | 31,388 |
| 3 | 34,000 | 35,000 | 69,000 | 0.751 | 51,819 |
| 4 | 47,000 | 35,000 | 82,000 | 0.683 | 56,006 |
| 5 | 8,000 | 35,000 | 43,000 | 0.621 | 26,703 |
|  |  |  |  | NPV | 12,732 |

   (ii)  The net present value is positive so the project generates more cash inflows than outflows, in present value terms at the given discount rate. The project is therefore worthwhile.

Marks

| | | | | |
|---|---|---|---|---|
| (a) | (i) | 1 mark for each | | 3 |
| | (ii) | Formula for constituents | 1½ | |
| | | Calculation | 1½ | |
| | | | | 3 |
| (b) | (i) | Depreciation | 1½ | |
| | | Depreciation adjustment | 2½ | |
| | | Discounting | 2½ | |
| | | Net present value | 1½ | |
| | | | | 8 |
| | (ii) | Worthwhile | 1 | |
| | | NPV positive at required rate of return | 1 | |
| | | | | 2 |
| | | | | 16 |

# 45 Compulsory written question: Minimum contract price and NPV

**Helping hand**

This was the longest of the Section B Questions - there were 19 marks allocated here. As such ensure that you spend proportionally longer on this question.

The amount of information may be, at first sight, rather daunting. It is worth taking time to read the question twice. All the information for requirement (a) is contained within '1 Contract W' and all the information for requirement (b) is contained within '2 Sub-contract work'.

For (a) make sure you label your workings very clearly so the marker can follow your arguments and award you maximum marks. In part (a) incremental costs are also known as marginal or extra costs. Some of these costs are nil. In your answer write 'nil' or '0' to show the marker that you know it is nil.

In part (b) remember that the discount factor for Period 0 is 1 ($1 received or spent today is worth $1!). If you used a tabular approach then there were very easy marks available for the calculation of the NPV.

**What the Examiner said**

Many candidates had problems calculating the relevant material costs in part (a) and establishing the relevant investment amount in part (b). Overall some candidates showed a lack of knowledge and understanding of the principles regarding relevant costs for decision making.

|  |  | **Marks** |
|---|---|---|
| (a) | Dept X labour | 1½ |
|  | Dept Y labour | 1 |
|  | Materials | 3 |
|  | Production overhead | 3 |
|  | Non-production overhead | 1½ |
|  |  | 10 |
| (b) | Opportunity cost of machinery | 2 |
|  | Cash inflows | 1 |
|  | Exclusion of depreciation | 2 |
|  | Disposal value of machinery | 1 |
|  | Discounting & NPV | 3 |
|  |  | 9 |
|  |  | 19 |

(a) **Contract W**

Incremental costs:

|  | $ |
|---|---|
| Labour    – Department X (W1) | nil |
|            – Department Y (W2) | 2,400 |
| Materials (W3) | 5,588 |
| Production overhead (W4) | 972 |
| Non-production overhead (W5) | nil |
|  | 8,960 |

Minimum price to quote for Contract W is $8,960.

*Workings*

1    No additional operatives will be taken on. The costs won't change.

2    Additional labour will cost $2400

3    *Materials*

|  | $ |
|---|---|
| Replacement Cost | 5,740 |
| Less replacement value of Material M already in stock | |
| 80 units × (replacement cost – scrap value) | |
| 80 × ($6.50 – $4.60) | 152 |
|  | 5,588 |

4    *Production overheads*

120% of direct labour costs

|  | $ |
|---|---|
| Dept X (1.2 × $7.50 × 220) | 1,980 |
| Dept Y (1.2 × $2,400) | 2,880 |
|  | 4,860 |

Incremental part (20%) = 4,860 × 0.2 = $972

5    None of the non-production costs are incremental.

(b) **Sub-contract work**

| Time | Cash flow $ | Discount factor 10% | Present value $ |
|---|---|---|---|
| 0 | (120,000) | 1.000 | (120,000) |
| 1 | 40,000 | 0.909 | 36,360 |
| 2 | 55,000 | 0.826 | 45,430 |
| 3 | 70,000 | 0.751 | 52,570 |
| | | | 14,360 |

Net present value of keeping the machinery for sub-contract work is $14,360.

# 46 Compulsory written question: NPV and IRR

**Helping hand**

You are required to explain and describe aspects of discounted capital investment appraisal and to use a graph to illustrate net present value and internal rate of return. Make sure you describe *how* the net present value is used (ie the positive/negative decision).

**What the Examiner said**

A significant number of candidates failed to realise that present values were given in the question and wasted time calculating values already provided in the graph.

(a) Discounting cash flows

The principle of discounting cash flows in capital investment project appraisal is on the basis that an amount of cash received sometime in the future is worth less than the same amount of cash received now. This is because of its earning capacity overtime and is referred to as the time value of money.

(b) Net present value

Cash flows expected at different times over the life of a capital investment project are first estimated. The net present value method of capital investment project appraisal then requires the estimated cash flows to be discounted. Discounting applies a factor to a future expected cash flow to reduce it to an equivalent value now. The factor applied will depend both upon the interest rate per time period and the number of time periods into the future when the cash flow is expected to occur. The higher the interest rate, and the greater the number of periods ahead, the lower will be the equivalent cash value now and vice versa. The net present value method discounts all the cash flows (both inflows and outflows), expected to arise during the lifetime of the investment, using the required rate of return (cost of capital %) as the discount rate. A different factor will be applied to each period's net cash flow. If the net total of the discounted cash flows (referred to as the net present value) is positive (i.e. if the present value of the cash inflows exceeds the present value of the cash outflows), the investment is acceptable. If it is negative, the investment is unacceptable.

(c) *Workings*

NPV at 10% = 261.3 – 224 = 37.3
NPV at 20% = 199.6 – 224 = (24.4)

Graph of investment project NPVs:

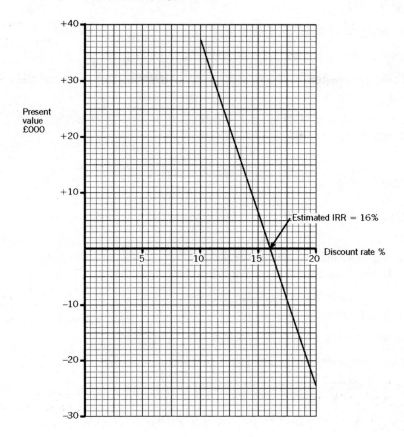

# 47 Mixed bank 1 (6/06)

1    C    The report will aid management in decision-making.

2    D    Useful management information is clear, accurate and relevant for its purpose.

3    D    An interlocking bookkeeping system is where separate accounts are kept for cost accounting and for financial accounting.

4    B    Job costing is most appropriate when production is carried out in accordance with the special requirements of each customer.

5    B    $y = a + bx$

$156,980 = a + (12.20 \times 7,400)$
$156,980 = a + 90,280$
$a = 156,980 - 90,280$
$a = 66,700$

6    C    Total cost of 6,000 units = 42,000 + 60,000 = 102,000
Cost per unit = 102,000/6,000 = $17

Total cost of 8,000 units = 50,000 + 76,000 = 126,000
Cost per unit = 126,000/8,000 = $15.75

Reduction in total cost per unit = 17 − 15.75 = $1.25

7    C    A materials returned note is used to record materials sent back.

8    D    The inventory used in production is valued at $6,500/500 = $13 per kg
410 kgs is valued at 410 × $13 = $5,330
Work-in-progress is debited and material stock credited when material is issued.

9    A    Re-order level is calculated as maximum usage × maximum lead time to avoid stock-outs.

10   B    $EOQ = \sqrt{\dfrac{2cd}{h}}$

$800 = \sqrt{\dfrac{2 \times c \times 12,000}{1.5}}$

$640,000 = \dfrac{2 \times c \times 12,000}{1.5}$

$960,000 = 24,000 \times c$

$c = 40$

11   D    Time sheets and job cards may be used to allocate costs to cost units.

12   D    The production volume ratio is calculated as standard hours for actual output ÷ budgeted hours.

13   A    Capital expenditure is the cost of acquiring or enhancing non-current assets.

14   D

|  | A | B | C | D |
|---|---|---|---|---|
| Overhead expenditure | 18,757 | 29,025 | 46,340 | 42,293 |
| Direct labour hours | 3,080 | 6,750 | | |
| Machine hours | | | 3,380 | 2,640 |
| Overhead absorption rate | $6.09 | $4.30 | $13.71 | $16.02 |

| 15 | C | Production cost per unit = $3.60 + ($258,000/60,000) = $7.90 |
|---|---|---|

Profit = 700,000 − (56,000 × 7.90) − 144,000 = $113,600

|  | $ | $ |
|---|---|---|
| Revenue |  | 700,000 |
| Production costs: |  |  |
| Variable |  |  |
| (56,000 + 4,000) × $3.60 | 216,000 |  |
| Fixed | 258,000 |  |
| Closing stock (4,000 × $7.90) | (31,600) |  |
|  |  | (442,200) |
|  |  | 257,600 |
| Fixed non-production costs |  | (144,000) |
|  |  | 113,600 |

16    C    Inventory levels have increased so marginal costing will result in higher profits and lower inventory values than absorption costing.

17    B    Contribution = 17.50 − (7.60 + 1.40) = $8.50 per unit

Contribution/sales ratio = 8.5/17.5 × 100 = 48.6%

18    B

|  | A | B | C | D |
|---|---|---|---|---|
|  | $ | $ | $ | $ |
| Variable manufacturing costs | 6.00 | 8.00 | 9.00 | 11.50 |
| Bought-in price | 11.00 | 11.50 | 13.00 | 16.00 |
| Difference | 5.00 | 3.50 | 4.00 | 4.50 |

Component B has the lowest difference between the cost of manufacture and the cost of buying it in. This would therefore have the smallest effect on profit.

19    A    $IRR = a\% + [\frac{A}{A-B} \times (b-a)]\%$

where   a is one interest rate
        b is the other interest rate
        A is the NPV at rate a
        B is the NPV at rate b

$IRR = 14\% + \left[ \frac{16,000}{(16,000+10,500)} \times (20-14) \right]\%$

= 14% + 3.6%

= 17.6%

20    C    Present value = $8,000 + ($8,000 × 3.791) = $38,328

# 48 Mixed bank 2 (12/06)

1    A

2    B    Statement (i) is not true as the benefit and cost of management information should be compared. Statement (iii) is not true because the cost of providing very detailed and accurate information may exceed the potential value of that information.

3    C

4    D

5    B    Low production is in period 2. High production is in Period 1. A change in production units must lead to the change in costs ie variable costs.

$$\frac{198,968 - 187,739}{129,440 - 117,620} = \frac{11,229}{11,820} = 0.95$$

6    C    FIFO (LIFO or weighted average) is used to value issues from inventory and also to calculate the value of inventory at a period end.

7    C    (1.0 / 0.8) = 1.25 kg

> **Helping hand**
>
> As a check or indeed as a way to find the correct solution take the answer and then calculate 20% of that value = 0.25 kg. Take this from the 1.25 kg to give 1 kg.

8    C

9    A    By definition.

10    B    Statement (iii) is not true as a balancing charge, which is the opposite to a balancing allowance, would be made.

11    C    65% of SCC1 Total Overheads and 35% of SCC2 overheads

($32,170 × 0.65) + ($24,850 × 0.35) = $29,608

12    B    The company manufactures less than it sells therefore inventory levels are falling.

> **Helping hand**
>
> It is often helpful to put some simple numbers into the example.

13    D    All jobs except Job 2 are complete. Therefore for Job 2:

|  | $ |
|---|---|
| WIP at beginning of period | 3,170 |
| Direct materials | 4,650 |
| Direct labour | 3,970 |
| Production overheads | |
| 11,430 × (3,970/12,700) | 3,573 |
|  | 15,363 |

14    C

15    C

|  | $ |
|---|---|
| Costs incurred in the process | 61,600 |
| less: scrap proceeds (440 × 1.80)] | (792) |
|  | 60,808 |

Per unit (/ 21,560) = $2.82 (to the nearest cent)

| 16 | D | All raw materials were input | = 10,000 units |
|---|---|---|---|

Conversion cost equivalent units = 10,000 − (800 × (100% − 75%))
= 9,800 units

17   A   Total joint costs = $87,500

Calculation of share for product X:

|  |  | $ |
|---|---|---|
| Sales value of X | $6 × 10,000 = | 60,000 |
| Sales value of Y | $8 × 15,000 = | 120,000 |
|  |  | 180,000 |

(60 / 180) × $87,500 = $29,167

18   D   Total costs divided by total number of occupied rooms

$104,976 / (60 × 0.8 × 90) = $24.30

19   D

|  | $ |
|---|---|
| Fixed costs ($56,000 + $38,000) | 94,000 |
| Required profit | 6,000 |
| Total contribution | 100,000 |

Contribution per unit ($7.00 − $4.20) = $2.80

Therefore number of units = 100,000/2.80 = 35,714

Sales revenue = 35,714 units × $7 = $250,000 (to the nearest $'000)

20   C

|  | $ |
|---|---|
| Initial Investment | 81,000 |
| NPV | 8,683 |
|  | 89,683 |

Divided by annuity factor

for Yrs 1-4 (3.037) = $29,530

OR:

| Initial investment | 81,000 |
|---|---|

Divided by annuity factor

At IRR rate (2.743) = $29,530

# 49 Mixed bank 3 (6/07)

1  D

2  A

3  A

4  B
5  D

6  C

7  C
8  B

9  C

10  D  ($17,600 + 450 + 760 + 2,780 + 1,100)

11  A

12  A

13  C

14  B  {$22/unit − 11.6 − [($7,200 + 16,400) ÷ 4,000 units]} × 100 ÷ 22

15  B  [200 units × ($7·5 − 4.8)/unit]

16  D  [(630 ÷ 0.9 hours) × $12/hour)]

17  C  {[$216,720 − (1,200 units × $2/unit)] ÷ (24,000 − 1,200 units)}

18  B  {$194,860 ÷ [11,400 + (1,200 × 0.6) units]}

19  D

20  B  [$65,124 ÷ (30 × 9 × 15 × 4 × 0.6 customers)]

# 50 Mixed bank 4 (12/07)

| | |
|---|---|
| 1 | D |
| 2 | D |
| 3 | B |
| 4 | C |
| 5 | B |
| 6 | A |
| 7 | C |
| 8 | D |
| 9 | A |
| 10 | D |
| 11 | B |
| 12 | C |
| 13 | D |
| 14 | C |
| 15 | A |
| 16 | B |
| 17 | A |
| 18 | C |
| 19 | C |
| 20 | B |

Workings to computational MCQs:

5 ($52,000 ÷ 5,000 units) + {[($760,000 − (50,000 units × $10.40/unit)] ÷ 54,000 units}

7 [(8 units × $260/unit) + (12 units × $270/unit)]

8 [(3,400 kg + 600 kg) ÷ 2]

11 [($44,210 × 1.4) + $3,190]

12 {[$4,250 ÷ (420 units good output + 20 units abnormal loss)] × 20 units}

14 {$71,628 ÷ [9,000 + (1,000 × 0.4) units]}

16 [($39,420 + $11,880) ÷ 5,400 units]

20 {11% + [4% × ($35,170/$29,130)]}

# Appendix tables

# Present value table

Present value of 1 ie $(1+r)^{-n}$

where    r = discount rate

           n = number of periods until payment

**Periods**                              **Discount rates (r)**

| (n) | 1% | 2% | 3% | 4% | 5% | 6% | 7% | 8% | 9% | 10% |
|---|---|---|---|---|---|---|---|---|---|---|
| 1 | 0.990 | 0.980 | 0.971 | 0.962 | 0.952 | 0.943 | 0.935 | 0.926 | 0.917 | 0.909 |
| 2 | 0.980 | 0.961 | 0.943 | 0.925 | 0.907 | 0.890 | 0.873 | 0.857 | 0.842 | 0.826 |
| 3 | 0.971 | 0.942 | 0.915 | 0.889 | 0.864 | 0.840 | 0.816 | 0.794 | 0.772 | 0.751 |
| 4 | 0.961 | 0.924 | 0.888 | 0.855 | 0.823 | 0.792 | 0.763 | 0.735 | 0.708 | 0.683 |
| 5 | 0.951 | 0.906 | 0.863 | 0.822 | 0.784 | 0.747 | 0.713 | 0.681 | 0.650 | 0.621 |
| 6 | 0.942 | 0.888 | 0.837 | 0.790 | 0.746 | 0.705 | 0.666 | 0.630 | 0.596 | 0.564 |
| 7 | 0.933 | 0.871 | 0.813 | 0.760 | 0.711 | 0.665 | 0.623 | 0.583 | 0.547 | 0.513 |
| 8 | 0.923 | 0.853 | 0.789 | 0.731 | 0.677 | 0.627 | 0.582 | 0.540 | 0.502 | 0.467 |
| 9 | 0.914 | 0.837 | 0.766 | 0.703 | 0.645 | 0.592 | 0.544 | 0.500 | 0.460 | 0.424 |
| 10 | 0.905 | 0.820 | 0.744 | 0.676 | 0.614 | 0.558 | 0.508 | 0.463 | 0.422 | 0.386 |
| 11 | 0.896 | 0.804 | 0.722 | 0.650 | 0.585 | 0.527 | 0.475 | 0.429 | 0.388 | 0.350 |
| 12 | 0.887 | 0.788 | 0.701 | 0.625 | 0.557 | 0.497 | 0.444 | 0.397 | 0.356 | 0.319 |
| 13 | 0.879 | 0.773 | 0.681 | 0.601 | 0.530 | 0.469 | 0.415 | 0.368 | 0.326 | 0.290 |
| 14 | 0.870 | 0.758 | 0.661 | 0.577 | 0.505 | 0.442 | 0.388 | 0.340 | 0.299 | 0.263 |
| 15 | 0.861 | 0.743 | 0.642 | 0.555 | 0.481 | 0.417 | 0.362 | 0.315 | 0.275 | 0.239 |

**Periods**

| (n) | 11% | 12% | 13% | 14% | 15% | 16% | 17% | 18% | 19% | 20% |
|---|---|---|---|---|---|---|---|---|---|---|
| 1 | 0.901 | 0.893 | 0.885 | 0.877 | 0.870 | 0.862 | 0.855 | 0.847 | 0.840 | 0.833 |
| 2 | 0.812 | 0.797 | 0.783 | 0.769 | 0.756 | 0.743 | 0.731 | 0.718 | 0.706 | 0.694 |
| 3 | 0.731 | 0.712 | 0.693 | 0.675 | 0.658 | 0.641 | 0.624 | 0.609 | 0.593 | 0.579 |
| 4 | 0.659 | 0.636 | 0.613 | 0.592 | 0.572 | 0.552 | 0.534 | 0.516 | 0.499 | 0.482 |
| 5 | 0.593 | 0.567 | 0.543 | 0.519 | 0.497 | 0.476 | 0.456 | 0.437 | 0.419 | 0.402 |
| 6 | 0.535 | 0.507 | 0.480 | 0.456 | 0.432 | 0.410 | 0.390 | 0.370 | 0.352 | 0.335 |
| 7 | 0.482 | 0.452 | 0.425 | 0.400 | 0.376 | 0.354 | 0.333 | 0.314 | 0.296 | 0.279 |
| 8 | 0.434 | 0.404 | 0.376 | 0.351 | 0.327 | 0.305 | 0.285 | 0.266 | 0.249 | 0.233 |
| 9 | 0.391 | 0.361 | 0.333 | 0.308 | 0.284 | 0.263 | 0.243 | 0.225 | 0.209 | 0.194 |
| 10 | 0.352 | 0.322 | 0.295 | 0.270 | 0.247 | 0.227 | 0.208 | 0.191 | 0.176 | 0.162 |
| 11 | 0.317 | 0.287 | 0.261 | 0.237 | 0.215 | 0.195 | 0.178 | 0.162 | 0.148 | 0.135 |
| 12 | 0.286 | 0.257 | 0.231 | 0.208 | 0.187 | 0.168 | 0.152 | 0.137 | 0.124 | 0.112 |
| 13 | 0.258 | 0.229 | 0.204 | 0.182 | 0.163 | 0.145 | 0.130 | 0.116 | 0.104 | 0.093 |
| 14 | 0.232 | 0.205 | 0.181 | 0.160 | 0.141 | 0.125 | 0.111 | 0.099 | 0.088 | 0.078 |
| 15 | 0.209 | 0.183 | 0.160 | 0.140 | 0.123 | 0.108 | 0.095 | 0.084 | 0.074 | 0.065 |

# Annuity table

Present value of annuity of 1, ie $\dfrac{1-(1+r)^{-n}}{r}$

where     r = discount rate
             n = number of periods.

| Periods (n) | Discount rates (r) | | | | | | | | | |
|---|---|---|---|---|---|---|---|---|---|---|
| | 1% | 2% | 3% | 4% | 5% | 6% | 7% | 8% | 9% | 10% |
| 1 | 0.990 | 0.980 | 0.971 | 0.962 | 0.952 | 0.943 | 0.935 | 0.926 | 0.917 | 0.909 |
| 2 | 1.970 | 1.942 | 1.913 | 1.886 | 1.859 | 1.833 | 1.808 | 1.783 | 1.759 | 1.736 |
| 3 | 2.941 | 2.884 | 2.829 | 2.775 | 2.723 | 2.673 | 2.624 | 2.577 | 2.531 | 2.487 |
| 4 | 3.902 | 3.808 | 3.717 | 3.630 | 3.546 | 3.465 | 3.387 | 3.312 | 3.240 | 3.170 |
| 5 | 4.853 | 4.713 | 4.580 | 4.452 | 4.329 | 4.212 | 4.100 | 3.993 | 3.890 | 3.791 |
| 6 | 5.795 | 5.601 | 5.417 | 5.242 | 5.076 | 4.917 | 4.767 | 4.623 | 4.486 | 4.355 |
| 7 | 6.728 | 6.472 | 6.230 | 6.002 | 5.786 | 5.582 | 5.389 | 5.206 | 5.033 | 4.868 |
| 8 | 7.652 | 7.325 | 7.020 | 6.733 | 6.463 | 6.210 | 5.971 | 5.747 | 5.535 | 5.335 |
| 9 | 8.566 | 8.162 | 7.786 | 7.435 | 7.108 | 6.802 | 6.515 | 6.247 | 5.995 | 5.759 |
| 10 | 9.471 | 8.983 | 8.530 | 8.111 | 7.722 | 7.360 | 7.024 | 6.710 | 6.418 | 6.145 |
| 11 | 10.368 | 9.787 | 9.253 | 8.760 | 8.306 | 7.887 | 7.499 | 7.139 | 6.805 | 6.495 |
| 12 | 11.255 | 10.575 | 9.954 | 9.385 | 8.863 | 8.384 | 7.943 | 7.536 | 7.161 | 6.814 |
| 13 | 12.134 | 11.348 | 10.635 | 9.986 | 9.394 | 8.853 | 8.358 | 7.904 | 7.487 | 7.103 |
| 14 | 13.004 | 12.106 | 11.296 | 10.563 | 9.899 | 9.295 | 8.745 | 8.244 | 7.786 | 7.367 |
| 15 | 13.865 | 12.849 | 11.938 | 11.118 | 10.380 | 9.712 | 9.108 | 8.559 | 8.061 | 7.606 |

| Periods (n) | 11% | 12% | 13% | 14% | 15% | 16% | 17% | 18% | 19% | 20% |
|---|---|---|---|---|---|---|---|---|---|---|
| 1 | 0.901 | 0.893 | 0.885 | 0.877 | 0.870 | 0.862 | 0.855 | 0.847 | 0.840 | 0.833 |
| 2 | 1.713 | 1.690 | 1.668 | 1.647 | 1.626 | 1.605 | 1.585 | 1.566 | 1.547 | 1.528 |
| 3 | 2.444 | 2.402 | 2.361 | 2.322 | 2.283 | 2.246 | 2.210 | 2.174 | 2.140 | 2.106 |
| 4 | 3.102 | 3.037 | 2.974 | 2.914 | 2.855 | 2.798 | 2.743 | 2.690 | 2.639 | 2.589 |
| 5 | 3.696 | 3.605 | 3.517 | 3.433 | 3.352 | 3.274 | 3.199 | 3.127 | 3.058 | 2.991 |
| 6 | 4.231 | 4.111 | 3.998 | 3.889 | 3.784 | 3.685 | 3.589 | 3.498 | 3.410 | 3.326 |
| 7 | 4.712 | 4.564 | 4.423 | 4.288 | 4.160 | 4.039 | 3.922 | 3.812 | 3.706 | 3.605 |
| 8 | 5.146 | 4.968 | 4.799 | 4.639 | 4.487 | 4.344 | 4.207 | 4.078 | 3.954 | 3.837 |
| 9 | 5.537 | 5.328 | 5.132 | 4.946 | 4.772 | 4.607 | 4.451 | 4.303 | 4.163 | 4.031 |
| 10 | 5.889 | 5.650 | 5.426 | 5.216 | 5.019 | 4.833 | 4.659 | 4.494 | 4.339 | 4.192 |
| 11 | 6.207 | 5.938 | 5.687 | 5.453 | 5.234 | 5.029 | 4.836 | 4.656 | 4.486 | 4.327 |
| 12 | 6.492 | 6.194 | 5.918 | 5.660 | 5.421 | 5.197 | 4.988 | 4.793 | 4.611 | 4.439 |
| 13 | 6.750 | 6.424 | 6.122 | 5.842 | 5.583 | 5.342 | 5.118 | 4.910 | 4.715 | 4.533 |
| 14 | 6.982 | 6.628 | 6.302 | 6.002 | 5.724 | 5.468 | 5.229 | 5.008 | 4.802 | 4.611 |
| 15 | 7.191 | 6.811 | 6.462 | 6.142 | 5.847 | 5.575 | 5.324 | 5.092 | 4.876 | 4.675 |

# Mock Exam 1

# CAT

# Intermediate Paper 4
# Accounting for Costs

# Mock Examination 1

# June 2008

| Question Paper | |
| --- | --- |
| Time allowed | **2 hours** |
| **This paper is divided into two sections** | |
| Section A | ALL TWENTY questions are compulsory and MUST be answered |
| Section B | ALL FOUR questions are compulsory and MUST be attempted |

**DO NOT OPEN THIS PAPER UNTIL YOU ARE READY TO START UNDER EXAMINATION CONDITIONS**

# Section A – ALL TWENTY questions are compulsory and must be attempted

Each question in this section is worth 2 marks.

1 Which of the following are characteristics of management accounting information?

(1) Forward looking
(2) Legally required
(3) Concerned with cost control
(4) Follows clearly defined standards

A 1 and 3 only
B 2 and 4
C 1, 3 and 4
D 1, 2 and 3

---

2 Which of the following best describes an investment centre?

A Part of a business that uses fixed assets
B Part of a business that provides a service for other parts of the business
C Part of a business where management is only responsible for investment costs
D Part of a business where management is responsible for capital investment as well as profit

---

3 Consider the following four accounts:

(1) Cost ledger control
(2) Financial ledger control
(3) Receivables control
(4) Work-in-progress control

Which of the accounts are features of an integrated accounting system?

A 1 and 2 only
B 1, 2 and 3
C 2, 3 and 4
D 3 and 4 only

---

4 When goods are sold, what double-entry would be made to record the transfer of costs?

| | Debit | Credit |
|---|---|---|
| A | Finished goods account | Cost of sales account |
| B | Sales account | Cost of sales account |
| C | Cost of sales account | Sales account |
| D | Cost of sales account | Finished goods account |

---

5 An extract from the list of accounts of a chemical processor follows:

| | Cost codes |
|---|---|
| Direct materials | 001 to 099 |
| Direct labour | 100 to 199 |
| Indirect materials | 200 to 299 |
| Indirect labour | 300 to 399 |

Which of the following items is coded INCORRECTLY?

| | Description | Code |
|---|---|---|
| A | Chemical C6 used in process | 061 |
| B | Wages of process supervisor | 106 |
| C | Chemicals used for cleaning | 229 |
| D | Wages of maintenance engineer | 345 |

6   Which of the following may be used for capturing or storing management accounting data by computer?

    (1)   Scanner
    (2)   Printer
    (3)   CD
    (4)   Bar code reader

    A     1 and 2 only
    B     3 and 4 only
    C     1, 3 and 4 only
    D     All four items

7   Which of the following would be regarded as a stepped-fixed cost in the annual operation of a motor vehicle?

    A     Hire purchase payments
    B     Insurance
    C     Petrol
    D     Tyre replacement

8   The cost per unit of an expense item at different levels of activity is shown below:

    | Activity (units) | Cost per unit ($) |
    | --- | --- |
    | 200 | 12.00 |
    | 300 | 8.00 |
    | 400 | 7.00 |
    | 500 | 5.60 |

    What is the behavioural classification of the expense item?

    A     Fixed cost
    B     Semi-variable cost
    C     Stepped-fixed cost
    D     Variable cost

9   A particular cost is classified as being semi-variable.

    What is the effect on the TOTAL COST if activity increases by 20%?

    A     Stays the same
    B     Decreases by less than 20%
    C     Increases by 20%
    D     Increases by less than 20%

10  Analysis of the gross wages in a factory reveals the following:

    | | Direct operatives ($) | Indirect operatives ($) |
    | --- | --- | --- |
    | Normal hours worked at basic rate | 36,260 | 14,320 |
    | Overtime hours at basic rate | 4,112 | 1,760 |
    | Overtime premium | 1,028 | 440 |

    Overtime working is a usual aspect of running the business.

    What amount would be recorded as a direct cost?

    A     $36,260
    B     $40,372
    C     $41,400
    D     $41,840

11    The production volume ratio for a period was 95%.

      What could have caused this?

      A    Actual hours worked being greater than budgeted hours
      B    Actual hours worked being less than budgeted hours
      C    Standard time for actual output being greater than budgeted hours
      D    Standard time for actual output being less than budgeted hours

12    A cost centre is charged with the following actual overhead costs for a period:

      Allocated costs                      $28,720
      Apportioned costs                    $10,260

      Overheads were absorbed in the cost centre over the period on 1,760 actual labour hours at a predetermined
      absorption rate of $21·50 per hour. Actual labour hours worked in the period were 90 hours above budget.

      What was the overhead over/under absorption in the cost centre?

      A    $1,140
      B    $1,935
      C    $3,055
      D    $9,120

13    A company sells more than it manufactures in a period.

      Which of the following explains the difference in profit between absorption and marginal costing in the
      above situation?

      A    Absorption costing profit is higher because of the difference in inventory levels
      B    Absorption costing profit is lower because of the difference in inventory levels
      C    Absorption costing profit is higher because of overhead over-absorption
      D    Absorption costing profit is lower because of overhead under-absorption

14    The production cost of Job J6 was $12,600. Administration costs are charged to jobs at 30% of production
      cost. The amount charged to the customer is calculated to provide a GROSS PROFIT MARGIN of 40%.

      What is the net profit on Job J6?

      A    $1,260
      B    $4,620
      C    $10,920
      D    $15,120

15    The following information relates to a process for a period:

      Input costs                                              $45,705
      Output passing inspection                                9,600 units
      Normal inspection loss              300 units (sold for $2.00 per unit)
      Abnormal inspection loss            100 units (sold for $2.00 per unit)

      What was the cost per unit (to two decimal places of $)?

      A    $4.49
      B    $4.56
      C    $4.65
      D    $4.76

16    A process produces two joint products, X and Y, with selling prices of $10 per litre and $20 per litre respectively. In a period, joint costs were $56,000 and finished output was:

Product X                    5,000 litres
Product Y                    2,000 litres

The sales value method is used to apportion joint costs.

What amount of joint costs should be apportioned to Product Y?

A    $16,000
B    $24,889
C    $31,111
D    $37,333

---

17    What is the effective annual rate of interest of 4·3% compounded every six months?

A    8.60%
B    8.78%
C    9.25%
D    10.88%

---

18    Net cash flows, estimated for a capital investment project, have been discounted at four discount rates with the following results:

| | Discount rate | | | |
|---|---|---|---|---|
| | **5%** | **10%** | **15%** | **20%** |
| Net present value ($000) | 92·9 | 39·1 | (4·8) | (40·9) |

What is the best estimate of the IRR using only the above data as appropriate?

A    13.6%
B    14.5%
C    15.4%
D    15.7%

---

19    A project, investing in new machinery, has an estimated five year life. The cost of capital is 10% per annum.

Estimated cash flows are:

Time                          Cash flows
0                             (cost) ($186,000)
1 to 5                        (inflows) $56,000 per annum
5                             (residual value) $10,000

The cumulative discount factor at 10% for Time 1 to 5 is 3·79. The discount factor at 10% for Time 5 is 0·62.

What is the net present value of the project?

A    $16,240
B    $20,040
C    $32,440
D    $36,240

---

20    A capital investment project requires an initial investment sum. The investment returns are expected to be a constant amount in each year of the life of the investment.

How is the payback period for the investment calculated?

A    Investment sum ÷ net cash inflow per annum
B    Investment sum ÷ net profit per annum
C    (Investment sum + residual value) ÷ net cash inflow per annum
D    (Investment sum + residual value) ÷ net profit per annum

**(40 marks)**

# Section B – ALL FOUR questions are compulsory and MUST be attempted

1    At the beginning of Month 2, the balance in the stores ledger for Material M27 was 2,400 kg at $3·60 per kg. The movements of the material in Month 2, and the prices per kg, were as follows:

| Day | Receipts | | Issues | |
|---|---|---|---|---|
| | Quantity kg | Price $/kg | Quantity kg | Price $/kg |
| 4 | 5,000 | 3·65 | | |
| 6 | | | 4,000 | 3·65 |
| 17 | 6,000 | 3·70 | | |

*Required*

(a)    State the pricing method used to value the material issues on Day 6.    **(2 marks)**

(b)    Calculate the closing inventory value at the end of Month 2.    **(3 marks)**

In Month 3, no further purchases of Material M27 were made. Issues in the month were:

Day 2               3,200 kg
Day 10           4,300 kg

*Required*

(c)    Prepare the inventory record for Material M27 for Month 3, showing both the quantity AND the value of:

       (i)    each of the issues; and    **(4 marks)**

       (ii)    the balance remaining after each issue.    **(4 marks)**

                                                **(Total = 13 marks)**

2    A company manufactures two products, Product A manufactured in Process Y and Product B manufactured in Process Z. The following information is available for a period:

| | Process Y | Process Z |
|---|---|---|
| Opening work-in-progress | Nil | Nil |
| Raw materials input | $162,180 (18,000 kg) | $210,090 |
| Conversion costs | $94,050 | $287,760 |
| Waste material | 1,000 kg (Note 1) | Nil |
| Sales value of waste material | $1.60 per kg | Nil |
| Output of finished product | 17,000 kg | 12,600 units |
| Closing work-in-progress | Nil | 1,500 units (Note 2) |

*Note 1*

In Process Y the normal amount of waste material is 5% of the weight of raw materials input.

*Note 2*

In Process Z the closing work-in-progress is 100% complete as to raw materials and 60% complete as to conversion costs.

*Required*

(a)    For Process Y, calculate the:

       (i)    cost per kg of the expected production of Product A; and    **(8 marks)**
       (ii)    total cost of the finished output of Product A.    **(2 marks)**

(b)    For Process Z, calculate the equivalent units of production of Product B in respect of conversion costs.    **(3 marks)**

                                                  **(Total = 13 marks)**

**3** Three of the cost items that are included in the production overhead budget for a factory for a period are:

| | |
|---|---|
| Machine maintenance labour | $33,600 |
| Power | $26,000 |
| Rent and rates | $39,800 |

Production overheads are currently absorbed using a single factory-wide rate.

It has been suggested that a separate overhead absorption rate should be calculated for each of the three groups of machines in the factory. The following additional budgeted data has been collected for the period:

| | Machine Group | | | Total |
|---|---|---|---|---|
| | MG1 | MG2 | MG3 | |
| Floor area (m2) | 1,600 | 1,400 | 1,000 | 4,000 |
| Machine values ($'000) | 320 | 250 | 230 | 800 |
| Kilowatt hours ('000) | 220 | 110 | 110 | 440 |
| Machine maintenance (labour hours) | 600 | 400 | 600 | 1,600 |
| Number of indirect workers | 4 | 4 | 2 | 10 |
| Machine hours | 8,200 | 5,600 | 4,900 | 18,700 |

*Required*

(a) Briefly explain one reason why a separate overhead absorption rate for each machine group would be preferable to a single factory-wide rate. **(2 marks)**

(b) Apportion each of the three items of budgeted overhead cost (machine maintenance labour, power and rent and rates) to the three machine groups. **(7 marks)**

The totals of ALL budgeted production overhead cost items, allocated and apportioned to the three machine groups, are as follows:

| | |
|---|---|
| MG1 | $129,560 |
| MG2 | $107,520 |
| MG3 | $119,070 |

*Required*

(c) Calculate an appropriate absorption rate for each machine group. **(3 marks)**

(d) Calculate the production overhead that would be charged to Job J21 which requires five hours on MG1 machines, two hours on MG2 machines and three hours on MG3 machines. **(3 marks)**

**(Total = 15 marks)**

**4** (a) Define the term 'limiting factor' and give an example. **(3 marks)**

(b) A company manufactures three products (X, Y and Z). All direct operatives are the same grade and are paid at $11 per hour. It is anticipated that there will be a shortage of direct operatives in the following period, which will prevent the company from achieving the following sales targets:

| | |
|---|---|
| Product X | 3,600 units |
| Product Y | 8,000 units |
| Product Z | 5,700 units |

Selling prices and costs are:

| | Product X | Product Y | Product Z |
|---|---|---|---|
| | $ per unit | $ per unit | $ per unit |
| Selling prices | 100.00 | 69.00 | 85.00 |
| Variable costs: | | | |
| Production* | 51.60 | 35.00 | 42.40 |
| Non-production | 5.00 | 3.95 | 4.25 |
| Fixed costs: | | | |
| Production | 27.20 | 19.80 | 21.00 |
| Non-production | 7.10 | 5.90 | 6.20 |
| *includes the cost of direct operatives | 24.20 | 16.50 | 17.60 |

The fixed costs per unit are based on achieving the sales targets. There would not be any savings in fixed costs if production and sales are at a lower level.

*Required*

(i) Determine the production plan that would maximise profit in the following period, if the available direct operatives' hours total 26,400. **(11 marks)**

(ii) Calculate the total net profit in the following period based on the production plan in (b) above.

**(5 marks)**

**(Total = 19 marks)**

# ACCA examiner's answers to Mock Exam 1

# Section A

1   A
2   D
3   D
4   D
5   B
6   C
7   D
8   C
9   D
10  B
11  D
12  A
13  B
14  B
15  C
16  B
17  B
18  B
19  C
20  A

Workings to calculation MCQs:

10  ($36,260 + $4,112)

12  [($28,720 + $10,260) − (1,760 units × $21.50 per unit)]

14  [($12,600 ÷ 0·6) − ($12,600 × 1.3)]

15  {[$45,705 − (300 units × $2.00 per unit)] ÷ 9,700}

16  [$56,000 × ($40,000 ÷ $90,000)]

17  [$(1.043)^2 − 1$]

18  {10% + [(15 − 10%) × (39.1 ÷ 43.9)]}

19  [($56,000 × 3.79) + ($10,000 × 0.62) − $186,000]

# Section B

1    (a)    Material pricing method

Last-in First-out (LIFO) – because the issue on day 6 is at the latest price (ie the price of the receipt on Day 4 rather than the price of the opening inventory).

(b)    End Month 2 closing inventory value – Material M27

[(2,400 kg at $3·60) + (1,000 kg at $3·65) + (6,000 kg at $3·70)] = $34,490

(c)    Month 3 inventory record – Material M27

| | | Issues | | | Balance | |
|---|---|---|---|---|---|---|
| Day | Quantity kg | price $/kg | Value $ | Quantity kg | price $/kg | Value $ |
| 1 | | | | 2,400 | 3·60 | 8,640 |
| | | | | 1,000 | 3·65 | 3,650 |
| | | | | 6,000 | 3·70 | 22,200 |
| | | | | 9,400 | | 34,490 |
| 2 | 3,200 | 3.70 | 11,840 | 2,400 | 3.60 | 8,640 |
| | | | | 1,000 | 3.65 | 3,650 |
| | | | | 2,800 | 3.70 | 10,360 |
| | | | | 6,200 | | 22,650 |
| 10 | 2,800 | 3.70 | 10,360 | | | |
| | 1,000 | 3.65 | 3,650 | | | |
| | 500 | 3.60 | 1,800 | | | |
| | 4,300 | | 15,810 | 1,900 | 3.60 | 6,840 |

2    (a)    (i)    Cost per kg of expected production of Product A

Expected output  = 18,000 kg × 0.95

             = 17,100 kg

| | $ | |
|---|---|---|
| Total costs: | | |
| Raw materials | 162,180 | |
| Conversion costs | 94,050 | |
| | 256,230 | |
| Sales value of waste | (1,440) | (normal waste 900 kg × $1·60/kg) |
| Net cost | $254,790 | |

Cost per kg  = $254,790 ÷ 17,100 kg

               = $14·90 per kg

(ii)    Total cost of finished output of Product A

17,000 kg × $14·90 per kg

= $253,300

(b)    Equivalent units of production of Product B

| | Conversion costs (units) | |
|---|---|---|
| Completed output | 12,600 | |
| Closing work-in-progress | 900 | (1,500 × 0.6) |
| Equivalent units | 13,500 | |

3    (a)    Overhead absorption

A separate overhead absorption rate for each machine group, rather than a single factory-wide rate, would be better because separate rates will reflect the resources consumed in each group. This will then be charged appropriately to jobs according to their relative consumption of the resources in each group.

(b)    Overhead cost apportionment

|  | Machine group | | | |
|  | MG1 | MG2 | MG3 | Total |
| --- | --- | --- | --- | --- |
|  | $ | $ | $ | $ |
| Machine maintenance labour (apportioned on machine maintenance labour hours) | 12,600 | 8,400 | 12,600 | 33,600 |
| Power (apportioned on kilowatt hours) | 13,000 | 6,500 | 6,500 | 26,000 |
| Rent and rates (apportioned on floor space) | 15,920 | 13,930 | 9,950 | 39,800 |

(c)    Overhead absorption rates

|  | Machine group | | |
|  | MG1 | MG2 | MG3 |
| --- | --- | --- | --- |
| Total allocated and apportioned ($) | 129,560 | 107,520 | 119,070 |
| Machine hours | 8,200 | 5,600 | 4,900 |
| Absorption rate ($ per machine hour) | 15.80 | 19.20 | 24.30 |

(d)    Production overhead charged to Job J21

|  | $ |
| --- | --- |
| MG1 5 machine hours at $15·80 = | 79.00 |
| MG2 2 machine hours at $19·20 = | 38.40 |
| MG3 3 machine hours at $24·30 = | 72.90 |
|  | 190.30 |

4    (a)    Limiting factor

The limiting factor is the factor (aspect of business/resource) that limits a business organisation's activities. For many businesses this may frequently be the level of sales that can be achieved but at other times a business may be limited by a shortage of a resource (as in the situation described in the next part of this question, where a scarcity of labour prevents the business from achieving its sales potential).

(b)    (i)    Production plan

|  | Product X | Product Y | Product Z |
|  | $ per unit | $ per unit | $ per unit |
| --- | --- | --- | --- |
| Selling price | 100.00 | 69.00 | 85.00 |
| Variable costs | 56.60 | 38.95 | 46.65 |
| Contribution | 43.40 | 30.05 | 38.35 |
|  | 43.40 | 30.05 | 38.35 |
| Contribution per £ of direct operative cost* | 24.20 | 16.50 | 17.60 |
|  | = $1.793 | = $1.821 | = $2.179 |
| Production priority | 3 | 2 | 1 |
| *or: |  |  |  |
| Direct operative hours per unit | 24.20 | 16.50 | 17.60 |
|  | 11.00 | 11.00 | 11.00 |
|  | = 2.2 hrs | = 1.5 hrs | = 1.6 hrs |
| Contribution per direct operative hour | 43.40 | 30.05 | 38.35 |
|  | 2.2 | 1.5 | 1.6 |
|  | = $19.73 | = $20.03 | = $23.97 |
| Production priority | 3 | 2 | 1 |

Production plan:

| | | Units | | Hours |
|---|---|---|---|---|
| Product Z | | 5,700 | x 17.6/11 | 9,120 |
| Product Y | | 8,000 | x 16.5/11 | 12,000 |
| Product X | | 2,400 | x 24.2/11 | 5,280 |
| | | | | 26,400 |

(ii) Net profit

| | | $ | $ |
|---|---|---|---|
| Contribution: | | | |
| Product X | 2,400 units at $43·40 | 104,160 | |
| Product Y | 8,000 units at $30·05 | 240,400 | |
| Product Z | 5,700 units at $38·35 | 218,595 | 563,155 |
| Fixed costs: | | | |
| Product X | 3,600 units at $34·30 | 123,480 | |
| Product Y | 8,000 units at $25·70 | 205,600 | |
| Product Z | 5,700 units at $27·20 | 155,040 | 484,120 |
| Net profit | | | 79,035 |

# Mock Exam 2

# CAT

# Intermediate Paper 4
# Accounting for Costs

# Mock Examination 2

# December 2008

| Question Paper | |
| --- | --- |
| Time allowed | **2 hours** |
| **This paper is divided into two sections** | |
| Section A | **ALL TWENTY questions are compulsory and MUST be answered** |
| Section B | **ALL FOUR questions are compulsory and MUST be attempted** |

**DO NOT OPEN THIS PAPER UNTIL YOU ARE READY TO START UNDER EXAMINATION CONDITIONS**

# Section A – ALL TWENTY questions are compulsory and must be attempted

Each question within this section is worth 2 marks.

1   Consider the following incomplete statements relating to features of management information:

    (1)    Communicated in writing
    (2)    Presented in report format
    (3)    Supported by calculations
    (4)    Timely and clear to the user

Which of the above are necessary features of useful management information?

    A    (1) and (4)
    B    (1), (2) and (3)
    C    (4) only
    D    (2) and (3) only

---

2   Which of the following performance measures would be appropriate for an investment centre rather than a profit centre or a cost centre?

    A    Contribution/sales ratio
    B    Cost per unit
    C    Labour efficiency ratio
    D    Residual income

---

3   Which of the following describes the term 'cost unit'?

    A    A basis for cost classification
    B    A production or service department
    C    A unit of product or service
    D    The cost of a unit of output

---

4   The cost accounts of a business are kept separate from the financial accounts but the two sets of accounts are reconciled each period.

What accounting system is being described?

    A    Cost control accounts
    B    Cost ledger accounts
    C    Integrated accounts
    D    Interlocking accounts

---

5   Cost Z is fixed in total for a period.

If the level of activity in the period is increased by 50% what change would occur in Cost Z per unit of activity?

    A    Decrease by a third
    B    Decrease by a half
    C    Increase by a third
    D    Increase by a half

---

6    In a factory, a team of six maintenance staff are paid a guaranteed weekly wage.

Which of the following is the most appropriate cost classification for their wages?

A    Direct labour cost
B    Indirect labour cost
C    Semi-variable cost
D    Variable overhead cost

7    Production costs incurred in the manufacture of 2,400 units of a product in a period are:

|  | $ |
|---|---|
| Direct costs | 19,680 |
| Variable overheads | 3,120 |
| Fixed overheads | 14,640 |

What would be the expected total cost of manufacturing 2,300 units of the product in a period?

A    $35,880
B    $36,490
C    $36,620
D    $37,310

8    The following documents are used in the process of purchasing and using raw materials:

(1)    Despatch note
(2)    Goods received note
(3)    Materials requisition
(4)    Purchase order
(5)    Purchase requisition

Which of the documents would be used to update the stores ledger accounts?

A    (2) only
B    (2) and (3)
C    (1), (2), (4) and (5)
D    (1), (3), (4) and (5)

9    A company produced 6,200 units of a product in a period. The product used 80 kg of material per 100 units of output. The inventory holding of the material reduced by 380 kg in the period.

What quantity of material was purchased in the period?

A    4,580 kg
B    4,960 kg
C    5,340 kg
D    7,370 kg

10    A firm has used the economic order quantity (EOQ) formula to arrive at an EOQ for Component C1 of 400 units. Annual demand for Component C1 is 12,000 units and the cost of placing an order for the component is $40.

What is the cost of holding one unit of Component C1 in inventory for one year?

A    $0.17
B    $0.33
C    $3.00
D    $6.00

11    'Materials Stores' is one of the service cost centres in a factory.

What would be the most appropriate basis for the reapportionment of the overheads of Materials Stores to the cost centres it serves?

A      Number of materials requisitions
B      Number of purchase requisitions
C      Reorder level of each material
D      Value of materials inventory

---

12    Production cost centre X absorbs overheads on the basis of machine hours and has the following budgeted and actual figures:

| | Budget | Actual |
|---|---|---|
| Overheads | $20,290 | $19,110 |
| Machine hours | 560 | 514 |

What is the predetermined production overhead absorption rate in production cost centre X (to two decimal places)?

A      $34.13
B      $36.23
C      $37.18
D      $39.47

---

13    There are two production cost centres in a factory. Production overhead absorption rates are:

Cost centre A      $10·60 per direct labour hour
Cost centre B      $36·20 per machine hour

Product P requires the following hours per unit of finished product in each cost centre:

| | Cost centre | |
|---|---|---|
| | A | B |
| Direct labour hours | 3.0 | 0.5 |
| Machine hours | 0.2 | 1.3 |

What is the total production overhead cost per unit of Product P?

A      $78.86
B      $91.40
C      $99.08
D      $234.00

---

14    Consider the following statements:

(1)     The difference between the profit reported by absorption costing and that reported by marginal costing is due to over or under absorption of overhead

(2)     Absorption costing profit will be higher than marginal costing profit if sales units exceed production units

Are the above statements true or false?

| | Statement (1) | Statement (2) |
|---|---|---|
| A | True | True |
| B | True | False |
| C | False | False |
| D | False | True |

15    In which of the following would job costing be most appropriate?

    A    College
    B    Hospital
    C    Car repairer
    D    Chemical manufacturer

16    Manufacturing process costs total $179,070 for a period. 9,000 kg of raw materials were processed with the following result:

| | |
|---|---|
| Completed good output | 8,100 kg |
| Normal loss | 1,200 kg |
| Abnormal gain | 300 kg |

What was the cost per kg (to two decimal places)?

    A    $19.90
    B    $21.32
    C    $22.11
    D    $22.96

17    Consider the following two descriptions:

    (1)    A product which is incidental to the main purpose of a process
    (2)    A product which has an insignificant value relative to other products from a process

Do the above describe a by-product?

| | Description (1) | Description (2) |
|---|---|---|
| A | No | No |
| B | No | Yes |
| C | Yes | No |
| D | Yes | Yes |

18    Which of the following statements is true of service costing?

    A    A composite cost unit may be used
    B    Indirect costs normally represent a small proportion of total costs
    C    Output is often tangible
    D    The cost of direct materials tends to be high in relation to other costs

19    Budgeted sales of a company's single product in a period are 20,000 units, producing a total contribution of $180,000 at a selling price of $24 per unit. Fixed costs are $6 per unit based on the budgeted sales quantity.

What is the budgeted variable cost per unit?

    A    $3
    B    $9
    C    $15
    D    $18

20    A firm makes a single product. Budgets have been prepared for the year ahead and include production and sales of 60,000 units with a break-even point of 45,000 units.

What is the margin of safety ratio?

    A    25%
    B    33%
    C    75%
    D    133%

**(40 marks)**

# Section B – ALL FOUR questions are compulsory and MUST be attempted

1   A company is considering whether to add a new product to its range. Machinery costing $280,000 would have to be bought at the start of the project (Year 0). The project life would be five years with no disposal value at the end of the project.

Sales of the new product are forecast at 12,000 units in each of Years 1 and 2, rising to 15,000 units in each of Years 3, 4 and 5. The selling price per unit will be $15 in Year 1 and $16 thereafter. Variable costs are estimated at $9 per unit.

Straight-line depreciation of the machine would be $56,000 in each year. No other future incremental fixed costs would be incurred. However, the company has already incurred expenditure of $6,000 for a market research survey and has decided to write this off against profits made in the first year if the investment takes place.

Assume that all cash flows, apart from the investment in machinery, occur at the end of each year.

The cost of capital is 14% per annum. Discount factors at 14% are:

| Year 1 | 0.877 |
|--------|-------|
| Year 2 | 0.769 |
| Year 3 | 0.675 |
| Year 4 | 0.592 |
| Year 5 | 0.519 |

*Required*

(a)   Calculate the net cash flows for each year of the project (Year 0 to 5).          **(8 marks)**

(b)   Calculate the net present value of the project (working in $000).                   **(6 marks)**

(c)   State whether the internal rate of return is above or below 14% and justify your conclusion.
                                                                                          **(2 marks)**

                                                                              **(Total = 16 marks)**

2   A garage operates a vehicle repair service. Space is limited and, although the garage is usually busy, the owner is concerned about the amount of profit that can be generated. Summarised data concerning vehicle repairs follows:

| Average number of repairs per period | 85 |
|--------------------------------------|------|
| Average variable cost of each repair | $126 |
| Average sales value of each repair   | $210 |

The owner is considering extending the garage opening hours. This would result in an increase in fixed costs from $6,972 to $7,728 per period. The average variable cost and the average sales value of each repair would be expected to remain the same.

*Required*

(a)   For the current situation, calculate per period the:

   (i)    profit;                                                                          **(3 marks)**
   (ii)   break-even sales revenue.                                                        **(4 marks)**

(b)   For the proposed extended opening hours, calculate the average number of repairs required per period to achieve the current level of profit.                                      **(4 marks)**

                                                                              **(Total = 11 marks)**

3    The following data is provided for a chemical process for a period:

Materials input                   29,000 kg (kilograms) at a total cost of $162,342
Conversion cost                   $74,700
Opening work-in-progress          Nil
Closing work-in-progress          3,000 kg, 60% complete as to conversion costs

There is a preparation loss at the start of the process operation. Actual losses in the period were at the normal level of 10% of the materials input.

*Required*

For the period:

(a)    Calculate the cost per kg (kilogram) of production.                    **(6 marks)**
(b)    Prepare the process account (showing kg as well as value).             **(9 marks)**

**(Total = 15 marks)**

4    (a)    Describe briefly how the following are used in the accounting for labour:

       (i)    Time sheets;                                                    **(3 marks)**
       (ii)   Job cards.                                                      **(3 marks)**

     (b)    The following details relate to the labour in a production cost centre for a period:

|  | Direct personnel | Indirect personnel |
|---|---|---|
| Hourly rates of pay: | | |
| Basic | $10·00 | $7·00 |
| Overtime | $13·00 | $9·10 |
| Payroll hours: | | |
| Productive | 310 | 118 |
| Idle | 18 | 4 |
| Total | 328 | 122 |

Additional information:

1.    The basic rates of pay apply to a normal working week of 38 hours
2.    There are eight direct personnel and three indirect personnel in the cost centre
3.    Overtime is worked from time to time to meet the general requirements of production
4.    Idle time is regarded as normal.

*Required*

Calculate the total amounts:

(i)    Paid to the direct personnel and the indirect personnel respectively;          **(6 marks)**

(ii)   Charged as direct wages to work-in-progress and indirect wages to overheads respectively (show clearly the make-up of the indirect charge).                                **(6 marks)**

**(Total = 18 marks)**

ACCA examiner's answers to
Mock Exam 2

Section A

| | |
|---|---|
| 1 | C |
| 2 | D |
| 3 | C |
| 4 | D |
| 5 | A |
| 6 | B |
| 7 | B |
| 8 | B |
| 9 | A |
| 10 | D |
| 11 | A |
| 12 | B |
| 13 | A |
| 14 | C |
| 15 | C |
| 16 | D |
| 17 | D |
| 18 | A |
| 19 | C |
| 20 | A |

Workings for calculation MCQs:

7   $(22{,}800 \times 23/24) + 14{,}640$

9   $(6{,}200 \times 0.8) - 380$

10   $(2 \times 40 \times 12{,}000) \div 400^2$

12   $20{,}290/560$

13   $(3.0 \times 10.60) + (1.3 \times 36.20)$

16   $179{,}070/7{,}800$

19   $24 - (180{,}000/20{,}000)$

20   $15/60$

Section B

1   (a)   Net cash flows:

Year 0       ($280,000)                          =   ($280,000)
Year 1       12,000 units x ($15 – $9) per unit  =   $72,000
Year 2       12,000 units x ($16 – $9) per unit  =   $84,000
Years 3–5    15,000 units x ($16 – $9) per unit  =   $105,000 per annum

    (b)   Net present value (NPV):

| Year(s) | Cash flow $000 | Discount factor 14% | NPV $000 |
|---|---|---|---|
| 0 | (280) | 1·000 | (280) |
| 1 | 72 | 0·877 | 63 |
| 2 | 84 | 0·769 | 65 |
| 3–5 | 105 | 1·786 | 188 |
| | | | 36 |

    (c)   The internal rate of return is above 14% because the NPV is positive when discounted at 14%.

2   (a)   Current situation per period:

        (i)    Profit = Contribution $7,140 [85 repairs x ($210 – $126) per repair] less fixed costs $6,972

               = $168

        (ii)   Break-even sales revenue = Fixed costs ÷ C/S ratio

               = $6,972 ÷ 84/210

               = $17,430

    (b)   Extended working hours: required number of repairs per period

        = Required contribution $7,896 ($7,728 + $168) ÷ contribution per repair $84

        = 94 repairs

3   (a)   Equivalent units of production:

|  | Materials | Conversion costs |  |
|---|---|---|---|
| Completed output | 23,100 | 23,100 | |
| Closing WIP | 3,000 | 1,800 | (3,000 x 0·6) |
| | 26,100* | 24,900 | |

* 29,000 kg input x 0·9. Therefore, completed output = 26,100 – 3,000.

Cost per kg:

|  | $ |  |
|---|---|---|
| Materials | 6·22 | ($162,342 ÷ 26,100) |
| Conversion costs | 3·00 | ($74,700 ÷ 24,900) |
| Total cost | $9·22 | |

    (b)   Process account:

| | kg | $ | | kg | $ |
|---|---|---|---|---|---|
| Materials | 29,000 | 162,342 | Output | 23,100 | 212,982 |
| Conversion costs | | 74,700 | Normal loss | 2,900 | – |
| | | | Closing WIP | 3,000 | 24,060 |
| | 29,000 | 237,042 | | 29,000 | 237,042 |

Workings:

Output        23,100 kg x $9·22 =   $212,982

Closing WIP   3,000 kg x $6·22 =    $18,660
              1,800 kg x $3·00 =     5,400
                                    $24,060

**4 (a) (i)** Time sheets are completed by individual employees. Each employee, on his/her time sheet, will record the time spent on each of various tasks/jobs.

**(ii)** A job card is prepared for each job. When an employee works on a job he/she records the time spent on that job's card. The card shows how long various employees spend on a particular job and at what cost.

**(b) (i)** Wages paid:

| | Direct personnel | $ | Indirect personnel | $ |
|---|---|---|---|---|
| Normal hours | 8 x 38 = 304 at $10 = | 3,040 | 3 x 38 = 114 at $7 = | 798 |
| Overtime hours | 328 − 304 = 24 at $13 = | 312 | 122 − 114 = 8 at $9·10 = | 72·80 |
| | | $3,352 | | $870·80 |

**(ii)** Wages charged:

| | Direct charge (to WIP) | $ | Indirect charge (to prod o'hd) | $ |
|---|---|---|---|---|
| Direct personnel | 310 hours at $10 = | $3,100 | Idle time 18 hours at $10 = | 180 |
| | | | O'time premium 24 hours at $3 = | 72 |
| | | | | 252 |
| Indirect personnel | | | | 870·80 |
| | | | | $1,122·80 |

**ACCA Certified Accounting Technician Examination – Paper T4**
**Accounting for Costs**

| | | | | | |
|---|---|---|---|---|---|
| **1** | **(a)** | | Non-inclusion of depreciation | 2 | |
| | | | Non-inclusion of market research | 2 | |
| | | | Year 0 | 1 | |
| | | | Years 1–5 | 3 | 8 |
| | | | | | |
| | **(b)** | | Year 0 | 1 | |
| | | | Years 1–5 | $3^1/_2$ | |
| | | | NPV | $1^1/_2$ | 6 |
| | | | | | |
| | **(c)** | | Conclusion | | 2 |
| | | | | | 16 |
| | | | | | |
| | | | | | |
| **2** | **(a)** | **(i)** | Contribution | 2 | |
| | | | Profit | 1 | 3 |
| | | | | | |
| | | **(ii)** | Break-even formula | 1 | |
| | | | Sales value | 3 | 4 |
| | | | | | |
| | **(b)** | | Number of repairs | | 4 |
| | | | | | 11 |
| | | | | | |
| | | | | | |
| **3** | **(a)** | | Completed output | 2 | |
| | | | Closing WIP | 2 | |
| | | | Cost per kg | 2 | 6 |
| | | | | | |
| | **(b)** | | Output | $1^1/_2$ | |
| | | | Closing WIP | 3 | |
| | | | Debit entries | $1^1/_2$ | |
| | | | Credit entries | 3 | 9 |
| | | | | | 15 |
| | | | | | |
| | | | | | |
| **4** | **(a)** | **(i)** | Time sheets | | 3 |
| | | **(ii)** | Job cards | | 3 |
| | | | | | |
| | **(b)** | **(i)** | Direct personnel – normal hours | $1^1/_2$ | |
| | | | – overtime hours | $1^1/_2$ | |
| | | | Indirect personnel – normal hours | $1^1/_2$ | |
| | | | – overtime hours | $1^1/_2$ | 6 |
| | | | | | |
| | | **(ii)** | Direct charge | $1^1/_2$ | |
| | | | Indirect charge – direct personnel | 3 | |
| | | | – indirect personnel | $1^1/_2$ | 6 |
| | | | | | 18 |

# REVIEW FORM & FREE PRIZE DRAW

All original review forms from the entire BPP range, completed with genuine comments, will be entered into one of two draws on 31 July 2009 and 31 January 2010. The names on the first four forms picked out on each occasion will be sent a cheque for £50.

Name: _____     Address: _____

_____

Date: _____     _____

### How have you used this Practice & Revision Kit?
*(Tick one box only)*

☐ Home study (book only)

☐ On a course: college _____

☐ With 'correspondence' package

☐ Other _____

### Why did you decide to purchase this Practice & Revision Kit? *(Tick one box only)*

☐ Have used complementary Interactive Text

☐ Have used BPP Texts in the past

☐ Recommendation by friend/colleague

☐ Recommendation by a lecturer at college

☐ Saw advertising in journals

☐ Saw website

☐ Other _____

### During the past six months do you recall seeing/receiving any of the following?
*(Tick as many boxes as are relevant)*

☐ Our advertisement in *ACCA Student Accountant*

☐ Other advertisement _____

☐ Our brochure with a letter through the post

### Which (if any) aspects of our advertising do you find useful?
*(Tick as many boxes as are relevant)*

☐ Prices and publication dates of new editions

☐ Information on Practice & Revision Kit content

☐ Facility to order books off-the-page

☐ None of the above

**Have you used the companion Interactive Text for this subject?**     ☐ Yes     ☐ No

**Your ratings, comments and suggestions would be appreciated on the following areas**

|  | Very useful | Useful | Not useful |
|---|---|---|---|
| Introductory section (How to use this Practice & Revision Kit) | ☐ | ☐ | ☐ |
| 'Do You Know' checklists | ☐ | ☐ | ☐ |
| 'Did You Know' checklists | ☐ | ☐ | ☐ |
| Possible pitfalls | ☐ | ☐ | ☐ |
| Objective test questions | ☐ | ☐ | ☐ |
| Short-form questions | ☐ | ☐ | ☐ |
| Content of answers | ☐ | ☐ | ☐ |
| Mock exams | ☐ | ☐ | ☐ |
| Structure & presentation | ☐ | ☐ | ☐ |
| Icons | ☐ | ☐ | ☐ |

|  | Excellent | Good | Adequate | Poor |
|---|---|---|---|---|
| Overall opinion of this Kit | ☐ | ☐ | ☐ | ☐ |

**Do you intend to continue using BPP Interactive Texts/Kits?**     ☐ Yes     ☐ No

**Please note any further comments and suggestions/errors on the reverse of this page.**

**Please return to: Mary Maclean, BPP Learning Media Ltd, FREEPOST, London, W12 8BR**

## REVIEW FORM & FREE PRIZE DRAW (continued)

**Please note any further comments and suggestions/errors below**

**FREE PRIZE DRAW RULES**

1   Closing date for 31 July 2009 draw is 30 June 2009. Closing date for 31 January 2010 draw is 31 December 2009.

2   Restricted to entries with UK and Eire addresses only. BPP employees, their families and business associates are excluded.

3   No purchase necessary. Entry forms are available upon request from BPP Learning Media Ltd. No more than one entry per title, per person. Draw restricted to persons aged 16 and over.

4   Winners will be notified by post and receive their cheques not later than 6 weeks after the relevant draw date.

5   The decision of the promoter in all matters is final and binding. No correspondence will be entered into.